W0044191

Language, Limits, and Beyond

Language, Limits, and Beyond

Early Wittgenstein and Rabindranath Tagore

Priyambada Sarkar

OXFORD
UNIVERSITY PRESS

OXFORD

UNIVERSITY PRESS

Oxford University Press is a department of the University of Oxford.
It furthers the University's objective of excellence in research, scholarship,
and education by publishing worldwide. Oxford is a registered trademark of
Oxford University Press in the UK and in certain other countries.

Published in India by
Oxford University Press
22 Workspace, 2nd Floor, 1/22 Asaf Ali Road, New Delhi 110002, India

© Indian Institute of Advanced Study, 2021

The moral rights of the author have been asserted.

First Edition published in 2021
All rights reserved. No part of this publication may be reproduced, stored in
a retrieval system, or transmitted, in any form or by any means, without the
prior permission in writing of Oxford University Press, or as expressly permitted
by law, by licence, or under terms agreed with the appropriate reprographics
rights organization. Enquiries concerning reproduction outside the scope of the
above should be sent to the Rights Department, Oxford University Press, at the
address above.

You must not circulate this book in any other form
and you must impose this same condition on any acquirer.

ISBN-13 (print edition): 978-0-19-012397-0
ISBN-10 (print edition): 0-19-012397-4

ISBN-13 (ebook): 978-0-19-099087-9
ISBN-10 (ebook): 0-19-099087-2

Typeset in Scala Pro 10/13
by Tranistics Data Technologies, Kolkata 700 091
Printed in India at Rakmo Press Pvt. Ltd.

To my near and dear ones
Baba, Pradip, and Titir

Contents

Preface

This book has long been in the making. What had the greatest impact on my mind when I first encountered the philosophy of Wittgenstein in my master's class was his simple ascetic lifestyle. I was awestruck by the fact that he lived almost a life of a *sanyāsi*, renouncing his entire inheritance away for noble causes, and by his astounding humility, which allowed him to take up the profession of a primary school teacher or of a hospital orderly.

Later, when I came to know about his reading of poems from the *Gitānjali* (Tagore 1913a) in Vienna circle meetings, I was struck by questions: How could Wittgenstein, an influential thinker on the tradition of Gottlob Frege and Bertrand Russell in the philosophy of language, be so deeply attracted by Rabindranath Tagore, the greatest mystical poet of India? Could there be some similarities in the ideas and attitudes of these two men?

Then I found a more detailed reference to Wittgenstein's fascination with Tagore in Ray Monk's book *Wittgenstein: The Duty of Genius* (1990), where I came to know about Wittgenstein's translation of Tagore's allegorical play entitled *The King of the Dark Chamber*. Not only that, Wittgenstein along with his student, Smythies, read *The King of the Dark Chamber* once again before he delivered his lectures on aesthetics, psychology, and religious belief in 1937 (Wittgenstein 1966).

Paul Engelmann's memoir (1967) and Janik and Toulmin's (1973) contention that the *Tractatus* (1922) had been fundamentally misunderstood by the logical positivists and that the real message and climax of the work was to be found in the last 10 pages certainly confirmed my hunches regarding the mysticism of the work. Then I got engrossed with the solipsistic remarks of Wittgenstein—with which he concerned himself throughout his life—for my PhD dissertation under the able supervision of Professor James Hopkins, King's College London, United Kingdom (UK).

After a break of almost 20 years when I again started working on my dream project of Wittgenstein and Tagore personally, I received a fellowship from Indian Institute of Advanced Study (IIAS), Shimla. Initially, I had planned to investigate the religious points of views of both the thinkers, hence I looked into their journeys of life, that is, the journey from the religious to the spiritual. During that period, I had a most helpful and thought-inspiring discussion with Professor Nirmalangshu Mukherjee, University of Delhi, one day, who pointed out that instead of devoting my time and energy to an anthropological survey of their background, I should rather attempt to find out the similarities in their basic philosophical views.

That was the beginning of a journey. It was not easy, for the first difficulty was that Tagore was reluctant to be treated as a philosopher; whereas Wittgenstein was a highly acclaimed philosopher in the Frege-Russell tradition of analytic philosophy. A comparison between them would sound like a comparison between chalk and cheese!

The second difficulty was the dearth of secondary literature on this topic. I had traced only two papers on the Tagore–Wittgenstein concourse (Choudhary, 2006) (Chakrabarty, 2012). Of them, the latter was unpublished. I thank Professor Sitangshu Chakrabarti, erstwhile professor of philosophy at the University of Burdwan, West Bengal, for giving me his copy of the unpublished paper.

So my exploration began. I never would have expected that so many points of contact could exist between a poet and a philosopher! In fact, I venture to add that such important points of contact will help one to arrange the pieces of the Tractarian jigsaw puzzle in a manner where all the pieces of logic, language, world, and the mystical will fall into place and form a coherent picture.

Acknowledgements

On a personal note, I would like to express my gratitude to my elder sister, Suchismita Sarkar, an erudite Tagore scholar working in silence at Santiniketan, who had offered me a select bibliography on the philosophy of Tagore before I joined IIAS. Later also, it was due to her only that I had access to the Rabindra Bhavan library and various primary source materials from the Śāntiniketan archive.

I take this opportunity to offer my profound gratitude to my parents whose unfailing support, love, encouragement, and values made me what I am today.

Big thanks are due to Pratichi, my daughter, and her energetic and vibrant friends (Shruthi, Jyoti, Tanvi, and Rajeev from Jawaharlal Nehru University [JNU]) who made their occasional visits to Shimla and my visits to JNU most enjoyable during the fellowship period.

I am thankful to IIAS which contributed to the fruition of my long-cherished dream of writing on Wittgenstein and Tagore. I am thankful to Professor Peter Ronald De Souza and Professor Chetan Singh, the directors of IIAS during 2012–14, for their unflinching support and utmost care for a peaceful living at the institute. I am grateful to my fellow participants of the Thursday seminars for their demanding questions, criticisms, and, finally, animated discussions in coffee shops and the dining hall, which I found most inspiring.

Among the fellows, special thanks are due to Dr Amit Ranjan Basu, Professor Kunal Chakrabarti, Sumanta Banerjee, Professor Nirmalāngshu Mukherjee, Dr Alexandra Wenta, Dr Aruna Bommareddy, and Dr Amvalika Jacob for making my stay pleasant and satisfying at the institute. On this occasion, I would like to extend my blessings and thanks to Prachi Srivastava and Rupinder Singh for all the help and service extended to me during those years.

I would also like to thank all the staff members who supported me in all respects so that I could speculate on the philosophy of Tagore and Wittgenstein amidst the natural beautiful surroundings of the institute.

Additionally, I wish to thank Harish Pedaprolu, who finally helped me in copyediting and formatting the manuscript before submission.

Last but not least, thanks are due to my husband, Pradip Kumar Mahapatra, for being with me throughout the journey and helping me, often translating Tagore's songs for my project.

Finally, I am grateful to OUP, India, for their interest in bringing out this book.

Priyambada Sarkar
7 April 2020

Language, Limits, and Beyond

Introduction

It is a well-known fact that Wittgenstein, while resenting the questions asked by the members of the Vienna Circle, often turned his back on them and read the poems of Rabindranath Tagore. A few Wittgenstein scholars such as W.W. Bartley (1973), Ray Monk (1990), and Rudolf Haller (2003) have written about Wittgenstein's fascination for Tagore's poems and his special liking for some of his symbolic plays such as *The King of the Dark Chamber* (1914e). It is learnt from Ray Monk that Wittgenstein along with his student, Smythies, began translating this particular play in English as he thought that the original English translation[1] by Tagore was not capable of expressing the deeper religious significance of the play. But so far no one has explored the reasons for Wittgenstein's interest in Tagore's writing, nor has anybody ventured to find out the influence, if any, of the former on the latter, though many of them have given hints about Tagore's influence on his thought. In this monograph, there will be an attempt to bring out the parallels between Tagore's thinking and that of Wittgenstein with regard to his views on the threshold of language, its meaning, and beyond.

In pursuing this project, my method had been to draw from Wittgenstein's and Tagore's own statements about the ideas and experiences which drove their creative, philosophical, and religious lives. In Tagore's case, we find ample sources in his autobiography and reminiscences, apart from a huge number of his literary publications. Wittgenstein's case is different. Wittgenstein had only one book and an article published during his lifetime, although many of his books are being published posthumously by his students and literary executors. Wittgenstein's biographers have done a commendable job in bringing out the details of his early life, both personal and intellectual. Moreover, many personal correspondences, secret diaries, and notebooks of the philosopher are still being discovered these days. For me, these first hand materials were helpful in bringing out the similarities in their structure of thinking as far as the concept of limits of language is concerned.

In this endeavour, I have consciously avoided mentioning the various debates among learned literary critics on interpretations of Tagore's ideas as they, though vast, are not aimed in this direction. Additionally, they have the potential to take us away from our original motivation and lead us to a completely different terrain altogether. So, I have preferred to depend upon Tagore's own testaments and remarks.

The case is slightly more complicated in the case of Wittgenstein. The book *Tractatus Logico-Philosophicus* is famous for its most dense and cryptic remarks. Commentators differ even regarding the most fundamental question: How to read the book? Is it nonsense, pure and simple? Should we completely discard it after reading the book, as the author advised? Or does the book manifest the most fundamental truth of language and reality through its nonsensical propositions? It has been almost 30 years since Cora Diamond and James Conant offered their resolute interpretation of the *Tractatus* against the background of metaphysical interpretations (*The Realistic Spirit: Wittgenstein Philosophy and the Mind* [1991]). Since then, Wittgenstein scholarship hinges on two broad lines of interpretations: resolute and non-resolute. They also have many variations within their own groups. Of the resolutists, some are strong while others are mild. Some believes that the *Tractatus* does not illuminate metaphysical truths; rather they elucidate some interesting philosophical points. Similarly, there are variations and subgroups even among the metaphysical interpreters.

However, according to traditional metaphysical interpreters, the *Tractatus* has metaphysical commitments. Some interpret Wittgenstein as a committed realist, some as an anti-realist, some as a linguistic idealist, and some again as a solipsist in a special sense. Peter Hacker interprets *Tractatus* as containing utterances which, though nonsensical, are still illuminating. They do not belong to the category of utter nonsense as they illuminate the essential features of the world and of representation, of thoughts and self (Hacker 1986). Roger White interprets the book as advocating realism though he denies that nonsensical propositions of the book are illuminating (White 2006).

According to resolute interpretationists, Wittgenstein did not want to convey ineffable metaphysical truths via the nonsensical utterances of the *Tractatus*. Rather, his aim was to argue against such ineffable truths of metaphysics by showing that the propositions of the *Tractatus*, though they look like propositions of philosophical importance, are not really so. After reading the book, the reader ultimately realizes that the propositions of the *Tractatus* are simply nonsensical. This realization will ultimately act as therapy against the human urge to philosophize, that is, to explain things where there is no need to.

My interpretation of the *Tractatus* in this endeavour is not resolute as I feel resolute interpreters have not given due importance to what the author himself had suggested in his letters to Bertrand Russell and Ludwig Von Ficker. Wittgenstein candidly expressed himself by saying that the main thrust of the book is to distinguish between what can be said and what cannot (Monk 1990, 164). Again, at the same time, he passionately believed that 'what we cannot talk about is most important' (Engelmann 1967, 97).

Wittgenstein's remarks on the mystical, the contrast between saying and showing, and the inexpressible also raise questions for the resolute interpreters. For me, the non-resolute reading of the *Tractatus* seems to be more pertinent as the publication of private notebooks and diaries speak in favour of the view that war-time experience had a toll on the body and mind of young Ludwig. It prompted him to stress on the inexpressibility of deep questions on life and death, values, and God in scientific terms, and brought him closer to the thoughts of the sage-poet of India, Rabindranath Tagore.

Before one goes deep into the parallels between the ideas of these two great thinkers of their time, one must first answer the question: Why Wittgenstein and Tagore? The question is important because Wittgenstein is known to be a revolutionary philosopher of language who was originally a student of aeronautical engineering at the University of Manchester and also an illustrious student of Bertrand Russell and G.E. Moore in the field of mathematical logic and analytic philosophy; whereas Tagore was an artistic and literary genius who was reluctant to be referred to as a philosopher. However, the works of Tagore and Wittgenstein are generally considered to be of crucial importance within their respective fields, Tagore's in the field of literature and Wittgenstein's in philosophy.

Tagore was acclaimed as a 'poet of the world'[2] who wished to foster a philosophy of harmony in his innumerable writings, whereas the early Wittgenstein was a philosopher of language trying to sort out the relationship between thought, language, and reality. They are conventionally seen as having very different interests and are usually studied separately. The separation between the two thinkers has become even more pronounced due to the thinking that poets and philosophers are opposed to each other. As we often hear from poets that 'philosophy can clip an angel's wings' and that 'all charms fly at the cold touch of philosophy' (Naravane 1977a, 26).

So why should one be bothered to compare a philosopher with a poet? To answer this, one will have to go back to the time when Wittgenstein was thinking of publishing his manuscript of *Tractatus Logico-Philosophicus*.[3] He had sent the manuscript first to Gottlob Frege, his mentor, who advised Wittgenstein to study philosophy under Russell at Cambridge. Frege was not happy with the manuscript. He asked:

> After reading the preface one didn't really know what to make of the first proposition and wouldn't it be better to make clear to which problems the book was supposed to provide a definitive solution? (Monk 1990, 176)

Wittgenstein was thoroughly disappointed. He wrote a letter to Russell saying:

> He [Frege] does not understand a single word of my work and I am thoroughly exhausted from giving what are purely and simply explanations. (Monk 1990, 164)

Then, Russell comforted Wittgenstein by saying that he would write an introduction to his manuscript, which would facilitate Wittgenstein to find a publisher. Ludwig was happy at the beginning but when he looked through the introduction, he was completely disheartened. He wrote in a letter to Russell on 10 October 1919:

> There is so much of it that I am not in agreement with, both when you are critical of me and also where you are simply trying to elucidate my point of view. ... Now I'm afraid you haven't really got hold of my main contention to which the whole business of logical propositions is only corollary. The main point is the theory of what can be expressed (*gesagt*) by propositions, i.e. by language (and, which comes to the same thing, what can be thought) and what cannot be expressed by propositions, but only shown (*gezeigt*); which I believe is the *cardinal problem of philosophy*. (Monk 1990, 164; emphasis mine)

Logical positivists on the other hand regarded the *Tractatus* as petrifying their own rejection of metaphysical doctrines. Members of the Vienna Circle such as Friedrich Waismann, Rudolf Carnap, Herbert Feigl, and Moritz Schlick all believed that he had finally managed to nail down the coffin of traditional metaphysics and religion.

Wittgenstein was initially irritated with such gross misinterpretations. Then, in October 1919, he explained the 'point' of the book in a letter to his friend Ludwig Von Ficker. He stated:

> The book's point is an ethical one. I once meant to include in the preface of the book which is not in fact there now, but which I will write out for you here, because it will perhaps be a key to the work for you. My work consists of two parts: the one presented here plus all that I have not written. And it is precisely the second part that is the important one. ... I would recommend you to read the preface and the conclusion, because they contain the most direct expression of the point of the book. (Engelmann 1967, 143–4)

At the same time, the preface of the book tells us:

> The whole meaning of the book can be summed up in the following way: What can be said at all can be said clearly; and what we cannot talk about, we must pass over in silence.
> Thus, the aim of the book is to draw a limit to thought, or rather ... not to thought, but to the expressions; for in order to be able to draw a limit to thought, we should have to find both sides of the limit thinkable (i.e. we should have to be able to think what cannot be thought).

> It will therefore only be in language that the limit can be drawn, and what lies on the other side of the limit will simply be nonsense. (Wittgenstein 1922, 3)

In the conclusion, he repeated the same thing and stated:

> What we cannot talk about, we must pass over in silence. (Wittgenstein 1922, 74)

The preface and the conclusion of the book emphasize that the project is all about drawing the boundary of what can be sensibly thought. But that cannot be done, for in that case we have to embrace a contradiction, that is, to think the unthinkable. The only way out of this impasse, Wittgenstein thought, is to draw a limit to language, which in a way will draw a boundary to thought as well. It is possible to draw a limit to language by distinguishing sensible expressions in language from nonsensible ones.

Now, how does one distinguish sensible expressions in language from nonsensible ones? The question will be addressed properly in the ensuing chapters, but at the present moment it will be sufficient if one mentions that to Wittgenstein of the *Tractatus*, an expression is sensible if and only if it depicts or describes a particular state of affair of the world. From this it follows logically that expressions that are not descriptions of states-of-affair cannot be expressed in sensible language. Here, Wittgenstein's advice is that it is better not to talk about them but to pass them over in silence.

Herein lies the similarity between a poem and the *Tractatus*. In a poem, everything is not stated—one has to grasp or feel what is not stated by looking at what is stated. In fact, Wittgenstein in his letter to Ludwig Von Ficker declared,

> The work [*Tractatus Logico-Philosophicus*] is strictly philosophical and at the same time literary. (Engelmann 1967, 78)

In *Culture and Value*, one again finds him talking about literature when he said:

> I believe I summed up where I stand in relation to philosophy when I said 'Philosophy really ought only to be composed in the way in which a work of literature is'. (Wittgenstein 1980d, 28)

Not only that, he wanted to publish his work (*Tractatus Logico-Philosophicus*) in a literary journal called *Der Brenner* as he himself treated it as a literary work.

Poets often stress on the indirect meaning of words conveyed through the use of symbols, suggestions, and metaphoric meanings. They believe that most of the time the value of language lies in its being non-discursive. Similarly, in the *Tractatus* there are important things that cannot be stated in factual language, but the unstated items manifest themselves indirectly within what is stated. What links the *Tractatus* with other works of literature is the kind of demand that Wittgenstein places on readers that 'they respond to what is not there', that is, the inexpressible in discursive language.

It seems that if one gives importance to what Wittgenstein himself had said about the *Tractatus* and try to read it accordingly as a literary work, it might be possible for one to solve the major riddle of the book, that is how to harmonize the logical aspect of the *Tractatus* with the mystical and the ethical. And in this venture, understanding Tagore's views on language and creativity will be of much help to the readers.

However, before one moves on with the project of finding parallels between Wittgenstein's thinking and that of Tagore, one should explore the relationship of Tagore to the people of Germany in the 1920s. In 1913, Tagore was awarded the Nobel Prize for literature and by 1920 German translations of his writings were available.[4] Tagore had visited Germany quite a few times, but his visits in 1921, 1922, 1926, and 1930 are especially significant, because during this period he was literally swayed by the 'frenzied ovations' of the people of Germany. German intellectuals such as Rainer Maria Rilke, Albert Schweitzer, Thomas Mann, Stefan Zweig, Hozmann Hesse, and many others had dialogues with Tagore and they were moved by his intellectual quality along with the innermost spirituality of his thoughts. Not only intellectuals, Germany's common masses were also influenced by him to a large extent. To quote Martin Kämpchen,

The immense popular enthusiasm, the frenzied ovations, which built up to a Tagore-mania in 1921 resulting in the sale of one million copies of Tagore books by the end of 1923 are seen as a proof of the poet's tremendous appeal to the masses and the success of his mission of peace and understanding between the people of 'East' and 'West'. (Kämpchen 1991, 12)

In 1922, Tagore's 61st birthday was celebrated in Germany with much enthusiasm and ovation (Kämpchen 1991, 14). Engelhard presented a 450-page biography of the poet with unadulterated admiration and devotion. The publication of his collected works (in eight volumes) in 1922 by Kurt Wolff Verlag and its success give evidence of 'Tagore-mania' in Germany.

Against this background, one can well imagine why Wittgenstein had admired the poems of Tagore. And when he recited poems of Tagore to the members of the Vienna Circle, the reason does not seem to be casual or non-deliberate. Rather, I think Ray Monk seems to be right when he points out:

> [Wittgenstein endeavoured] to emphasize to them [members of the Vienna Circle], as he [Wittgenstein] earlier explained to Von Ficker, that what he had not said in the *Tractatus* was more important than what he had said. (Monk 1990, 131)

Wittgenstein perhaps thought that reading these poems could be an effective way of teaching them 'what one cannot speak of, one must pass over in silence'.

This is something that is constitutive of the most fundamental similarity between the poet and the philosopher in the midst of their legitimate differences. Both Tagore and Wittgenstein agreed to the fact that there are limits to rational thought and language. But none of them was ready to believe that these limits are the ultimate, those which no one can transgress. They believed that there is 'a beyond', that is inexpressible. And the distinction between what is expressible in sensible language (*vyakta*) and what is not (*avyakta*) formed the central focus of their respective philosophies.

In the first chapter, what I hope to show is that more sense can be made of Wittgenstein's controversial remarks about the distinction between the expressible (what can be said) and the inexpressible (what cannot be said, but be shown), if one juxtaposes them with the thoughts of Tagore.

Both Tagore and Wittgenstein wanted to stress the importance of what cannot be expressed in sensible language, regarding which one should remain silent. The second chapter will highlight the fact that both of them believed that there are limits to language, limits on what can be factually or scientifically articulated. For both, remaining 'silent' plays an important role in their respective discourses, although each has a unique approach to arriving at the same conclusion—Tagore through literature and Wittgenstein through logic.

There is another important factor in their congruence of beliefs: 'indirect communication'. Both of them rely on indirect methods of communication where straightforward communication is impossible. To elucidate, the domain of the inexpressible incorporates ethics, aesthetics, metaphysics, and religion. But one can somehow grasp them by the suggestiveness of language, by indirection, and by bending of meanings through poems, music, drawing, and painting. In fact, this parallel of methodology (that is, bending of meanings through poems and other forms of art instead of referring to direct meaning) shows that there are important connections between the poet and the philosopher, which is striking but overlooked in the history of secondary literature on Wittgenstein.

However, in the *Tractatus*, ethics, aesthetics, metaphysics, and religion come under the head of 'what cannot be spoken about' on the one hand and nonsensical (*unsinnig*) on the other. These propositions are nonsensical as they attempt to express something that cannot be expressed in sensible language. Here one might think that in this respect the *Tractatus* is in complete accordance with the views of logical positivists.

But Wittgenstein differed from logical positivists in his attitude to such nonsensical discourses. About these, he shared his feelings with his friend Ludwig Von Ficker. To quote from the letter:

I see now that these non-sensical expressions were not non-sensical because I had not yet found the correct expressions but that their non-sensicality was their very essence. For all I wanted to do with them was just to go beyond the world and that is to say, beyond significant language. But this is just impossible. My whole tendency and the tendency of all men who ever tried to write or talk ethics or religion was to run against the boundaries of language. This running against the walls of our cage is perfectly, absolutely hopeless. Ethics, so far as it springs from the desire to say something about the ultimate meaning of our life, the absolute good, the absolute valuable, can be no science. What it says does not add to our knowledge in any sense. But it is a document of a tendency in the human mind which I personally cannot help respecting deeply and I would not for my life ridicule it. (Wittgenstein 1965, 11–12)

Not only that, once Wittgenstein told his student, M.O.C. Drury:

> Don't think I despise metaphysics or ridicule it. On the contrary, I
> regard the great metaphysical writings of the past as among the noblest
> productions of human mind. (Drury 1967, 70)

Wittgenstein had a lifelong interest in all these things of which
one must be silent. *Notebooks 1914–1916* and the *Tractatus* contain
thoughts of a religious nature, and what is interesting at this point
is that he clubbed ethics, aesthetics, and religion together. It entails
what is religious is also ethical and aesthetical, and vice-versa. They
are all connected by being ineffable on the one hand and being connected with 'viewing the world from eternity' (sub specie aeternitatis)
on the other.

In the third chapter, the domain of the ineffable, the ethical and the
aesthetic will be dealt with. In this chapter, there will be an attempt to
establish that, to Wittgenstein, the discourse of ethics was extremely
important because it is 'the enquiry into the meaning of life', or
'into what makes life worth living', or 'into the right way of living'
(Wittgenstein 1965, 5). The chapter will deal with the problems of
ineffability along with nonsensicality of ethics in the *Tractatus*. There
will also be an attempt to interpret Wittgenstein's remarks on ethics
and aesthetics in the light of the poems of Tagore and find out how
such a characterization of ethics follows from the philosophy of both
Tagore and Wittgenstein separately.

In the fourth chapter, I treat 'the religious' within the domain of
the ineffable separately as, since the publication of *Nachlass*, much
has been written on the religious views and interests of Wittgenstein.
Reflection on the literature based on reminiscences, letters, anecdotes,
and remarks in coded diaries make it evident that Wittgenstein was
occupied with questions of a religious nature throughout his life. The
same is true of Tagore. Although not belonging to any particular creed,
he was out and out a spiritual person throughout his life. In this
chapter, there will be an attempt to explore how both Wittgenstein and
Tagore were not 'religious' in the traditional sense of the term, while
studying the journey of their lives. At the same time, I would like
to wade through textual remarks to discover how they 'couldn't help
seeing every problem from a religious point of view' (Drury 1984, 86).

It will be surprising to note that 'this religious point of view' for both of them incorporates ethical and aesthetical points of views.

In the fifth chapter, we will see the reflections of 'religious points of views' of both the thinkers condensed in a play entitled *The King of the Dark Chamber* by Rabindranath Tagore. Here juxtaposition of the content of *The King of the Dark Chamber*, the play by Tagore (which was Wittgenstein's favourite), with the cryptic passages on ethics and religion from *Notebooks 1914–1916*, *Tractatus Logico-Philosophicus*, and 'A Lecture on Ethics' will finally reveal that these passages make perfect sense together in light of the ideas contained in the play. And probably because of this, Wittgenstein was drawn so close to the play of the Indian mystical poet.

Finally, in the concluding chapter there will be an attempt to show that Wittgenstein looked well beyond the threshold of language and meaning in the *Tractatus* even at the cost of being paradoxically labelled as a transgressor of limits.

Notes

1. Apparently, the play was translated by a Bengali student, Kshitish Chandra Sen, though Macmillan had published it with the name of Tagore as the translator; Wittgenstein also thought that it was translated by Tagore. We will discuss this translation controversy in Chapter 5.
2. Brahmabandhab Upadhyāy referred to Rabindranath Tagore as 'world-poet of Bengal' in *Sophia*, a monthly catholic journal (which he edited during 16 June 1900–8 December 1900), on 1 September 1900 for the first time; thereafter this phrase has become quite common in the Indian subcontinent.
3. Hereafter, *Tractatus* will stand for *Tractatus Logico-Philosophicus*. And a paragraph/tract will be represented by the number with capital T (representing the *Tractatus*) at the beginning.
4. Many German translations of Rabindranath Tagore's works were published between 1913 and 1927.

1

Crossing the Threshold of Language
Early Wittgenstein and Rabindranath Tagore

Norman Malcolm (1958, 59) tells us and Ray Monk (1990, 412) confirms that Wittgenstein had read *Gitānjali* (*Song Offerings*) and *Rājā* (*The King of the Dark Chamber*); though it seems that Wittgenstein might have read much more of Tagore's works than these two books. But, so far, this has not been given the attention it deserves. What I hope to show in this chapter is that more sense can be made of Wittgenstein's controversial remarks about the distinction between saying and showing, which he thinks is 'the cardinal problem of philosophy'[1] (which also shows how human beings attempt to go beyond language), if one juxtaposes them with Tagore's thoughts regarding these matters. With this end in view, I have divided the chapter into three sections. In the first section, I give a brief exposition of Wittgenstein's distinction between saying and showing in the *Tractatus*, which will portray the limits of language and of thought on the one hand and the tendency of human beings to transcend those limits on the other. Then I will sketch out what Tagore has to say on these matters in the second section, and I will attempt to bring the two together in the concluding section.

Saying and Showing: *Notebooks 1914–1916* and the *Tractatus*

The distinction between saying and showing is fundamental to Wittgenstein's early philosophy and clarification of it is essential for any interpretation of *Notebooks 1914–1916* and the *Tractatus*. It is especially important as Wittgenstein has regarded ethics, religion, metaphysics, and various other branches of knowledge as inexpressible in sensible language, that is, they go beyond the limits of sensible discourse. He treats them as nonsensical. In fact, we need to understand now why Wittgenstein treats these discourses as inexpressible on the one hand and nonsensical on the other. What exactly does he mean by the terms 'inexpressible' and 'nonsensical'? In fact, during the period of the *Tractatus*, Wittgenstein held that there is a sharp distinction between what can be stated sensibly in language (*sinnvoll*) and what cannot (*sinnlos* and *unsinn*). If someone used a sentence meaningfully, he used it to picture a state of affairs, and this meant that there was a special kind of correlation between psychic elements in his mind, elements of language, and objects in the world. A sentence that in this way pictures a state of affairs would be true or false depending on whether the state of affairs actually obtained in the world or not (depending upon whether or not the sentence pictures a fact).

This idea of what had to be the case for a sentence to make sense also led to the view that many collections of words which might seem in one way or other to be sensible sentences, were not so. This was because they were not pictures or representations of states of affairs in this sense. According to Wittgenstein, these are pseudo-propositions (*Scheinsätze*) as they say nothing about the world. Among these pseudo-propositions, he identifies different kinds: *bedeutungsloss* (meaningless), *sinnlos* (senseless), and *unsinnig* (nonsense) in the following passages of the *Tractatus*:

> T3.328: If a sign is useless, then it is meaningless. That is the point of Occam's maxim (if everything behaves as if a sign had meaning, then it does have meaning).

This is an application of Occam's principle that entities should not be multiplied unnecessarily. Wittgenstein states:

> T5.47321: Occam's maxim is of course, not an arbitrary rule, nor one that is justified by its success in practice: its point is that unnecessary units in a sign language mean nothing.
>
> Signs that serve one purpose are logically equivalent, and signs that serve none are logically meaningless.

In another paragraph he gives an example:

> T5.4733: Thus the reason why 'Socrates is identical' says nothing is that we have not given *any adjectival* meaning to the word 'identical'. For when it appears as a sign for identity, it symbolises in an entirely different way.

Many commentators have interpreted this passage as an early indication of his emphasis on use as mostly determining the meaning of a word in his later years; though we can also interpret it as emphasizing on Occam's principles and treat *bedeutungslos* as some words which have no use in ordinary language. Now this might include a violation of syntax; that is, 'the table penholders the green' as being utter nonsense. One cannot extract any sense from such nonsensical combinations of words.

There are propositions of logic and propositions of mathematics that do not picture any situations of the world. To Wittgenstein, they are also senseless. This sort of senselessness is the direct consequence of the peculiarity of the theory of language and meaning of the *Tractatus*, which demands that a sensible proposition should have the possibility of being true or false. Having these two poles, that is, being true and being false, is integral to the sense of a proposition; whereas the propositions of logic lack this:

> T4.461: Tautologies and contradictions show that they say nothing.
> A tautology has no truth conditions, since it is unconditionally true: a contradiction is not true under any condition.
> Tautologies and contradictions lack sense.
> (For example I know nothing about the weather when I know that it is either raining or not raining).

Now, tautologies are true and contradictions are false in all possible worlds. So they lack the above-mentioned bi-polarity of sense. This is the same as the point that they do not represent any fact or situation as opposed to any other. Wittgenstein, however, remarks:

T4.4611: Tautologies and contradictions are not, however, non-sensical.

Tautologies and contradictions are not nonsensical, meaning they are not senseless combinations of words. They also are not attempts to express what is inexpressible. They lack sense because they do not picture anything.

But they are not unimportant. They are part of the symbolism, much as '0' is part of the symbolism of arithmetic (T4.4611). Although they do not say anything, they show, and showing is important. Wittgenstein says:

T4.1212: What can be shown cannot be said.

This distinction is very important in Wittgenstein's writings (not only in the *Tractatus*, but also in his later writings) as confusion of this distinction causes 'misunderstanding of the logic of our language' (Wittgenstein 1972 [1921], 3). In the *Tractatus*, he stated that proper understanding of the logic of our language demands that philosophers should be apprised of the distinction between what can be said in a language and what cannot; otherwise it will generate philosophical puzzles.

Now what are the things that tautologies or contradictions show? What does a contradiction 'p.not-p' show? It shows something about the rules that reflect logical form, that is what a proposition must have in common with reality if it intends to represent a fact.

The distinction between 'sayability' and 'unsayability' thus is quite peculiar to the *Tractatus* itself. In the *Tractatus*, language is synonymous with descriptive language (that is, any proposition that depicts, represents, or describes possible situations of the world is a sensible proposition).Thus, the totality of true propositions is the whole of natural science. So, what can be said is identified with the propositions of natural science or empirical propositions (T4.11).

But what are the characteristic features of the propositions of ethics, aesthetics, religion, metaphysics, and even those of the *Tractatus* itself? These are all, according to the *Tractatus*, nonsensical, but their nonsensicality is different from that of the propositions of logic in

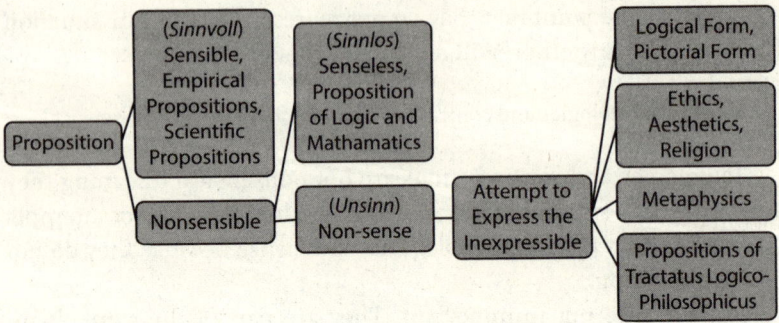

Figure 1.1   Distinction between Sensible and Nonsensible Propositions
Source: Author.

the sense that the former attempts to say something that is unsayable whereas the latter do not. Here, to elucidate the distinction, I have drawn the above diagram after the *Tractatus*.

The nature and criteria of sensible sentences in accordance with the ideas of early Wittgenstein has already been discussed earlier, and the senselessness of logical and mathematical propositions, under the head 'sinnlos' in the diagram, has also been dealt with in the previous paragraph.

Now we will turn to various things that fall under the heading 'attempt to express the inexpressible'.[2] Here, listing the items which are unsayable but show themselves is necessary, as this will make the discussions of nonsense, as an attempt to say the unsayable, more precise.

1. Logical Form, Pictorial Form
2. Causal Propositions and the Laws of Science
3. Ethics, Aesthetics, and Religious Experience
4. Metaphysics
5. The Propositions of the *Tractatus*.

Logical Form, Pictorial Form

T4.121: Propositions cannot represent logical form: it is mirrored in them. What finds its reflection in language, language cannot represent. What expresses *itself* in language, *we* cannot express by means of language.

Now what is logical form? Logical form is what a proposition must have in common with reality in order to be able to represent it. We cannot represent this logical form.

Pictorial form is an instance of logical form. Logical form is the minimum similarity or commonness and pictorial form is the maximum similarity or commonness existing between the picture and the pictured. Wittgenstein uses these two notions together in using the term logico-pictorial form. He says:

> T2.2: A picture has logico-pictorial form in common with what it depicts.

Why are logical and pictorial forms not picturable? Picturing or representing, according to the *Tractatus*, is a two-termed relation. It holds between two complexes when they are related in a certain way, that is, when one is projected onto, or used as a projection of the other.

But given this account of picturing, only a fact-complex can be pictured. One proposition-complex can be a picture of a fact-complex. The picturing relation between complexes cannot be pictured. One complex can be a picture of another if it is related to it by a rule of projection. But this does not allow a rule of projection to be pictured. A rule of projection is neither a complex proposition nor a complex fact. So it cannot be related to a complex by another law or rule of projection. So no complex can be a picture of a law of projection or of a relation that two complexes must have if one is to picture the other.

The Tractarian account of picturing therefore leads immediately to the idea that the picturing relation itself cannot be described.

Causal Propositions and the Laws of Science

> T6.36: If there were a law of causality, it might be put in the following way: There are laws of nature. But of course that cannot be said: It makes itself manifest.

Here, Wittgenstein is saying that the idea of a law of causality is the idea that there are natural laws. The contents of the causality statements are to be understood in terms of natural laws, that A causes

B entails that there are laws of which that transition is an instance. Again he says:

> T5.1361: We cannot infer the events of the future from those of the present. Superstition is nothing but belief in the causal nexus.
> T6.37: There is no compulsion making one thing happen because another has happened. The only necessity that exists is logical necessity.

What he suggests here is that it may be a general law that A-type event can cause B-type events. But it is a superstition to think that it is logically necessary that if A-type event occurs, then B-type event *must* occur. Wittgenstein distinguishes sharply between logic and matters of fact. In logic, everything is necessary and the laws of logic do have logical necessity, whereas, outside logic, there are empirical statements that are utterly contingent. But the law of causality is neither logically necessary nor like ordinary contingent statements. So to explain it, he says that it is the form of a law.

> T6.32: The law of causality is not a law but the form of a law.

By the form of a law he probably suggests that it does not tell us anything about the world. Nor is it a tautology, that is, a proposition of logic. What this means becomes clear in T6.34.

> T6.34: All such propositions, including the principle of sufficient reason, the laws of continuity in nature and of least effort in nature, etc. etc.—all these are a-priori insights about the forms in which the propositions of science can be cast.

Wittgenstein's idea is that someone who puts forward the law of causality is expressing an a priori insight about our mode of representation of the world. This, again, is not a picture of a fact. If it were to be a picture, it could only be a picture as to how language may picture the world. And, as we have seen, this sort of thing does not count as a picture in the *Tractatus* sense.

Ethics, Aesthetics (T6.421), and Religious Experience (T6.45)

> T6.421: It is clear that ethics cannot be put into words. Ethics is transcendental (Ethics and Aesthetics are one and the same).

T6.42: So too it is impossible for there to be propositions of Ethics. Propositions can express nothing that is higher.

But why cannot ethics be put into words? According to the *Tractatus*, what can be put into words are only the factual propositions of natural science. The task of language is, according to the *Tractatus*, to describe only this factuality and all propositions are, in a sense, descriptions of 'this is how things stand' (T6.432).

The propositions of ethics are not factual statements by any means. They are concerned with values. Hume and Wittgenstein agree in this respect: both deny that moral utterances are propositions. But Hume accounts for them in terms of sentiments. Wittgenstein does not seem to be doing that. He seems to suggest that moral utterances seek to refer to something that is not within the world of natural science.

At this point one feels like asking: If it is really impossible for there to be propositions of ethics, then what about the status of our moral science, ethics, as a branch of philosophy that can be put into words? What does 'higher' signify in this context?

These two important questions will be dealt with in the third chapter of this book, 'The Domain of the Ineffable: The Ethical and the Aesthetic', taking his lecture on Ethics into account.

Generally, both ordinary people and philosophers attach the notion of right conduct to ethics. Wittgenstein is also not an exception. He says:

T6.422: When an ethical law of the form 'thou shalt' ... is laid down, one's first thought is 'and what if I don't do it'? There must indeed be some kind of ethical reward and ethical punishment. But they must reside in the action itself.

Although Wittgenstein referred to ethical conduct in this passage, still it seems that he conceived the true centre of ethical interest lying in the investigations of 'the meaning of life' or 'the sense of the world'. As to the sense of the world, Wittgenstein says 'The sense of the world must lie outside the world' (T6.41). Answers to the questions concerning the sense of the world must necessarily take us beyond the world (that is, all that is the case).

In consonance with saying that no value exists in the world, he says:

T6.41: If there is any value that does have value, it must lie outside the whole sphere of what happens and is the case. For all that happens and is the case is accidental.

> What makes it non-accidental cannot lie within the world, since if it did, it would itself be accidental.
> It must lie outside the world.

Again in T6.43 he goes on to say:

> Here what is obvious is the fact that good will or bad will affects the world, the whole world, not a part of it. Hence it does not say anything about any event of the world, if the good or bad exercise of the will does alter the world, it can alter only at the limits of the world and not the facts—not what can be expressed in language.
> In short, the effect must be that it becomes an altogether different world. It must, so to speak, wax and wane as a whole.

Now changing the unhappy world into a happy one is something that cannot be pictured, hence it lacks *sense* from the perspective of the *Tractatus*. We could say that on Wittgenstein's idea of sense, the sense of anything must lie outside itself. This may not reflect what he means here, but in any case we can see that the sense of life or the world will be something that cannot be pictured. All that can be pictured are actual or possible states of affairs, the sorts of things that make up the world, nothing beyond the world can be pictured. So language cannot be used with sense in ethics. But what about the discourses on aesthetics and religious experiences? Wittgenstein says that ethics and aesthetics are one and the same, and about religion or religious experience he also says that he will call something as genuinely good which is divine. Now, how the characterization of ethics will apply equally well to aesthetics and religious experiences will be considered in Chapters 3 and 4.

Metaphysics

> T4.003: Most of the propositions and questions to be found in philosophical works are not false but non-sensical. Consequently, we cannot give any answer to questions of this kind, but can only establish that they were non-sensical. Most of the propositions and questions of philosophers arise from our failure to understand the logic of our language.

Hence, we find Wittgenstein treating earlier philosophies as full of nonsensicalities generated out of the confusions of the use of words in the language. Generally, what we do in our ordinary life is that we use the same sign in different ways to signify different things.

Sometimes we use the same sign for different symbols. Thus, a lot of confusions arise from such misuses of language.

T3.324: In this way the most fundamental confusions are easily produced (the whole of philosophy is full of them).

As a metaphysical position, Wittgenstein discusses solipsism and shows how the solipsists confuse grammatical statements with experiential statements and come up with the entirely false view that 'I and my ideas alone exist'. But what they mean (that is, that the world is my world), although nonsensical, still serves to show something—the coincidence of limits of 'the world' and 'my world'. Wittgenstein says:

T5.62: For what the solipsists mean is quite correct: Only it cannot be said, but makes itself manifest. The world is my world: This is manifest in that the limits of language (the only language that I understand) mean the limits of my world.

It is obvious that this cannot be sensibly put into words as it is neither a fact nor an event to be pictured, yet it manifests itself in the coincidence of the limits of language (the only language that I understand) and the limits of the world. In our classification of sense and nonsense, it falls under the broad category of 'nonsensible' as they (solipsists) say nothing about the world. And then it falls under the head 'attempts to say the unsayable' as the truth of solipsism lies in the coincidence of the limits of 'the world' with those of 'my world', which is inexpressible in sensible language. Still one is attempting to express it in language and thus committing oneself to nonsensicalities.

Propositions of the *Tractatus*

T6.54: My propositions serve as elucidations in the following way: Anyone who understands me eventually recognises them as non-sensical, when he has used them—as steps—to climb up beyond them. (He must, so to speak, throw away the ladder after he has climbed up it.)

He must transcend these propositions, and then he will see the world aright.

This passage is extremely difficult and it invites several opposite interpretations that condemn Wittgenstein's position in the *Tractatus* as self-defeating. Here, I will discuss some interpretations. Rudolf Carnap says:

In the first place, he seems to be inconsistent in what he does. He tells us that one cannot state philosophical propositions and that whereof one cannot speak, one must be silent; and then instead of keeping silent, he writes a whole philosophical book. (Carnap 1935, 37–8)

G. Pitcher, in his book, says:

In the course of the *Tractatus*, he has said certain things about the relationship about propositions and situations, that one is a logical picture of the other, that they have the same structure, and so on. We understand these doctrines, we weigh their merits and demerits, and no doubt, take a stand on them, either accepting or rejecting them. But at the end we are told that they are all non-sense, and that such doctrines cannot be stated. That they merely try to say something that can only be shown and that cannot be said. This evaluation cannot be accepted; Wittgenstein has said these things and therefore they can be said. What is non-sensical is to deny that what has been said can be said. (Pitcher 1964, 155)

Frank Ramsey also meant the same when he said:

What we cannot say, we cannot say, we can't whistle it either. (Ramsey 1931, 238)

All these remarks, I think, are the results of the misunderstanding of the use of the term 'nonsense' and the doctrine of 'saying and showing'. The propositions of the *Tractatus* fall under the head of 'an attempt to express the inexpressible', hence they are nonsensical. And it is not the case that Wittgenstein never realizes this position. In fact, because of this, he says that these propositions of the *Tractatus* are nonsensical.

Moreover, this position is not self-defeating. Wittgenstein's task in the *Tractatus* is to show the distinction between what can be said and what cannot be said. In order to show how he accomplishes this and how it is connected with the discussion of T6.54 and T7, one will have to discuss some other passages that hint at the aim of the book.

In the preface, one sees him eliciting his intentions: 'the aim of the book is to set a limit to thought ... and what lies on the other side of the limit is non-sense'. But it is logically impossible since to draw a boundary on thought would be to lead one to think the unthinkable.[3] Hence, the only way that one can signify what cannot be said, Wittgenstein recommends, is by presenting clearly what can be said (T4.115). For early Wittgenstein, 'The correct method in philosophy will really be the following: To say nothing except what can be said, i.e., that is natural science' (T6.53). On the other hand, 'A philosophical work consists essentially of elucidations. Philosophy does not result in "philosophical propositions" but rather in the clarification of propositions' (T4.112). Hence, the *Tractatus* fits the bill of a philosophical text as he concludes the book by saying:

> T6.54: My propositions serve as elucidations in the following way: Anyone who understands me eventually recognises them as non-sensical.

Thus, the propositions of the *Tractatus* did not really say anything that is unsayable.

Rather the work elucidates some important things which manifest themselves. While clarifying what he means by elucidations, he remarks:

> T3.263: Elucidations are propositions that contain the primitive signs. So they can only be understood if the meanings of those signs are already known.

It implies that if philosophy is the activity of elucidating, then it must clarify and illuminate something that is already known, or that which is already there, but unclarified. Hence, for early Wittgenstein, philosophy is the activity of making such things as the logical form of language, thought, and the world, the coincidence of their limits, and so on more clearly manifest. In attempting to make things manifest, they are not stating or picturing anything about the world; hence in the strict sense of the term 'proposition', they are not propositions at all. They lack sense as they say nothing about the world. But they also have a positive point. Unlike the propositions of metaphysicians, they are not generated out of the confusion of the logic of our language. They have a point precisely in that they show how these confusions arise and how they can be avoided. Hence, we can say that the *Tractatus* has gotten a hold of the language–world relation in the right way, that is, it is there, but it cannot be pictured. It will succeed if the reader gets it and so sees that Wittgenstein's sentences are meaningless. Although he held that there are no significant philosophical propositions in the sense that philosophy is not a body of doctrines; he nevertheless thought that philosophy is an important and useful activity (T4.112). He said that it can, in effect, clarify thoughts logically and it can show that problems arise from our failure to understand 'the logic of our language' (Preface, 3; T4.003).

So what the philosophy of the *Tractatus* tries to do is to put an end to confused philosophical talk. Since the *Tractatus* shows that metaphysical propositions are all nonsense, that is, they represent nothing in the world, it becomes useless once it serves its purpose. Then it must be thrown aside like a ladder.

Thus, the concluding remark of the *Tractatus* does not contradict itself. Rather, T6.54 is a natural conclusion of the whole book. The reader must transcend the propositions of the book, only then he will see the world aright. The implication is that he did not see the world aright before climbing those steps (before reading the *Tractatus*). So he gains something important, he sees the world rightly—the boundary between what can be said and what cannot be said has become clear to him.

The book, as proposed in the preface, seems to have been able to draw a limit to thought, or rather to its expressions, that is, to the language, and thus showed that what lies on the other side of the limit is simply nonsense. This distinction between sense and nonsense in the realm of language corresponds well with the important distinction between saying and showing in the *Tractatus*. What is within the limit, that is, what is sensible, is sayable, and what lies on the other side of the limit, what is beyond the domain of the sensible, that is, the nonsensible, is that which is showable. It shows itself. Here an important question might arise regarding the nature of the distinction between sensible and nonsensible, between saying and showing. Is the distinction sensible or nonsensible? Is the distinction sayable or showable? From the point of view of the *Tractatus*, this distinction falls into the domain of the nonsensible and showable. Here, one cannot draw the boundary sensibly as the distinction peeps beyond the boundedness of language.

From the above discussion, it follows that, in the *Tractatus*, Wittgenstein distinguished clearly between the domain of the necessary and the domain of the contingent, the domain of the significant and that of the insignificant. The world as a totality of facts is contingent and devoid of value or significance; but logic and ethics as 'the conditions of the world' belong to the domain of necessity and significance. Yet the two domains are not mutually exclusive, they are linked by the doctrine of showing. The facts of the world reveal the logic and value of the world. Herein lies the fundamental importance of the doctrine of showing.

This distinction, one might argue, carries the basic philosophy of the *Tractatus*, which actually is the journey from the form to the formless. To elucidate, one can point out that the notion of form plays a very crucial role in the *Tractatus*. Young Wittgenstein was convinced about the infallibility of a priori knowledge and believed that the world has a priori forms and so does language and thought. Communication is possible only because of the coincidence of these forms. In order to elucidate how these forms coincide, Wittgenstein says that their limits merge. The limits of the world coincides with the limits of language, the limits of language with those of logic, the limits of logic with those of thinking, which finally coincide with the limits of the self. Now these limits cannot be *in* the world, hence they cannot be described or pictured. They are the boundaries, hence, in a sense, they are formless. Whatever is *in* the world has some form or other. While discussing how a proposition pictures a state of affairs, Wittgenstein talked about logical form, pictorial form, and representational form.

These forms are important for the sensible representation of facts, but they themselves cannot be represented in terms of facts. Outside the domain of facts, there lies a huge corpus of discourses (which include ethics, aesthetics, religion, metaphysics, and, above all, the *Tractatus*) that our sensible languages cannot express. This is why Wittgenstein thinks that values such as truth, beauty, and goodness are supernatural, that is, they cannot be described in terms of facts, which are considered to be natural. But then how can one become aware of these values? To Wittgenstein, the answer is simple. One can be aware of them because they manifest themselves. They are manifest in the structure and the limits of the world, which are formless.

Hence the journey for Wittgenstein in the *Tractatus* was, one can say, from the form to the formless. In fact, the limits of language, thought, and reality are, so to speak, formless—at which the forms can only hint. What is most important here is to see that the formless is manifest in the form. Facts, in order to be represented as facts, in order to depict the reality, must possess pictorial form and logical form. But these forms do not depict or picture the world; hence they fail to be facts themselves. But their importance lies in the fact that they manifest the formless, the limits of the world and those of language. Hence, we can conclude that according to the philosophy of the *Tractatus*, the formless is valuable and is manifest in the forms but it cannot be uttered or expressed in ordinary, sensible language. It is, thus, inexpressible. Facts are contingent and, in a sense, valueless as values are beyond the world of facts; yet our factual world, though valueless from the point of view of the *Tractatus*, can be value laden when seen from an ethical/aesthetical point of view, and also can be shown through the facts. These points will be discussed extensively in subsequent chapters.

One important point to note over here is that under the head of the inexpressible, we have on the one hand the logical aspect of the *Tractatus*, that is, logical form, pictorial form, the form of a law, and the form of the world, and on the other hand ethics, aesthetics, religion, and metaphysics, which Wittgenstein simply refers to as 'the mystical'. This creates problems for the interpreters: they feel puzzled as to why a treatise on the philosophy of logic should contain remarks on *Das Mystische* (the translation of which, as the author preferred, is 'the mystical') and also how to reconcile the logical and the mystical part of the *Tractatus*? This problem has often been regarded as 'the riddle of the *Tractatus*'. Here, I would like to claim that if one treats the *Tractatus* as a literary work and juxtaposes it with the works of Tagore, the riddle can be solved.

In the next section, the philosophy of Tagore will be sketched with special reference to the notion of expressibility versus inexpressibility of language.

Saying and Showing in Works of Rabindranath Tagore

In this section, I concentrate on Tagore's famous distinction between fact *and* truth in ontology on the one hand and its corresponding distinction between science *and* Art in epistemology on the other (Art with capital 'A' broadly includes literature, painting, drawing, sculpture, music, and dance, that is, all art forms as well as aesthetics, religion, and ethics). These distinctions, we will see later, will come closer to the Tractarian distinction between saying and showing and cast new light on the philosophy of manifestation of the formless in form. With this end in view, I would like to divide the section into two subsections:

1. Fact and Truth
2. Science and Art.

Fact and Truth

The distinction between fact and truth is fundamental to the philosophy of Tagore as it finally paves the path of his celebrated distinction between science and Art, between 'construction and creation'.

Now, what is a fact? Tagore defines a fact as

the characterisation of whatever exists, in the manner it exists.[4]

To state it clearly in Wittgensteinian terminology, a fact is the existence of state of affairs (T1.13, that is, a fact is an existent state of affairs). If the state of affair is of the form 'S is P' [that is, S has the characteristics P], the fact will be S is P and that S exists. From this definition it follows that a fact is something which is objective and impersonal. When we are talking about the fact that S is P, we are not talking about one's thinking or feelings for 'S' or 'P'. Thus, a fact being objective and impersonal becomes the base of our scientific discourse and inter-subjective communication.

Now it is very easy to verify or examine a picture or an object of art by reference to facts. What one will have to do is just find out whether it agrees with the state of affairs or not. If it does, it is true, if not, it is false. Tagore explains it with the example of a horse. It is not difficult to prove whether the picture of a horse is exact or not. As far as facts are concerned, there are very many points that one can compare with the picture and find out if it satisfies all the criteria or not. This again goes well with the view of the *Tractatus*. I quote:

> T2.201: A picture depicts reality by representing a possibility of existence and non-existence of states of affairs
> T2.21: A picture agrees with reality or fails to agree; it is correct or incorrect, true or false.
> T2.223: In order to tell whether a picture is true or false we must compare it with reality.

So far, the above discussion shows that there are close affinities in the views of early Wittgenstein and Rabindranath Tagore as far as facts are concerned.

Here, one might object by saying that:

> The suggested affinity between Tagore and Wittgenstein on the notion of facts can set off with the required significance in the background that both of them are realists, both of them seem to endorse a correspondence bsetween pictures, propositions and reality as scientifically determinable. This common admission will be significantly opposed to philosophers of the Idealist genre. While some idealists would refute mind-independent fact, others (Hegel) would also emphasise that any such purported fact is already invaded by the whole. Such theories will make the logical atoms, their recursion in various combinations to forge atomic facts, notionally impossible, thus leading on to a falsification of analysis. As we know, this trend was taken up in different ways by Quine and later Wittgenstein himself. Now while one can safely categorise early Wittgenstein as a Realist, and Atomist, it is difficult to put Tagore under the standard philosophical brands of Realist or Idealist, Atomist or Holist.[5]

In order to answer this objection, I feel, one should have to be more careful about labelling these two thinkers as either a realist or an idealist in a straightjacketed format, respectively. It is customary to regard Tagore as an idealist and Wittgenstein as a realist, though it will be seen in a moment that none of them could be titled as such. Tagore, in his 'Kavyer Gadyariti' in *Rupam*, 1924 (cited in Naravane 1977b, 34), clearly states:

> Realism and idealism in the East do not have the same import as they have in the West. Realism in India is not absolute but comparative, as if it were a 'realism of idealism'.

Tagore does not think that realism and idealism are mutually exclusive. And his 'realism of idealism' ceases to appear paradoxical when we see it from two different perspectives. For Tagore, the world of facts constituting the domain of science and everyday life is not unreal or *māyā*. Nor would he prefer to call this domain as absolutely 'real' or 'true', as he considers 'fact' an abstraction, which makes it separate from the whole, the reality. His view is idealistic in the sense that he does not limit 'truth', the domain of which comprises that of beauty and goodness, to the realm of objectively verifiable reality. It is realistic to the extent that he regards facts as necessary and useful for our inter-subjective communication in everyday life.

Coming to Wittgenstein, one can ask: In what sense and to what extent is Wittgenstein a realist? I suggest that Wittgenstein's early works are uniquely characterized by a commitment to the structure of the world as derived from the analysis of the logic of our language. According to prevailing opinion, the *Tractatus* can be regarded as a prototypical realist theory.[6] But a careful analysis will show that Tractarian ontology is intended as a description of the structure of reality that is presupposed by language and thought. A most pertinent analysis of the realism/idealism controversy regarding the *Tractatus* comes from Stockhof, who maintains,

> Starting from an a priori fixed set of logical principles Wittgenstein undertakes a search for the conditions of any meaningful language to be possible. His aim was to provide us with a completely general characterization of its possibility. The picture theory of meaning is his answer and this theory contains as one of its essential elements a theory about the logical structure of reality, the totality of objects is the limit of the logical analysis of sentences, that is, a logical construction that shows how meaning is possible. So in whatever sense objects can be said to exist, it is in a different way than ordinary things and ordinary situations. That is why we neither have knowledge of objects, nor are able to state their identity criteria. As the ontology is tied to language, the question of realism as such need not arise. The world and the way it is built up, as it is described in 1–2.063, is the world as language and thought present it. It is the world in so far as we can know it and talk about it scientifically. (2002, 246)

The similarity with Tagore lies exactly here as the term *tothyo* denotes scientific and objective facts of the world in so far as we can know it.

But the notion of truth as Tagore explains in his writings appears to be far away from the views of Ludwig Wittgenstein. For Tagore, truth goes beyond the domain of facts in the sense that it is personal and subjective. His point of view will be clear if I quote an incident of his life from his writings:

> I had a servant whose looks or intelligence were hardly worthy of notice. He would go home at night, return the next morning and go about his chores with a dusting cloth on his shoulder. His major virtue was that he did not talk too much. I registered the fact of his presence on the day he did not turn up. That morning I found the water had not been drawn for my bath, the rooms had not been swept. He showed up around 10 in the morning. I asked in a rather brusque voice 'Where were you all the time?' He said 'My daughter died last night.' And he promptly picked up the dusting cloth and went quietly to work. My heart stopped for a moment. The veil of necessity that had covered the servant was lifted, revealing a father. Myself discovered its likeness with his. He became a perceptible presence, something distinctive. ... That day at the touch of the rasa of compassion that rustic man was united with the self that dwells in my heart: beyond the bounds of need, on the plane of imagination, Momin Mia became real for me. (Tagore 2001, 306–7)

What did Tagore mean by 'real for me'? 'Real for me' seems to mean that Momin Mia became personally related to Tagore's inner self by the touch of the *rasa* of compassion and, thus, become 'real' for him. Tagore elucidates,

> Where there is beauty in flowers, sweetness in fruits, where there is compassion for other living beings, where there is a feeling of surrendering oneself to the '*bhūmā*', we feel ourselves as being in an eternal personal relation with the universe. We call it 'real', as in reality truth is personal. (2001, 298)

Tagore treated the Ultimate Truth as 'the Truth of relationship, the Truth of harmony in the Universe, the fundamental principle of creation' (Tagore 1931c, 100). I will come back to this point again in Chapter 3. It will be sufficient for the present context if I suggest that Tagore equated this Truth with some 'inner value which is not in the extension in space and duration in time' (Tagore 1931c, 29), and this eludes factual representation. To elucidate, facts must be devoid of personal attachments, otherwise they cannot achieve objectivity in knowledge, but that also makes a fact an abstraction, makes it separate from the whole, the reality. Here one might object: facts are spatio-temporal and spatio-temporality is the characteristic feature of concrete things. Hence, how could we treat facts as abstract? This is alright but the sense in which Tagore uses the word 'abstract' is quite different. This abstraction for Tagore is, however, not an 'abstraction of events' as used commonly for 'facts'. Rather, the way a scientist focuses on pragmatic, impersonal, and objective aspects of an object (fact), disregarding other aspects, is the way that contributes, for Tagore, to its abstract nature. 'Abstraction' here connotes abstraction from its entirety, from its truth.

Regarding truth, Tagore thinks that it can be grasped only when one leaves the domain of facts, which is limited within the bounds of space–time and objectivity. Truth transcends those limits. He makes this distinction between fact and truth/reality clear in *The Religion of Man*.

> In the region of Nature by unlocking the secret doors of workshop department, one may come to that dark hall where the mechanics dwells and help to attain usefulness, but through it one can never attain finality. Here is the storehouse of innumerable facts and how-ever necessary they may be, they have not the treasure of fulfilment in them. But the hall of union is there, where dwells the lover in the heart of existence. When a man reaches it, he at once realizes that he has come to truth, to immortality, and he is glad with a gladness which is an end and yet which has no end. (Tagore 1931c, 106– 7)

Facts are necessary, facts are useful for our everyday life, but they cannot reach the truth, the eternal, which is also the personal. Tagore says:

> We must know that the evolution process of the world has made its progress towards revelation of its *truth*, that is to say some *inner value* which is not in the extension in space and duration in time. (1931c, 29)

It is clear that facts cannot grasp the realm of inner values, the realm of truth. Tagore while distinguishing between fact and truth has referred to Keats's famous poem 'Ode on a Grecian Urn' and quotes:

> Thou, silent form, dost tease us
> Out of thought, as doth eternity. (Keats 1919, 17)

Tagore explains it in his own words:

> When Keats said [this] in his Ode to a Grecian Urn ... he felt the ineffable which is in all forms of perfection, the mystery of the One, which takes us beyond all thought into the immediate touch of the Infinite. This is the mystery which is for a poet to realize and to reveal. (Tagore 1922, 14–15)

Thus, for Tagore, it is the ideal of perfect harmony pervading the outer as well as the inner world that a poet wants to realize and to reveal. For him, the Supreme One resides in our own inner selves. When He wants to create, wants to have pleasure out of creation, He manifests his oneness in the outside world through literature, paintings, drawings, songs, sculptures, and so on. Then there is the union of our own inner world with the outside world.

To elucidate the ideal of harmony, one can take an example of a rose. One feels happy when one sees a rose; one sees the beauty of harmony in colour, smell, and contour, that is, in the form of a flower. His inner self whom he terms as One, treats the rose as His own relative and, thus, the rose becomes valuable. It does not require any other value. The unity which we find residing in the colour, smell, and petals of a rose is the same unity that resides in the inner core of the world. The music of the world finds affinity with the tune of the rose. Thus, the inner One realizes Oneself in the unity of the outside world and this is called *ānandarūpa*, which I would like to translate as 'joy in itself'. Here one might ask: Why did Tagore call the harmony of the inner and the outer world joy in itself? And the answer might come from the teachings of the Upaniṣad, to which Tagore often used to refer. I quote:

> In our country the Supreme Being has been defined as *saccidānanda* (one who combines in his self being, consciousness and joy). *Ānanda* or joy is the last of the three terms, and there is no utterance beyond it. (2001, 264)

When the rose expresses truth, it expresses the infinite in finite and since the truth about expression inheres in joy, it becomes joy in itself, becomes beautiful, valuable, and, at the same time, a source of special delight.

He contrasts this *ānandarūpa* of a rose with the delight of a miser who in his aspirations to make more money strikes the unity or oneness of the world. Definitely, whatever a miser thinks and does is unified by one single thought, which is, of making money, but that unitary thought is narrow and cannot cover the unification of the whole world. A rich person distinguishes himself from the rest of the world as a wealthy being; but the unity of a rose, of a piece of art, a poem, is consistent with the unity of the world. They are the messengers of the One, the infinite and the eternal. Tagore says that Keats in his poem has spoken to us about this unity of the Grecian Urn with the whole world. This is the truth which is beautiful as well. Whenever one feels unity of the inner with the outer, one expresses truth and finally we get pleasure (*ānanda*) out of it.

Now this truth, which is beautiful, valuable, and joy in itself, has to be freed from the shackles of facts. When an artist draws pictures, he does not want to give us information. He takes as much or as little information as needed in creating the pure harmony of an Art object. Like the rose, an object of Art also displays a unity, and through this unity we get the pleasure of truth (*satyer ānanda*). That means if that object, say, for example, the picture or sculpture of a horse, possesses the beauty of the harmony of colour, painting, drawing, and music (*rūpa-rekha-gīter-susamājukta-oikya*), then one's heart recognizes it as real or true. If it fails to give accurate information, it does not really matter for the artist. But if it does not have this harmony of colour, painting, drawing, and music, then, however accurately it gives information about the object, it will be rejected by an artist as it fails to capture the truth. 'If the Formless, the Truth of rasa, is to manifest itself in the domain of form; it will have to be liberated from the dominion of facts'(Tagore 1980, 389; translation mine).

Now one can distinguish between fact and truth after Tagore as given in Table 1.1.

Table 1.1 Contrasting Paradigms of 'Facts' and 'Truth'

Facts	Truth
a. Abstract	a. Concrete
b. Impersonal	b. Personal
c. Objective	c. Subjective
d. Unrelated, not a harmonious whole	d. Harmonious whole
e. Incomplete	e. Complete
f. Relative	f. Absolute
g. Facts are determined by necessity and do not belong to the realm of *surplus*	g. Truth belongs to *the realm of surplus**

Note: *The important notion of 'surplus' will be defined and analysed in the next subsection, 'Science and Art'.
Source: Author.

What is important to note over here is that this distinction, however neat it appears, is not absolute. According to Tagore, what is a fact today may become truth tomorrow by being complete, by being related to the universe. He believes that we can get an inkling of what truth is, only indirectly via suggestiveness (*vyanjanā*) of language. It is clear that the truth, the One, the Supreme Person, is indescribable as far as our factual, scientific language is concerned. But it gets manifested in Art: literature, music, and dance. However, in whatever form, truth shows itself. It is indescribable in the sense that it cannot be expressed in ordinary scientific language, which depicts facts. Why can it not be stated in ordinary language? Because words used in ordinary language have some fixed reportive meanings that are usually compiled in a dictionary. Facts move around unquestioningly in this domain of reportive meaning and, thus, are limited by it. But truth lies outside this limit; hence the problem remains: How can one grasp the unbound, the unlimited? How can one express this unlimited through facts, which are limited by space–time, objectivity, and other factors? Here comes the notion of suggestiveness, indirection, and bending of meaning. However, for Tagore, truth cannot be grasped or described in factual parlance. I will come back to this important notion of indescribability of truth within the domain of facts again at the end of this chapter.

Now, corresponding to this distinction between fact and truth at the ontological level, we have, in the writings of Tagore, the distinction between science and Art, which comprises ethics, aesthetics, religion, and metaphysics at the level of epistemology. In the next subsection, this epistemological distinction will be highlighted.

Science and Art

According to Tagore, what science deals with is not truth but facts. In Bengali, 'science' is termed as *vijñāna*, which etymologically analysed signifies a special kind of knowledge. If one analyses the 'speciality' of scientific knowledge, one can find the following three important characteristic features of it:

• Scientific objects are independent of human mind, hence in that sense they are ontologically real.
• Science always wants to build a theory or system, which is amenable to logic or reason, which anyone on earth can grasp or understand. This makes scientific knowledge universal as well.
• Science gives importance to quantity, that is, it offers a quantitative account of the universe. (Ganguly 1968, 47; translation mine).

Here one notices that such knowledge can only be concerned with facts. The scientist seeks an impersonal principle of unification, which can be applied to all things. For instance, he destroys the human body, which is personal, in order to find out physiology, which is impersonal and general. When one treats a human body not as mine or yours, but as the object of anatomy or physiology, one looks at it from an objective point of view, which is at the same time universal. And it is because of this that one can learn or teach, can generalize and classify important facts about our body, or bodily organs, to be precise. 'Whereas the artist finds out the unique, the individual which is yet in the heart of the universal' (Tagore 1917, 35). When he looks upon a tree, he looks upon the tree as unique, not as the botanist who generalizes and classifies. It is the function of the artist to particularize that one tree. Such uniqueness of viewing of the artist as being related to viewing 'sub specie aeterni' will be elaborated in the third chapter.

A scientist can make known what he has learnt by analysis and experiment. But what an artist has to say, *he cannot express by merely informing and explaining*. There it has nothing to do with the facts or with laws; it deals with taste, which can be realized only by testing.

Tagore elucidates this by means of a poem where the lover praises his beloved by saying, 'It seems to me that I have gazed at your beauty from the beginning of my existence that I have kept you in my arms for countless ages, yet it has not been enough for me' (Tagore 1923c, 34).

To convey a feeling of attraction, the poet said, 'Her body's breeze dissolves the stone,' and again, 'The swaying glaze from the young body flows into the earth' (Tagore 2001, 338).[7] To take these words literally would be misleading. Words have been created to denote what is exact; 'hence in order to express what it is like, their meanings have to be extended and bent a little. The language of what it is like has not been codified in the dictionary; the poet has therefore to skilfully make do with ordinary language' (Tagore 2001, 298–9).

Judged from the standpoint of reason or science, these are exaggerations, which can never be true objectively. Hence, such exaggerations fail to be a piece of information in the scientific sense, but from the point of view of the poet, these come from the heart and are freed from the limits of facts. When facts are looked upon as mere facts, having their chain of consequences in the world of facts, they are rejected by Art. An object of Art does not want to deliver any information to us, rather it 'expresses' the truth, the beauty of the One. Tagore uses the word 'expression' here in a technical sense. Following the Upaniṣads, he maintains:

> There are three facets of human beings like, I am, I know, and I express corresponding to the three distinct selves of the absolute: *satyam*, *jñānam* and *anantam*. These together constitute an integral truth. The 'I am' aspect of truth motivates us to undertake activities such as gathering, preserving, and making. The 'I know' aspect persuades us to acquire knowledge and 'I express' is related to the wealth of the soul where one unites with the Infinite, with others. (Tagore 2001, 258)

Expressions have to do with surpluses. Our world of 'expressions' does not accurately coincide with the world of facts, because the world of expression surpasses facts on every side.

When one scientifically analyses a flower, the considerations whether the flower appears to be beautiful to one or many is completely irrelevant. One can actually give a pragmatic, impersonal, and objective description of a flower and that might suit a botanist's purpose, yet for the poet that description will be incomplete. Science has to abstract fact from the truth, has to neglect the whole, and thus it perverts the truth. Tagore argues with the example of a doctor who, while medicating his ailing son, might try to be impersonal and unaffected by emotion, but if he does it all the time that implies that he is not facing the truth. He elucidates this in *The Religion of Man:*

> The father has his personal relationship with his son; but as a doctor may detach the fact of son from that relationship and let the child become an abstraction to him, only a living body with its physiological functions. It cannot be said that if through the constant pursuit of his vocations he altogether discards the personal element in his relations to his son, he reaches a greater truth as a doctor than he does as a father. The scientific knowledge of his son is information about a fact, and not the *realization of a truth.* (1931c, 99–100)

How can he have realization of truth? What then is truth to the doctor? Tagore elucidates:

> In his intimate feeling for his son he touches an ultimate truth—'*the truth of relationship, the truth of harmony in the Universe, the fundamental principle of creation.* It is not merely the number of protons and electrons which represents the truth of an element; it is the mystery of this relationship which cannot be analysed. (Tagore 1931c, 100; emphasis mine)

Thus, Tagore's view of truth is different from those of the scientists. For him, harmony is the criterion of truth. If a scientist emphasizes a particular objective aspect while neglecting other aspects, his account will fail to represent the harmony of the whole. He narrates:

> I still remember the shock of repulsion I perceived as a child when some medical students brought to me a piece of a human windpipe and tried to excite admiration for his structure. (Tagore 1931c, 100)

Because of these reasons, he thought:

> In order to live efficiently man must know facts and their laws. In order to be happy he must establish harmonious relationship with all things with which he has dealings. (Tagore 1931c, 133)

Such views get confirmed when he writes,

> Our scientific world is our world of reasoning. It has its greatness, uses
> and attractions. We are ready to pay the homage due to it. But when it
> claims to have discovered the real worlds for us and laughs at the worlds
> of all simple-minded men, then we must say it is like a general grown
> intoxicated with his power, usurping the throne of his king. For the reality
> of the world belongs to the personality of man and not to reasoning, which
> is useful and great but which is not the man himself. (Tagore 1917, 70)

From the above discussion, one can find parallels between the
ontological distinction between facts and truth and the corresponding
epistemological distinction between science and Art. The reasons for
bringing all these studies under one head will be discussed elabo-
rately in subsequent chapters. Here it will be sufficient if I hint only
at the major reasons for it:

> When our universe is in harmony with man, the eternal, we know it
> as truth, we feel it as beauty. Religion realizes these truths and links
> them up with our deeper needs. ... Religion applies values to truth,
> and we know truth as good through our own harmony with it. (Tagore
> 2001, 297)

Coming back to the parallels one can point out that corresponding
to the characteristic features of facts, we find *science*, which is concerned only with facts, also to be abstract, objective, impersonal, and
thus incomplete and relative. Not only that, science also is determined
by necessity, be it causal or material whereas Art is free and belongs
to the domain of 'surplus'. But what is surplus? The notion of surplus is the central notion in the philosophy of Tagore. In order to
make us understand what he exactly means by 'surplus', he shows
us clearly how human beings are different from all other creatures of
the universe in the domain of surplus. Like animals, human beings
also have hunger, thirst, and bodily cravings, but what makes man different from animals is that apart from these bodily cravings, human
beings crave for completely different things. To elucidate, animals are
necessarily bounded by their needs and necessities, they cannot go
beyond them; but men, after fulfilling their needs, go beyond them.
Animals possess knowledge but that knowledge is employed for
useful purposes, such as how to build nests, how to jump on prey,

how to avoid danger, and so on. Human beings also have knowledge, which they often employ for immediate necessities in life, but they can go far beyond and declare that I am acquiring knowledge just for the sake of knowledge and not for anything else. Here they differ fundamentally from animals.

Animals possess certain altruistic tendencies such as parenting and taking interest in herd and hive. Humans also know that they have to be good because their goodness is necessary for their race, yet they go far beyond that. They can afford to say that goodness is for the sake of goodness. Animals also have emotions, which they use for self-preservation. 'Man has a fund of excess emotional energy that does not get satisfied with simple preservation. It seeks an outlet in creation of art, literature, music and dance. For man's civilization is built upon their surplus' (Tagore 1917, 20).

This surplus is something that distinguishes men from all other creatures. It is expressed in his poem.

The bird or animal cannot go beyond nature; they follow nature even in singing. Man goes beyond what is given to him, he creates. Man is given voice, yet he goes beyond it. He creates songs, he sings. (Tagore 1916c, 76)[8]

He can create because he has excess, he has surplus. His surplus gets manifested in the domain of Art.

When a man sees the world through music, through art, through literature, he understands it properly,[9] we know the world in the true sense of the term. The world then becomes an altogether different world, what was a trifle (akincitkar) becomes most valuable in the world.

Of all creatures only man knows himself because his impulse of knowledge comes back to him in its excess. Therefore in Art, man reveals himself, feels his personality more intensely than other creatures because his power of feeling is more than can be exhausted by his objects, Man as a knower is not fully himself. ... His mere information does not reveal him. (Tagore 1917, 21)

Here, one notices that there is a difference between description and revelation. Facts can be described but human excesses or surplus gets revealed only in art, literature, and other discourses, which can never be described in factual terms. In Tractarian terms, they are unsayable, but showable. They show themselves in art, literature, ethics, aesthetics, and religious discourses.

In the writings of Tagore, we find both ways of transition from facts to truth and truth to facts. On the one hand, the infinite, the formless, the feeling of the supreme, the personal truth gets manifested in the forms, and on the other form also abandons itself to feeling of the one and the formless. In his own words:

> Truth is expressed when the finiteness of form, like a lamp, lights up the flame of the infinite. The *invisible* [*arūpa*] has to be shown in the *visible* [*rūpa*], *form* [*rūpa*] has to be seen enveloped by the *formless* [*arūpa*]. (Tagore 2001, 268–9)

Hence, with Tagore, there is no riddle concerning how to reconcile the form and the formless, the finite and the infinite, they yearn to manifest and be manifested by each other. And their harmony constitutes truth. To illustrate this point, I would like to quote from a poem from the volume *Utsarga*:

> Feeling yearns to become a part of form. But form desires to surrender itself to feeling.
> The infinite wants the finite's intimate comradeship
> And the finite wishes to lose itself in the infinite.
> In creation and dissolution, through some mysterious contrivance,
> There is continuous coming and going between feeling and form.
> (Tagore in Naravane 1964, 123–4)

Rabindranath elucidates the relationship thus:

> Expression, properly speaking, is the expression of the truth within the fact. As expression is the basic function of literature and the arts, their chief task is to afford our minds the savour of truth in the vessel of fact. This savour is the savour of the one, of the unbounded. (Tagore 2001, 15)

It is clear that though Tagore had distinguished fact from truth, and science from Art, still he was keen on establishing that truth gets manifested in facts, even though there are differences and truth in a sense lies beyond the domain of facts. In his own words:

> The *Vīna* of the formless is being played secretly under the veil of forms. My world is filled with musical tunes where there is no distinction between far and near, between formless and form. (Tagore (1920) 2002, 42)[10]

Again, he stated clearly:

> In my writings there is no conflict between the finite and the infinite, they somehow merge together. The reason for that is not personal, nor does it lie on my personal self but it pervades the whole outside world. (Tagore in Letter to B. Seal, 1921, cited in Ghosh 2011, 135)

Again, he writes about the intimate companionship of the bounded and the unbounded, finite and the infinite, the form and the formless.

> Within the bounds play your own tune, oh the unbound. You express yourself through me, that's why it is so melodious. (Tagore (1910) 2002, 140)[11]

In this section, we have seen how the distinction between science and Art is related to the ontological distinction between fact and truth, how the domain of truth as revealed in Art eludes factual representation. It follows that truth revealed in art and literature, ethics, aesthetics, and religious experience is not describable in factual terms. They are, in that sense, indescribable, though they are showable.

Tagore in his writings had talked about different uses of language; of them, two types of uses are specially significant. One is the pragmatic and descriptive use of everyday language, which depicts or mirrors facts, and the other is the creative use reflected in the language of art, literature, music, and religion. It is obvious that he preferred the creative use of language to the pragmatic one. In *Bāngla-Bhāṣā-Parichay*, Tagore elucidates this distinction:

> The language of science or knowledge must be as clear as possible; the right word must bear its exact meaning. But in the poetic language, the language of feeling is to some extent inexplicit. Hence if, in the language of emotion and feelings, it does not express things with directness, if it has appropriate figures of speech, it is in fact more

effective. ... The language of knowledge (science) requires clarity of meaning: the language of feeling (art, poetry) needs indirection, perhaps with a bending of meaning. (Tagore 2001, 338)

According to him:

> Language is on the one hand the vehicle of clear statements and on the other hand of unclear statements as well. In one direction science has been proceeding along the stairway of language towards the uttermost bounds of language, and has arrived at formulaic symbols transcending language; in another direction, poetry too has reached the far end of ideation, step by step along the stairs of language, and finally begun to construct signals of thought, transgressing its own limited meanings. (Tagore 2001, 339)

Now I will move to the final section where I will strive to find out affinities (including affinities of opposition) between the ideas of Wittgenstein and those of Tagore as far as the distinction between saying and showing is concerned.

Similarities: A Portrayal of the Views of Wittgenstein and Tagore

Although it is not stated explicitly anywhere in Tagore's writings that science falls within the domain of the sayable in terms of facts, still it is obviously so. Same is the case with art, ethics, aesthetics, and religion, which are also unsayable in factual terms, but showable. One can easily notice the distinction between saying and showing implicit in the distinction between fact *and* truth, science *and* art. It is surprising to note over here that Tagore was keen on making this distinction in the early 1920s!

Not only that, what is more interesting is that both the thinkers had their reservations about scientism, scientific culture of society, and also the scientific notion of progress. It is true that in the *Tractatus*, Wittgenstein regarded empirical and scientific discourse as the only meaningful discourse and he was primarily a student of science and engineering who had 'an abiding interest in certain kinds of scientific investigations'. Still he rejected the belief in progress and abhorred societies' obsession with science, which he regarded as 'both a symptom and a cause of cultural decline' (Wittgenstein 1980a, 6–7).

Tagore values Art as an 'expression' of truth more than science, so does Wittgenstein. In a letter to Engelmann, Wittgenstein admits that through a work of art, the world may be captured 'sub specie aeterni'. And 'only the work of Art compels us—as one might say—to see it in the right perspective, but without Art the object is a piece of nature like any other and the fact that we may exalt it through our enthusiasm, does not give anyone the right to display it to us' (Wittgenstein 1998, 6–7).

Wittgenstein also expressed his worry that the advancement of science and technology 'marginalise ethics and the Arts and thereby endanger the human spirit' (Wittgenstein 1998, 69).

Wittgenstein's view became prominent in this regard in 1930, when he wrote the sketch for the foreword to *Philosophical Remarks*, which has since been published as part of the compilation *Culture and Value: A Selection from the Posthumous Remains*.

The book is written for those who are in sympathy with *the spirit* in which it is written. This is not, I believe, the main current of European and American civilization. The spirit of the civilization makes itself manifest in the industry, architecture and music of our time, in its fascism and socialism, and it is alien and uncongenial to the author. ...

The fact remains that I have no sympathy for the current of European civilization and do not understand its goals, if it has any. So I am really writing for friends who are *scattered throughout the corners of the globe* [emphasis mine].

It is all one to me whether the typical western scientist understands or appreciates my work, since he will not in any case understand *the spirit* in which I write. Our civilization is characterised by the word '*progress*'. Progress is its form rather than making progress being one of its features. Typically, it constructs. It is occupied with building an ever more complicated structure. And even clarity is sought only as a means to this end and not as an end in itself. For me, on the contrary, clarity, perspicuity is valuable in themselves I am not interested in constructing a building, so much as having a perspicuous view of the foundations of possible buildings. So I am not aiming at the same target as the scientists and my way of thinking is different from theirs. (Wittgenstein 1998, 8–9)

This long quotation shows Wittgenstein's aversion to the goal of sciences, the progress that the scientists want to make, and how it differs from his own views regarding progress. Here he distinguishes between construction and creation, which is also noticed in the writings of Tagore. To show the parallels in their ideas, I would also like to quote from Tagore:

> Science sets up an impersonal and unalterable standard of space and time which is not the standard of creation. Therefore at its fatal touch the reality of the world is so hopelessly disturbed that it vanishes in an abstraction where things become nothing at all. For the world is not atoms and molecules or radio activity or other forces, the diamond is not carbon and light is not vibration of ether. You can never come to the reality of creation by contemplating it from the point of view of destruction. (1923c, 50)

Tagore speaks candidly about the distinction between the world of science and the world of art:

> The world of science is not a world of reality. It is an abstract world of force we can use it by the help of our intellect but cannot realize it by the help of our personality. It is like a swarm of mechanics that though producing things for ourselves as personal beings, are mere shadows to us.
>
> But there is another world which is real to us, we see it, we feel it, we deal with it with all our emotions. Its mystery is endless because we cannot analyse it or measure it ... this is the world from which science turns away, and in which Art takes place. (Tagore 1917, 12–13)

Here we find Tagore emphasizing the creative use of language, which he calls 'expressions.' These cannot be accounted for, it cannot be surveyed or mapped. Facts are inadequate tools for the expression of truth. They are 'like wine cups that carry it, they are hidden by it, it overflows them. It is infinite in its suggestions; it is extravagant in its words. It is personal, therefore beyond science' (Tagore 1917, 48).

Although it is true that Wittgenstein would not subscribe to Tagore's idealism that 'to say that Truth as we see it, exists apart from humanity is really to contradict Science itself' (Tagore 1931c, 16). Still Wittgenstein also thinks in the same way as Tagore in very many important respects. Engelmann tells us that Wittgenstein brought the others (members of Olmütz circles) to see, by strict attention, that in contrast to the nature of science and mathematics the realm of religion (as well as ethics and aesthetics) was indeed inexpressible. In fact, in his 'A Lecture on Ethics', he draws the analogy of a cup that can have only a cupful of water but not a gallon of water. It is beyond the capacity of the cup to contain a gallon of water. Similarly all these discourses (that is, ethics, aesthetics, and religion) are beyond the expressibility of scientific language. They are inexpressible, they are unutterable. Like Uhland's poem (Engelmann 1967, 97) they are unutterably contained in the utterable. They show themselves in what is utterable.

As mentioned earlier, there is a persistent riddle in the *Tractatus*: How to reconcile 'the logical' and 'the mystical'? Wittgenstein also thought a lot about it. We find in the coded part of his diary (from Brenner archive) on 6 and 7 July 1916:

> Have thought a lot about everything possible. But strangely enough, I cannot establish the connection with my mathematical lines of thought. But the connection will be established ... what cannot be said, cannot be said. (McGuinness 2001, 226)[12]

Wittgenstein did find the connection in the realm of the 'unsayable but showable', and only because of this he, at the end of the *Tractatus*, advised us to throw away the book of nonsense. Now, one can get to his point, can see the connection 'rightly' if one reads the *Tractatus* as a literary work, as a poem, as expressing the 'truth'. Here one might ask: Did Wittgenstein use the word 'truth' as Tagore did in his writings? One might answer that Wittgenstein uses the word 'truth' (*die wahrheit*) in the domain of the sensible, in the context of propositions; as an operator, as when he talks about truth combination, truth condition, truth possibility, truth operation, truth function, truth type, and so on. But he used the word 'truth' (*die wahrheit*) in a different sense when he talked about what the solipsists mean (T5.62), what absolute value judgements point at (Wittgenstein 1965, 7), about viewing of the world as sub specie aeterni, and about feeling the world as a limited whole (T6.45). This was because he thought that the correct method in philosophy would really be to say nothing except what can be said, that is, propositions of natural science (T6.53). And because of this, he writes, 'we feel that even when all possible scientific questions have been answered, the problems of life remain completely untouched' (Wittgenstein 1922, 3).

Also because of this, the key to understanding the *Tractatus* lies in giving much importance to what cannot be talked about in the preface and the conclusion of the book.

Although Wittgenstein did not use the word 'truth', in the way Tagore did, yet it follows that he was looking for the connection between the logical and the mystical world as the totality of facts, and the world as a limited whole. Finally, he finds the connection, the harmony, through his doctrine of showing. He realizes that harmony is evident when facts are viewed sub specie aeternitatis and when facts manifest logical forms of language, thought, and the world. I will elaborate on this later and show how the logical merges with the mystical, the outer with the inner, where the limits of language, thought, and reality coincide. Here, Tagore's works will be of immense help in understanding this connection, in understanding that this connection eludes our speech—'our minds and words come back baffled from it' (From Tagore's letter to Bertrand Russell, 13 October 1912 in Griffin 2002).

Quoting the *Ishopaniṣad*, Tagore says:

> Those who pursue the knowledge of the finite for its own sake cannot find truth. This knowledge merely accumulates but does not illuminate. It is like a lamp without its light, a violin without its music. You cannot know a book by measuring and weighing and counting its pages, by analysing its paper. An inquisitive mouse may gnaw through the wooden frame of a piano, may cut all its strings to pieces and yet travel farther and further away from the music.
>
> This is the pursuit of the finite for its own sake. ...
>
> Similarly the absolute infinite is emptiness. The finite is something ... it may be a mere cheque book with no account in the bank. But the absolute infinite has no cash and not even a cheque book.
>
> The infinite and finite are one as song and singing are one. (Tagore 1917, 76)

If we apply this to Wittgenstein's distinction between saying and showing, between the language of science and that of ethics and aesthetics, we will see that the logical part in itself is informative but not illuminating in the sense that 'it is like a lamp without its light, a violin without its music'. The logical part of the *Tractatus* comes up with the general form of a proposition in T6:

> The general form of a truth function is: [p, ξ, N (ξ)]. This is the general form of a proposition.

This, in fact, justifies Tagore's saying, that 'in one direction science has been proceeding along the stairway of language towards the uttermost bounds of language, and has arrived at formulaic symbols transcending language' (Tagore 2001, 319). These formulaic symbols are obviously without content and because of this, these are termed as nonsensical (*sinnloss*) in the *Tractatus*. Again, as 'there are no a-priori order of things' (T5.634), scientific propositions are all about things and facts which can be true or false. Now these facts in order to be facts, in order to depict reality, must have logical form and pictorial form. Thus, facts that we can term as visible (*rūpa*) always manifest themselves in the form of the world and in the logical form, which is, so to speak, invisible (*arūpa*). It might be stated, by borrowing Kantian terminology and applying it to the distinction between form and content, that form without content is empty and content without form is blind. Hence, in the *Tractatus* we find harmony at this level of fact and form, but harmony also plays a very important role at the level of the inexpressible. While we were talking about nonsense (*unsinn*), we found on the one hand logical form, pictorial form, and the form of a law, and on the other ethics, aesthetics, metaphysics, religion, and the propositions of the *Tractatus*. They all come under one head because they all attempt to express what is inexpressible. The inexpressible, according to the *Tractatus*, 'is *to feel* the world as a limited whole' (T6.45), that is, the world as limited by the coincidence of the limits of language with those of thought and the self. I will elaborate on this notion of *feeling of a limited whole* in the following chapters. Here it will be sufficient if one simply mentions that this inexpressible, *the feeling* of the world as a limited whole, is the 'Truth' for Tagore, where

> feeling yearns to become a part of form.
> But form desires to surrender itself to feeling. (Tagore in Naravane 1964, 123–4)

Finally, one notices a kind of philosophy of harmony in the *Tractatus* that includes harmony of fact and form, of form and feeling, and, above all, of the expressible and the inexpressible, the sayable and the showable. This harmony of the infinite and the finite, the formless and the form, the showable and the sayable, sculpts the key concept of the philosophy of both Tagore and Wittgenstein. But one will have to accept that at the same time it is also beyond description or narration in terms of scientific factual language. As these are not sayable in ordinary scientific language, its unsayability and the mode of silence forms the important key theme in the *Tractatus* and also in the poems of Tagore.

With this background of the philosophy of both Tagore and that of early Wittgenstein, I can now move onto the analysis of the role of silence encapsulating 'what matters in life' for both the thinkers.

Notes

1. Wittgenstein writes in a letter to Russell:

    Now I'm afraid you haven't really got hold of my main contention to which the whole business of logical propositions is only corollary. The main point is the theory of what can be expressed (*gesagt*) by propositions, i.e. by language (and, which comes to the same thing, what can be thought) and what cannot be expressed by propositions, but only shown (*gezeigt*); which I believe is the *cardinal problem of philosophy*. (Cited in Monk 1990, 164; emphasis mine)

2. Wittgenstein did not use the expression 'attempt to express the inexpressible' in the *Tractatus*, though the notion is implicit in what he says there. The expression first appears in 'A Lecture on Ethics' (1929), a decade after the completion of the *Tractatus*.

3. When someone draws a boundary, he knows what lies on the other side of the boundary. Now, if one wants to set a limit to thought or what is thinkable, then one would have to know what lies beyond the boundary of what is thinkable. Logic cannot allow that, as in that case one will have to think the unthinkable.

4.

    Tathyo o satya,
      Sahityer pathe. (Tagore 1986, 387)

    Tagore has made a distinction between *tathyo* and *satya*. I have translated *tathyo* as 'fact'. 'Fact' is a loaded philosophical term referring often to 'meaning of a proposition'/'objects in relation'/'abstraction of events', and 'true state of affairs'. Here, I mean 'existent state of affairs which give us information' in the spirit of Tagore's writings.

5. This objection was raised by Dr Enakshi Mitra, University of Delhi, in a seminar at Indian Institute of Advanced Study, Shimla, in April 2014.

6. There are commentators such as Norman Malcolm (1989) who discern an independent ontology in the *Tractatus* and view the structure of language as derived from that. David Pears (1987, Vol. 1) defends a 'basic uncritical realism' as the proper interpretation, and Hintikka and Hintikka (1986) espouse a form of 'sense data realism'.

7. '*Dholo dholo kānchā angero lāboni abanī bohiyā jāi.*'

8. '*Pākhire diyecho gān, gai sei gān, tar besi kore nā se dān Amare diyecho swar, ami tār besi kori dān, ami gāi gān*' (Tagore 1916a, 76; translation mine).

9. '*Ganer bhitor diye jokhon dekhi bhubankhāni, tokhon tāre jāni*' (Tagore 1931, 221). 'Music offers a special vision of the world I see ... truly then, I feel it so near and dear to me' (Basu 1999, 7).

10. '*Arūpa vīna rūper arale lukiye bāje ...*
    Bhuban amar bhorilo sure, bhed ghuche jai nikot o dure' (translation mine).

11. '*Sīmār mājhe asīm tumi bājāo āpan sur*
    āmar modhye tomār prokāsh tāi eto modhur.'

12. Ludwig Wittgenstein: MS103, Trinity College Library, UK. Publication of code passages is planned by the Brenner Archive.

2

In Silence There Is Eloquence

It has already been made explicit in the earlier chapter how, for Wittgenstein, the notion of 'limits of language' has left a huge corpus of discourses as 'unsayable', in Tractarian terms. Not only that, the early Wittgenstein claims that philosophical problems arise only out of saying things about what cannot be said and these can be solved once and for all if we remain silent on such matters, that is, 'What we cannot talk about, we must pass over in silence' (T7).

In this chapter we will see that the idea that there are limits to language, limits on what can be factually or scientifically articulated, is also advocated, implicitly at least, by Rabindranath Tagore in various poems and essays. Both Wittgenstein and Tagore harp on a common theme. The theme is the ability of one to communicate or understand the inexpressible, that which remains beyond the limits of language through poems, music, and art. Both have a unique approach to arriving at the same conclusion, Tagore through literature and Wittgenstein through logic. However, for each remaining 'silent' plays an important role in their respective discourses.

Tagore, however, unlike Wittgenstein, was not concerned with representations of linguistic and cognitive structures. Rather, he was concerned with the problem of the articulation of truth in scientific language. In this chapter, I intend to demonstrate the striking similarities between early Wittgenstein and Rabindranath Tagore as far as the importance of silence is concerned.

There are numerous differences between these two geniuses of the twentieth century.

They employ different vocabulary to develop their respective concerns. Also, there are differences as far as the goals of their respective projects are concerned. Yet, despite such differences, there are similarities as far as the notion of silence is concerned.

The next two sections of this chapter will concentrate on the importance of silence in the works of the two thinkers, respectively.

Is Silence Eloquent in the *Tractatus*?: A Paradox.

The famous last sentence of the *Tractatus*, 'Whereof one cannot speak, thereon one must be silent', if noticed carefully, expresses a simple tautology. It sounds paradoxical as Wittgenstein has said a lot of things about what cannot be said in the book. Finally at the end, he declares that whatever he has said in the book is nonsensical, whereas in the preface he declared that the truth he found in this book is unassailable and definitive. If the whole book is nonsensical, then what exactly is the status of the distinction between sense and nonsense? Is it sensical or nonsensical? How can it be sensical when it does not claim to be a picture of any worldly state of affairs? If the distinction is nonsensical, then the question of being nonsensical does not arise.

Hence, this dramatic silence at the end of the book on the philosophical logic has created deep puzzlement among thinkers. Recent literature on Wittgenstein abounds with books and articles that attempt to demonstrate that there is nothing profound about which we can be silent, that nonsense is nonsense and that is that (Crary and Read 2000). On the one hand, we have philosophers such as Cora Diamond, James Conant, and Marie McGinn who think that this silence is not by any means pregnant, we just cannot say anything. To quote:

> The silence which Wittgenstein wishes to leave us at the end is one in which nothing has been said and there is nothing to say (of the sort we had imagined there to be); the silence we are left with is not a pregnant silence that comes with a conscious posture of guarding the sanctity of the ineffable. (Conant 1991, 344)

These philosophers who prefer the 'resolute reading'[1] of the *Tractatus*, take his remarks on nonsense quite literally and reject that there can be any metaphysics in the *Tractatus*. Put simply, their argument is as follows: Wittgenstein describes the aim of the book as one of drawing a limit to thought, or to the expression of thoughts (Wittgenstein 1972, 3). But in the *Tractatus* (T4.112), he remarks that 'the task of philosophy consists entirely of elucidations' and that 'it does not result in philosophical propositions'. 'It seems clear that, however we understand the philosophical activity of "elucidations", nothing substantial—nothing that could be taken as a philosophical answer to a philosophical question—should survive at the end' (McGinn 2001, 24).

James Conant and Cora Diamond have argued persuasively that any attempt to interpret the *Tractatus* as pointing to some inexpressible metaphysical truths 'whose unsayability precludes its being said, but which we can nevertheless grasp' (Diamond 2000, 152–3), fails to do justice to the radical nature of Wittgenstein's thought. If we take seriously Wittgenstein's claim that he deliberately avoids philosophical doctrines, then the only end of philosophical activity in which he is engaged must, they argue, be the realization that there are no philosophical insights expressible or otherwise to be had (McGinn 2001, 24). As per this reading, nothing is left standing at the end of the work: all philosophy including the remarks of the *Tractatus*, have been revealed as nonsensical.

On the other hand we have proponents of ineffability theory[2] who argue that the role of nonsense in the *Tractatus* is to make us grasp ineffable truths, which 'strictly speaking' cannot be said or thought. Again, Oskari Kuusela (2006) in his article 'Nonsense and Clarification in the Tractatus—Resolute and Ineffability Readings and the Tractatus' Failure' has shown the paradoxicality of both the resolute and the non-resolute interpretations. Moreover, a new genre of interpretations have come up following Wittgenstein's letters and diaries after the publication of *Wittgenstein's Vienna* (1973) by Janik and Toulmin who have forced Wittgenstein scholars to look into his biography to interpret his writings.

However, in this controversy I would like to side with Allan Janik and Stephen Toulmin who rightly claim that 'with the publication of more and more unpublished personal and philosophical writings of Wittgenstein, it has become clear that Wittgenstein himself really did consider the admonition to silence to be the crucial insight that philosophy provides' (Janik 2011, 1) and that insight came from his reflection on himself and the then contemporary society.

For me, the non-resolute reading of the *Tractatus* seems to be more pertinent as the publication of private notebooks and diaries speak in favour of the view that Wittgenstein had a great transformation during the time he spent serving in the war. I will elaborate in Chapter 4, 'The Domain of the Ineffable: The Religious', how war-time experience had taken a toll on the body and mind of young Ludwig, which prompted him to stress on the inexpressibility of deep questions on life and death, values, and God in scientific terms. It taught him that unstatability in scientific terms does not imply its irrelevance or insignificance. On the contrary, he passionately believed that what we cannot talk about is most important.

However, I think along similar lines as Engelmann, that there is no paradox in Wittgenstein's admonition to silence at the end. That admonition is meant for the scientists and philosophers alike, but not for the poets, musicians, or artists. Here one should remember that Wittgenstein wanted to treat the *Tractatus* as a literary work at the same time![3] Through the literary work, we can apprehend the unutterable. The unutterable is unutterably contained in their utterances; one can also say that in these art forms, the inexpressible manifest themselves. I will elucidate these ideas in a moment.

When Wittgenstein wrote to Ludwig Von Ficker that what he did not write in the book is most important, it was something that was most revolutionary for the readers and commentators. Because it implied that the *Tractatus* ultimately did not concern logic or language but rather those matters that the treatise ruled out from being talked about—namely, ethics, aesthetics, metaphysics, and religion—which the text 'points to'.

Engelmann confirms our presentiments when he states categorically:

Wittgenstein passionately believes that all that really matters in human life is precisely what, in his view, we must be silent about. (Engelmann 1967, 97)

Engelmann rightly elucidates, 'When he nevertheless takes immense pains to delimit the unimportant, it is not the coastline of that island which he is bent on surveying with such meticulous accuracy, but the boundary of the ocean' (Engelmann 1967, 97).

The domain of silence for early Wittgenstein thus follows from the boundedness of sensible language. For him, whatever does not fulfil the criteria of sensicality in the *Tractatus* is nonsensical on the one hand, and on the other hand he feels that these nonsensical items encompass 'the important'. But how did Wittgenstein know that '*what really matters in human life is precisely what, in his view, we must be silent about*'? Is it not paradoxical for one to characterize *something* as most important about which they must remain silent?

Herein lays the peculiarity of the notion of 'silence' in early Wittgenstein. The peculiarity consists in the fact that if one remains silent, that is, does not say what is unsayable, then it can be conveyed by what has been said. In elucidating this, an anecdote from Engelmann's memoir would be of help to us. In 1917, Engelmann read a poem by Uhland that touched him 'differently and more deeply'. He sent it to Wittgenstein. The poem is quoted below:

Count Eberhard's Hawthorn

Count Eberhard Rustle-beard,
From Wurttemberg's fair land,
On holy errand steer'd
To Palestina's strand.

The while he slowly rode
Along a woodland way;
He cut from the hawthorn bush
A little fresh green spray.

Then in his iron helm
The little sprig he plac'd;
And bore it in the wars,
And over the ocean waste.

And when he reach'd his home,
He plac'd it in the earth;
Where little leaves and buds
The gentle Spring call'd forth.

He went each year to it,
The count so braveand true;

And overjoy'd was he
To witness how it grew.

The count was worn with age
The sprig became a tree;
'Neath which the old man oft
Would sit in reverie.

The branching arch so high,
Whose whisper is so bland,
Reminds him of the past
And Palestina's strand.

(U'hland 1848, 348–9)

While commenting on the poem, Engelmann said:

Each one of Uhland's verses was simple—not ingenuous, but tersely
informative—so that none of them, taken by itself would cause delight.
But the poem as a whole, given in 28 lines, is the picture of a life.
The impression was so powerful that I understood that here was a
higher level of poetry and language which had previously eluded me.
(Engelmann 1967, 84–5)

He then sent it to Wittgenstein. In response, Wittgenstein said:

The poem by Uhland is really magnificent. And this is how it is: *If only
you do not try to utter what is unutterable, nothing gets lost. But the unutterable will be ... unutterably contained in what has been uttered.* (Engelmann
1967, 7)

Obviously there is no direct way to say what cannot be said. But
there are things that can be said that will 'contain' the unsayable: to
say these things is somehow to communicate what is in itself unsayable. A poem is an example of this phenomenon—it can communicate some ineffable truth about life while talking about the growth of
a sprig into a hawthorn bush.

'A poem may alter one's whole view of the world, making happy
what was unhappy; and it is no accident that the poem makes the
change possible' (Edwards 1985, 51).

It is curious to know that not only for Tagore, but also for
Wittgenstein, poems, music, painting, or any art form has the peculiar

capacity of communicating the incommunicable. It suggests that something lies beyond the threshold of factual language and meaning *does not* imply that (*a*) there is nothing beyond; (*b*) that we cannot have access to 'what is beyond'; and (*c*) that it is paradoxical to even conceive of accessing 'the beyond'.

Accessing 'the beyond' is not paradoxical as it can be done by indirect means, for instance, bending of meanings through indirection and suggestiveness, which are evident in the writings of Tagore.

Paul Engelmann mentions that for Wittgenstein, poetry is a mode of keeping silent (Engelmann 1967, 89). Clearly for Wittgenstein, all these art forms can express what philosophy cannot say—he has already stated in the preface of the book that confusing the grammar of utterable items of knowledge with unutterable ones had given rise to philosophical problems of nonsensicality. Without uttering anything, the unutterable becomes manifest in poems, music, architecture, painting, and drawing. The point is that such sentences that are essentially literary are ambiguous in the sense that they are not, truly speaking, propositions. Thus they are capable of showing something that cannot be said, that is, something essential that gets lost if we try to put it into scientific form (Engelmann 1967, 83). One can attempt to demonstrate this by means of explaining the difficulty of articulating our emotions in factual language.

In the play *King Lear*, when asked who doth love the king best, Cordellia says to herself:

> I'm sure my love is richer than my tongue. Love is silent but can be more vocal or communicative than a thousand words in most cases. (Janik 2011, 17)

How love is regarded as a value in ethics and aesthetics for both Wittgenstein and Tagore will be discussed in Chapter 3. In a way, the earlier discussion reveals that silence is also a kind of language and it can also be eloquent at times, which we can somehow grasp through poems and other art forms.

Now we can see that the *Tractatus* is an attempt to show the threshold of language and meaning. The scientific language in the *Tractatus* is limited, bounded by the totality of elementary propositions. But the matter does not end there. The *Tractatus* wants to convey through language, its boundary, its limit, and also, in a paradoxical sense, a glimpse of what lies on the other side of the boundary. According to the *Tractatus*, on the other side of the boundary is the realm of values, the domain of God, and the meaning of life and the world. Regarding all these things, Wittgenstein opines, philosophers should remain silent. It has two underpinnings. On the one hand the critics such as logical positivists, materialists, and others will not be allowed to criticize the domain of values for if they want to formulate their criticisms, they will fall into the trap of uttering nonsense. On the other hand, philosophers will not be able to defend the domain of values by means of arguments.

Thus the unutterable, of which one should remain silent, is beyond the argumentation of defenders or critics. It is beyond words of our ordinary language. Here one might say that it has, so to speak, got its own language, which shows us the nature of the deepest interconnection between 'the logical' and 'the mystical'. As on the one hand, the unutterable lies in the relations between language and the outside world, so on the other hand does it lie in the relation between language and the world of values.

In fact, Wittgenstein at one time endorsed the Quaker's 'silent rituals' for their mystically based religious movement. He once gave a copy of the journal of George Fox, the founder of this movement, to Norman Malcolm. 'The members of the congregation through observance of a silent waiting upon God, attempt to focus their attention away from worldly things in order to re-establish and renew contact with the transcendence of Inner Light'(Nieli 1987, 90). Admiration of 'silent rituals' though does not necessarily imply his faith in their presuppositions, still the thinking 'that silence is not just emptiness, but rather something that cannot be said, might account for Wittgenstein's reported admiration of George Fox' (Nieli 1987, 91).

Now, to conclude this section, I would like to draw attention to an important query. One knows from Engelmann's memoir that Wittgenstein visited Olmütz in 1916 and got involved with members of a Jewish circle (which I will elaborate on in Chapter 4). Surprisingly, during that period of time he discussed mainly those items of knowledge which he himself regarded as unutterable. In his memoir, Engelmann says:

> That the subject matter of discussion usually focused on two broad areas, one being the philosophical conceptions of the *Tractatus*, the

other religion and morality. Both are unutterable, that is, of both we should remain silent. (Engelmann 1967, 74–6)

So, how is it that Wittgenstein himself got involved in discussing those special areas of knowledge, of which he genuinely believed that 'one should remain silent'? Regarding silence, Nieli Russell comments, 'while it may sometimes be the best mode of communication for one's deepest thoughts and feelings, [it] is not necessarily so' (Nieli 1987, 169). It shows that early Wittgenstein had tensions regarding the status of these unutterable items of knowledge, which might have led the later Wittgenstein to dispose of the concept of the unutterable and the silent in his philosophical works.

Tagore and the Domain of the Inexpressible

In an article entitled '*Redrawing the Boundaries*', Uday Narayan Singh, a Tagore scholar, has stated categorically:

> The question that has bothered Tagore all his life is: Does *language* begin where silence ends; often slashing as waves against a vast coastline of content, or when all attempts are made to speak what an author such as Tagore always wanted to speak, resulting in a journey to nowhere? Does *silence* gain entry into our system of representation, and occupy the centre-stage of all semiotic activity? (2014, 1)

In fact, Tagore admitted both the domain of the expressible and that of the inexpressible and is of the opinion that the domain of the expressible is surrounded by that of the inexpressible. He says:

> Huge surge of the inexpressible has engulfed all day and night.[4]

What Tagore did not utter is not at all unmanifest; rather it manifests itself in emotions and feelings that can be represented in an indirect manner. Herein lies the similarity between the two geniuses. Corresponding to the distinction between fact and truth as explained in Chapter 1, there is a distinction between two different modes of representation in our language: the first one is a description of a fact, which can be true or false, and the other one is an attempt to represent truth that transcends our ordinary mode of representation. What is sensible, expressible in Tagorean terms is a scientific fact that is objective and impersonal. Regarding the inexpressible, which transcends beyond ordinary modes of representation, he often refers to the Upaniṣads. He quotes from Upaniṣad:

> I think not that I know him well or that I know him or even that I know him not. By the process of knowledge we can never know the infinite being. But if He is altogether beyond our reach, then He is absolutely nothing to us. The truth is that we know Him not, yet we know Him. (Tagore 1914d, 158)

This has been explained in another saying of the Upaniṣads:

> From Brahma words come back baffled as well as the mind, but he who knows him by the joy of him is free from all fears. (Tagore 1914d, 158–9)

It is important to note that though ordinary words cannot describe the infinite, still one can somehow grasp it—it may be inexpressible in words but that does not imply it is nothing; for one can know It/ Him. How does one know Him? This implies that though inexpressible in terms of scientific/everyday sentences, there are indirect ways of expressing it; there may be indirect expressions where the unsayable manifests itself. He continues:

> Knowledge is partial, because our intellect is an instrument, it is only a part of us, it can give us information about things which can be divided and analysed, and whose properties can be classified, part by part. But Brahman is perfect and knowledge which is partial can never be knowledge of Him. ...
> Therefore as the Upaniṣads say, *mind can never know Brahman, words can never describe Him,* and *He can only be known by our soul.* (Tagore 1914d, 159)

Here, one might argue that Tagore talks directly about infinite, about 'Brahman', of which Wittgenstein remained completely silent. This is true as they belong to two different cultural genealogies, and also one prefers to call himself a poet rather than a philosopher and the other is an established philosopher of language in Western analytical tradition. My purpose here is to elucidate the importance of what cannot be talked about but be shown in the works of both the thinkers.

Tagore used to believe in two different kinds of language: one is primary, intellectual, and factual and the other, the language of feeling, the language of art. He says:

> The language of intellection has found its fulfilment in science and Philosophy. The highest expressions of heart's impulses occur in poetry. There is a great deal of difference between these two kinds of languages. The language of knowledge must be as clear as possible; the right word must bear its exact meaning, unobscured by its frills and decorations. But if the language of feeling is to some extent inexplicit, if it does not express things with directness, if it has appropriate figures of speech, it is in fact more effective. The language of knowledge requires clarity of meaning; the language of feeling needs indirection perhaps with a bending of meaning. (Tagore 2001, 338)

Here are two distinct uses of language, one is for construction and the other is for creation as narrated by Tagore in his article 'Construction and Creation' (1988, 453). The language of construction is factual which serves the purpose of a scientific language with its clear and precise meaning, whereas the language of creation has to deal with items that do not have exact meaning and often lie beyond the scope of scientific language. Tagore gives an instance from a love ballad. To convey a feeling of attraction, the poet says:

> The liquid grace of his young form spreads over the earth. (Tagore 2001, 338)

To take these words literally would be misleading. Tagore explains it candidly:

> Had these words occurred in a scientific work, one would have understood that a certain kind of ray had been found in some person's body which had been named *lābani* (grace), which gradually diffuses itself across the ground because of the earth's pull. If one entirely trusts the meanings of the words, there is no alternative to this kind of explanation but here we are not talking about natural events, we are talking about what seems to be. Words have been created to denote what-is-exact; hence in order to express what-it-is-like, their meanings have to be extended and bent a little. The language of what-it-is-like has not been codified in the dictionary; the poet has therefore to skilfully make do with ordinary language. ... The poet therefore eschews the exact

denotation of the word *lābaṇya*, and says something he has made up, as though *lābaṇya* is a mountain spring that flows from the body onto the ground. There is an anxiety of expression here, following complete annihilation of the meaning of the word; while saying something, it is simultaneously been said 'I cannot say it.' By imparting the look of the unfamiliar to a familiar word, the denotative boundaries of language are extended indefinitely. (Tagore 2001, 338–9)

Here, the poet nicely articulates the spirit of 'I cannot say it while saying it'. This exactly is the position of Wittgenstein at the end of the *Tractatus*, where he is almost saying, 'I cannot say whatever I have said in the book.' But this is not giving rise to any inconsistency as everything is done on a different plane, on the plane of a poetic language, only when he can view the world 'sub specie aeterni'. Probably because of this, he told Engelmann that poetry is a mode of keeping silence and it can express what philosophers cannot. In the poetic language of creation, there are no fences around language, that is, no limits can be drawn around the language of creation.

In the *Tractatus*, one notices the domain of the ineffable, which includes the realm of art, aesthetics, ethics, metaphysics, and religion. That there is a domain of values, which words cannot reach, is something that gets nicely articulated in Tagore's following brief poems from *Fireflies* (Tagore 1928b, 272).

Poem no. 251

When the voice of the
Silent touches my words
I know him and therefore I know myself.

Poem no. 229

Those thoughts of mine that are never captured by words
Perch upon my songs and dance.

Poem no. 42

I touch God in my song
As the hill touches the far away sea
With its waterfall
In a whispered dialogue between the shore and the sea,
The shore begs 'Write to me what thy waves struggle to say.

The sea writes in foam again and again and wipes off the lines in a
boisterous despair.'

(Tagore 1928b, 216)

These poems manifest that 'theories, propositions, words and
utterances are futile attempts to convey the meaning of man's ultimate
experience' (Tuck 1974, 102–3). If words fail to convey the meaning
of the union of the finite with the infinite, the poet attempts to write
about silence in paradoxes of words. Attempting to set this expression
of silence in a context, Tagore speaks through the utterance of the
loving devotee, 'Now it is time to sit quiet, face to face with thee, and
to sing dedication of life in this silent and overflowing leisure' (Tagore
1913a, 27). The silence is not only on man's side of the union, but the
Personal Ultimate also remains silent. This does not dishearten or
disturb the man, for he sings, 'If thou speakest not I will fill my heart
with thy silence and endure it' (Tuck 1974, 102).

His union with the Personal Ultimate cannot be expressed wholly
by words, but when verbal forms are employed, song, dance, and
poetry breathe love, joy, and trust. Having exhausted verbal forms,
the religious and artistic man realizes that beyond the verbal barri-
ers there exists a sphere incapable of being pressed into words. How
can one speak of it? Tagore calls it 'silence' or 'silent salutation' (Tuck
1974, 103).

In the philosophy of the *Tractatus* as well as that of Rabindranath
Tagore, we have seen how knowledge is possible and how scientific
knowledge is confined to facts, but within the domain of truth, the
only way of expressing our 'feeling', which has the primary role in life,
is through Art: music, literature, and, above all, poetry.

However, although Wittgenstein stresses that 'whereof one cannot
speak, thereof one must be silent', he was not at all pejorative about
these items of which one should be silent. On the contrary, he believes
them to be very important and he also hints that being silent can also
be, in a certain sense, more communicative (they manifest the limits
of language along with that of reality) than being vocal. In this regard,
one can bring out some affinities between Wittgenstein's notion of
the role of silence in the *Tractatus* and that of Rabindranath Tagore
in *Gītāñjali* and *Stray Birds*. The importance of the role of silence in
the philosophy of Tagore has been noticed by an Egyptian poet-critic,

Muhammad Hesham (2008), in his blog post, 'Language of Eternal Silence: A Reading of Poems by Rabindranath Tagore (1861–1941)', which I have referred to in my subsequent discussion.

Let me turn to some of the poems of *Stray Birds* and *Gītāñjali* where the poet has shown the importance of the role of silence in human life and discourse.

Poem no. 286:

Lead me in the *centre of thy silence* to fill my heart with songs. (Tagore 1916c, 74; emphasis mine)

Songs are expressions of truth; they express the delight of the union of oneself with the outer universe. Here silence is depicted as the centre of the truth, which fills the heart of the poet with deepest feelings, that is, songs without sounds. Silence is said to contain beauty and the secret of love in the following poems:

Poem no. 298:

The silent night has the beauty of the mother and the clamorous day of the child. (Tagore 1916c, 77)

Poem no. 309:

Tonight there is a stir among the palm leaves, a swell in the sea, Full Moon, like the heart throb of the world. From what unknown sky hast thou carried in thy silence the aching secret of love? (Tagore 1916c, 80)

In *Gītāñjali*, God is described as the lord of silence to whom the poet requests:

Poem no. 39:

When tumultuous work raises its dins on all sides, shutting me out from beyond, come to me my lord of silence with thy peace and rest. (Tagore 1913a, 32)

Here, God is 'the lord of silence' and not the metaphysical God or the lord of creation but someone who is very close to one's heart and soothes one's mind when one is experiencing the stress and tensions of life.

In another poem (no. 12) of *Stray Birds*, this eternal silence is posed as the ultimate answer to the eternal quest of human beings.

Poem no. 12:

'What language is thine, O sea?'
'The language of eternal question.'
'What language is thy answer, O sky?'
'The language of eternal silence.' (Tagore 1916c, 4)

Silence is associated with 'the purity of heart and soul':

Poem no. 147:

The dust of the dead words clings to thee
Wash thy soul with silence. (Tagore 1916c, 39)

Poem no. 247:

'How may I sing to thee and worship, O sun?' asked the little flower.
'By the simple silence of thy purity.' Answered the sun. (Tagore 1916c, 64)

In another poem (no. 19) in *Gītāñjali*, the poet hints that the feeling of the truth, the merging of the infinite in finite, can be grasped only by silence:

If thou speakest not, I'll fill my heart with thy silence and bear it. I'll keep still and wait like the night with starry vigil and its head bent low with patience. (Tagore 1913a, 23)

And in Poem no. 65:

Is it thy delight to see thy creation through my eyes and to stand at the portals of my ears silently to listen to thy own eternal harmony thou givest thyself to me in love and then feelest thine own entire sweetness in me. (Tagore 1913a, 47)

One notices here the role of silence in grasping the harmony of the universe reflected in God-in-love, in union with man.

Hesham (2008) rightly interprets a poem in *Stray Birds*:

Silence demonstrates its irony, of being more competent and more communicative than speech. This ironic aspect is revealed through an analogy between the small truth and a little water, on the one hand, and between the great truth and the water in the sea, on the other (from Poem no. 176):

The water in a vessel is sparkling; the water in the sea is dark.

The small truth has words that are clear; the great truth has great silence. (Tagore 1916c, 56)

Here, as in other poems, the efficacy of language is called into question. Words can only describe simple things and emotions, while no language can encompass 'the great truth' which belongs to the world of 'great silence' (Hesham 2008, 3).

In a poem (no. 16) of *Gītāñjali*, the poet is saying that truth eludes our sensible representations in words:

Poem no. 16:

I have had my invitation in this world festival and thus my life has been blessed. My eyes have seen and my ears had heard.

It was my part at this feast to play upon my harp and I have done all I could. Now, I ask, has the time come at last when I may go in and see thy face and offer thee my silent salutation? (Tagore 1913a, 22–3)

What one can see or listen to in everyday life is translatable in words, but when one is with their innermost reality, 'one's lord of life', they fail to express it in words. This is probably the reason that one's salutations are always silent.

This, on the other hand, shows the expressive power of silence as far as the expression of truth is concerned. In the poem, what is spoken of suggests the 'doubled significance of what is not spoken of' (Hesham 2008, 2).

However, I would like to quote, finally, two poems (no. 100 and no. 67) from *Gītāñjali*, where he is explicit about the intimate companionship of the form and the formless, where the importance of silence has also been portrayed:

Poem no. 100:

I dive down into the depth of the ocean of forms, hoping to gain the perfect pearl of the formless. No more sailing from harbour to harbour with this my weather beaten bark. The days are long past when my sport was tossed on waves.

Into the audience hall at the fathomless abyss where swells up the music of the toneless strings I shall take this harp of my life. I shall tune it to the notes of forever, and, when it has sobbed out its last utterance, lay down my silent harp at the feet of the silent. (Tagore 1913a, 64)

Poem no. 67:

But there where spreads the infinite sky for the soul to take her flight in, reigns the stainless white radiance, there is no day, nor night, nor form, nor colour and *never never a word*. (Tagore 1913a, 48; emphasis mine)

All these poems point to the fact that when you are face to face with your innermost reality, words are inadequate tools for the expression of that ultimate communion. Now it is clear why instead of replying to the queries made by the members of the Vienna Circle, Wittgenstein preferred reading poems from Tagore's *Gītāñjali*.

Like the Tagore of *Personality* (1959), Wittgenstein had also used the simile of a cup to bring forth the right significance of that situation. Even if you genuinely want, you cannot pour a gallon of water into a small teacup. It is beyond the capacity of the cup to contain a gallon of water. Similarly, if you want to express your experience of communication with reality, words are incapable of doing that. We cannot sensibly express our communication with reality in words, this is sensibly inexpressible. One can arrive there silently and 'lay down one's silent harp at the feet of the silent'.

Finally, I would like to conclude the chapter by agreeing with Allan Janik that 'whether we like it or not, the *Tractatus* concludes with a genuinely *mystical silence* that permits *something which cannot be said* come into focus' (Janik 2011, 11; emphasis mine). And it is this *genuine mystical silence* that is highlighted in most early works of Rabindranath Tagore. That the important discourses such as ethics and aesthetics also belong to this domain of 'mystical silence' will be evident when one moves to the next chapter: 'The Domain of the Ineffable: The Ethical and the Aesthetic'.

Notes

1. Resolute reading is upheld in James Conant (1991; 2002) and Cora Diamond (1991; 1997), Conant and Diamond (2004), Brian McGuinness (1981), Ricketts (1996), and Peter Winch (1993).

2. The proponents of ineffability readings include G.E.M. Anscombe (1959), Anthony Kenny (1973), Norman Malcolm (1986; 1993), David Pears (1987), Bertrand Russell, (as reflected Russell's introduction in Wittgenstein 1972, ix–xxii), and currently most notably, P.M.S. Hacker (1986; 2000).

3. 'The work is strictly philosophical and at the same time literary', as he observes in a letter to Ludwig Von Ficker (as cited in Engelmann 1967, 78).

4. *'Abyakter birāt plabon beston koriā āche dibas rātrire'* (Tagore's poem, as quoted in Ganguly 1968, 37).

3

The Domain of the Ineffable

The Ethical and the Aesthetic

Wittgenstein's characterization of his own *Treatise on Philosophical Logic* (*Tractatus Logico-Philosophicus*) as a book on ethics[1] has baffled its interpreters right from the publication of his letter in which he described it as such to Ludwig Von Ficker (Engelmann 1967, 143–4), his closest confidante during the early period of his life. Even before that, Wittgenstein's dense and cryptic remarks on ethics and aesthetics in the last few pages of the *Tractatus* have puzzled and intrigued its commentators. How could a treatise on philosophical logic talk about 'the mystical', while also including remarks on ethics, aesthetics, and other such disciplines? Not only that, the remarks characterized ethics as (a) *transcendental* hence *beyond significant language* (b) *mystical* and *nonsensical* and (c) being *one and the same with aesthetics*. Early commentators were eager to brush aside these remarks as unimportant compared to the main thesis about language and meaning in the *Tractatus*.[2] Now, as I have mentioned earlier, with the publication of Wittgenstein's diaries, notebooks, letters, and other manuscripts, it has become evident that these remarks found in the last few pages are as important as those in the earlier pages, and that to ignore all these deliberately would contribute to the complete misunderstanding of the work.

In this chapter there will be an attempt to interpret Wittgenstein's remarks on ethics and aesthetics in the light of the poems of Rabindranath Tagore. However, my reference to Tagore is not intended to imply that Wittgenstein's view in this regard is a direct consequence of or is influenced by the writings of Tagore. Rather, I intend to point out that in spite of their different intellectual make-ups and their belonging to two different modernities, their visions regarding ethics and aesthetics overlap in significant respects. Hence, there' will be an attempt to bring out the parallels between Wittgenstein's and Tagore's thoughts on ethics and aesthetics in this chapter.

In earlier chapters, the readers are informed that the theory of language and meaning of the *Tractatus* demand that there are certain things that cannot be put into words, but make themselves manifest. It has already been mentioned that these include things such as logical form, pictorial form, the form of a law, the limit of the world, language, self, ethics, aesthetics, metaphysics, religion, and finally the propositions of the *Tractatus*. What is intriguing is that Wittgenstein characterizes these also as 'mystical'. I quote:

T6.522: There are indeed things that cannot be put into words. They make themselves manifest. They are what is mystical.

The incongruity of the above remark lies in making both the logical and the ethical items mystical at the same time. We have noticed earlier, that the inexpressibility of certain items of knowledge is in large part a consequence of the thesis of the *Tractatus* that describes language as a picture of reality, implying that various things about language and the world cannot be pictured. Thus, a proposition is sensible if it can picture a fact of the world. If it pictures accurately, it is a true proposition; if not, it is false. As language consists of the combination of complex sentences, so the world consists of a combination of highly complex facts. A complex proposition is the truth function of elementary propositions and an elementary proposition pictures an atomic fact. To elucidate the notions of 'elementary proposition' and 'atomic fact', if one analyses a complex proposition, one gets less complex propositions, and if one analyses a less complex proposition, one gets a simple proposition.

However, one can go on analysing simple propositions, and ultimately reach a proposition that cannot be further analysed.

Such propositions, Wittgenstein claims, are called elementary propositions.

On the other hand, the world, for early Wittgenstein, is the totality of facts, which are very complex. Now when one analyses a complex fact, one gets less complex facts; while analysing less complex facts, one gets simple facts; and on analysing simple facts, one ultimately reaches facts that cannot be further analysed into any other facts. Such facts are designated by Wittgenstein as atomic facts. According to the *Tractatus*, these elementary propositions picture atomic facts.

However, an elementary/atomic proposition consists of 'names'. 'Names' have been used technically in the *Tractatus* to denote indefinable, un-analysable logical atoms of language. Had they not been so, these names could have been analysed in terms of other propositions and they would not fit the criteria of being un-analysable. Similarly atomic facts are not composed of other facts, but they consist of objects. These objects are not our ordinary objects. 'Objects' also has been used in a special, technical sense. They are indefinable, un-analysable logical atoms of the world. Moreover, we do not have any example of a 'name' or an object in the *Tractatus*. Once, when asked about the reason for the absence of examples of 'names' and 'objects', Wittgenstein said that he had arrived at these logical atoms by adopting an a priori method and that as he is a logician, he is not supposed to give a concrete example of what he deduced as the conclusion of a deductive argument.

Hence, according to the *Tractatus*, if someone uses a sentence meaningfully he uses it to picture an atomic fact, and this means that there was a special kind of correlation between psychic elements in his mind, elements of the sentence in a language, and elements of the state of affairs of the world. A sentence which in this way pictures an atomic fact will be true or false depending upon whether the atomic fact obtained or not.

This idea of what had to be the case for a sentence to make sense also led to the view that many collections of words that might seem in one way or another to be sensible sentences are not so. This was because they are not representations of any state of affair. First of all, we have the notion of logical form and pictorial form. A logical form/pictorial form is the form that a proposition must have in common with reality in order to be able to represent it. This form cannot be pictured; as picturing itself is a two-termed relation. It holds between two complexes (that is, between a picture-complex and a fact-complex) when they are related in a certain way, that is, when one is projected onto or used as a projection of the other. But this does not allow a rule of projection to be pictured, for it is neither a complex picture, nor a complex fact, nor a state of affairs. So the rule of projection cannot be related to a complex picture or fact by another law of projection.

Thus these pictorial/logical/representational forms are indeed things that cannot be put into words. They make themselves manifest in a picture. They are 'the mystical'.

Similarly, propositions of ethics, aesthetics, metaphysics, religion, art, and so on are also not pictures of a worldly state of affairs. The criterion of meaning of the *Tractatus* makes all these propositions nonsensical although they manifest the meaning of life and the world. He believed that it is the tendency of human beings to try to go beyond the boundaries of language and say something that is unsayable (about the totality, the meaning of life, and the world) from the point of view of the *Tractatus*. In Chapter 4, one will be able to make out how the logical and the ethical merge consistently in being 'transcendental' and in 'being the condition of the world'.

It has been stated clearly in Chapter 1 how Wittgenstein himself wanted to stress that essentially formless in fact *manifests* the form in the realm of ethics, aesthetics, art, literature, and religion. It has also been hinted earlier that if the meeting can be understood via non-factual contemplation (silence), then it will establish also why ethical judgments are not meaningless, although they lack sense in terms of the criteria given in the *Tractatus*.

In this chapter there will be an attempt to establish that to Wittgenstein, the discourse of ethics was extremely important because it is 'the enquiry into the meaning of life' or 'into what makes life worth living' or 'into the right way of living'. The chapter is divided into three main sections in accordance with the characterization of ethics in the *Tractatus*, where views of both the thinkers are juxtaposed. The first section is about the inexpressibility/transcendentality of ethics, the second takes care of the mysticality and nonsensicality of ethics, and the third is on Wittgenstein's account of the sameness of ethics and aesthetics. Thereafter, I will demonstrate that Tagore's characterization of ethics and aesthetics was the same in his early and later works of Art, and finally I argue that the domain of the ineffable, that is, the ethical and the aesthetical as being one and the same, follows from the philosophy of both Tagore and Wittgenstein.

Inexpressibility/Transcendentality of Ethics and Aesthetics

In this section, I will begin with the remarks on ethics in the *Tractatus*, *Notebooks 1914–1916*, and 'A Lecture on Ethics',[3] the totality of which will represent the thoughts of early Wittgenstein. The *Tractatus* declares:

> T6.421: It is clear that Ethics cannot be put into words. Ethics is transcendental (Ethics and Aesthetics are one and the same).
> T6.42: So too it is impossible for there to be propositions of Ethics. Propositions can express nothing that is higher.

Early Wittgenstein had to maintain this as he believed that what can be put into words are only the propositions of natural science, that is, factual propositions. The propositions of ethics are not factual statements by any means. They are concerned with values. At this point, the most disturbing questions which one faces is: If one cannot talk about what is higher, what about the literature entitled as 'ethics' right from the days of sophists to the present day? How does one regard them as inexpressible? What does 'higher' signify in this context? Why should one treat value as transcendental and higher?

If one remains confined only within the remarks of the *Tractatus*, there is no clue as to how to answer these questions or how to explain the cryptic passages of the *Tractatus*. But in 'A Lecture on Ethics' we find Wittgenstein elucidating the reasons why he thought that ethics cannot be put into words and why ethics is transcendental. This lecture is the only public lecture that Wittgenstein delivered in Cambridge during his stay. It had been prepared sometime between September 1929 and December 1930. It is interesting to note over here that all the major works of Tagore had been translated in German language by this time!

While discussing ethical matters in this lecture, Wittgenstein distinguishes between relative value judgments and absolute value judgments. Relative value judgments are those for which we have factual criteria, which means that in each case in which the statement of relative value is true, there is a factual criteria in virtue of which it is true. In simple words, relative value judgments can be reducible to mere statements of facts. For example, we can consider these:

1. He is a good orator.
2. This is the right way to go to Alipore Campus, University of Calcutta.

For all these statements of relative value, there are factual statements which correspond to them. We can also say that these are the factual criteria for such judgments of value.

Corresponding to the first relative value judgment, the factual criteria are: he has got a command of the language and the topic he is giving a speech on, he can express his thoughts within a short period of time, his voice is appealing to the masses, and so on. But these are all contingent matters of fact, which may vary from one situation to another.

So is our second example. One could equally well describe it by 'this is the right way', that is, 'it is the shortest route, without traffic signals, and the condition of the road is smooth enough for a ride and so on, you have to go if you want to get to Alipore campus, University of Calcutta in the least time'.

In contrast to this, 'there are absolute judgments of value for which there are no factual criteria'. There will be no factual statements corresponding to these statements, which will serve as the criterion for making such judgments. For example, you ought not to tell lies; you ought to love your parents.

According to Wittgenstein, these absolute statements go beyond any facts. What would have to correspond to them if they were to be true, would be something like a necessary truth about the world. As he says:

> If one could talk about the absolutely right road, it would be the road which, everybody, on seeing it would, *with logical necessity*, have to go, or be ashamed for not going. And similarly, the absolute good, if it is a describable state of affairs, would be one, which everybody would

necessarily bring about or feel guilty for not bringing it about. And I want to say that such a state of affair is a chimera. (Wittgenstein 1965, 7)

Regarding these absolute value judgments Wittgenstein wants to make two important points: first of all, these judgments cannot be put into words, and if anyone tries to put them into words, the result would be a chimera. He elucidates:

> Suppose one of you were an omniscient person and suppose this man wrote all he knew in a big book, and then this book would contain the whole description of the world; and what I want to say is that this book would contain nothing that we would call an ethical judgment or anything that would logically imply such a judgment. It would of course contain all relative judgments of value and all true scientific propositions and in fact all true propositions that can be made. But all the facts described would, as it were, stand on the same level. (Wittgenstein 1965, 6)

From this quotation it follows that we cannot write a book on ethics as consisting of absolute judgments of value because that would contain facts, facts, and facts, and facts cannot express something that is *higher* and facts are all 'on the same level'.

In the *Tractatus*, Wittgenstein gives no hint regarding how to explain the word 'higher', but in 'A Lecture on Ethics' he is quite explicit. He says:

> There are no propositions which, in any absolute sense, are sublime, important and trivial. (Wittgenstein 1965, 6)

So, it seems, by 'higher' he meant something absolute and sublime, which he attached to his notion of ethics:

> Ethics, if it is anything, is supernatural and our words only express facts. ... So far as facts and propositions are concerned, there is only relative value and relative good, right etc. (Wittgenstein 1965, 7)

Now, the second point that he wants to emphasize is that our words, as we use them in science, are capable of conveying only facts that constitute the sense of the empirical and scientific propositions but they cannot express anything other than that. That is beyond their capacity as a teacup is incapable of containing a gallon of water; similarly a word is incapable of expressing anything other than facts. To quote from Wittgenstein:

> Our words will only express facts; as a teacup will only hold a teacup full of water even if I were to pour out a gallon over it. (Wittgenstein 1965, 6)

This reminds us of similar remarks made by Rabindranath in *Personality (Lectures Delivered in America)* and translated in German as *Persönlichkeit* by Helene Meyer-Franck in 1921. Both Tagore and Wittgenstein agree that words in our everyday language are incapable of expressing the higher truth. Tagore also wanted to stress that facts are inadequate tools for the expression of truth:

> They [facts] are like wine cups that carry it [truth], they are hidden by it, it overflows them. It is infinite in its suggestions; it is extravagant in its words. It is personal, therefore beyond science. (Tagore 1923c, 48)

It seems that for both the thinkers, ordinary words are incapable of expressing truth; hence they cannot be put into words. Not only that, both of them believed that ethics goes beyond scientific representation. In his letter to Ludwig von Ficker, Wittgenstein states clearly: 'Ethics ... does not add to our knowledge in any sense' (1965, 12). Obviously he means that it does not add to our factual scientific knowledge. It simply depicts human tendencies to run against the boundaries of language which, though fruitless, still deserve our deep respect and admiration.

At a meeting in Schlick's house on 17 December 1930, Wittgenstein said:

> At the end of my lecture on Ethics, I spoke in the first person. I think that this is something very essential. Here there is nothing to be stated anymore; all I can do is to step forth as an individual and speak in the first person. ... Running against the limits of language? Language is after all not a cage.
>
> All I can say is this: I do not scoff at this tendency in man; I hold it in reverence. And here it is essential that this is not a description of sociology but that I am speaking about myself. (Cited in Waismann 1979, 117–18)

Here, one finds Wittgenstein feeling within himself this tendency to run against the boundaries of language, since he personally feels that this is the only way one can understand or talk about ethics, aesthetics, religion, art, literature, and so on. These are not, however, statements of facts or events, hence they are 'not a description of sociology'. That means one cannot give a sociological description of ethics. Ethics, as depicted by Wittgenstein, lies beyond sociological description.

There is another puzzling point in the quotation. Here one sees Wittgenstein saying both that language is a cage and not a cage. He took language as a cage when he stated, 'This running against the walls of our cage is perfectly, absolutely hopeless,' and not a cage when he stated, 'Language is after all, not a cage.' To solve this puzzle one can refer to Cyril Barrett who solves it in the following way:

> Language is in one sense a cage and in another sense not a cage. As a cage it sets limits and establishes boundaries to what can be said. We run up against these boundaries when we try to say what cannot be said in the manner in which we try to say it. But in another sense it is not a cage; by using it obliquely or by just running up against it, we can transcend it and make ourselves understood. We are still not saying anything but we are communicating with one another and can therefore be understood. (Barrett 1991, 49)

This interpretation comes very close to the philosophy of Tagore for whom ethics belongs in the domain of surplus and beyond the domain of science, where man

> can amply afford to say that goodness is for the sake of goodness. And upon this wealth of goodness—*where honesty is not valued for being the best policy, but because it can afford to go against all policies*—man's ethics is founded. (Tagore 1917c, 19; emphasis mine)

While elucidating this notion of goodness for the sake of goodness, he points out: 'There is a division in man, a dualism in his consciousness of what is and what ought to be. In the animal this is lacking, man's conflict is between what is desired and what should be desired. "What is desired" dwells in the heart of the natural life that we share with animals [the domain of facts]; but "what should be desired" belongs to a life that is far beyond it [the domain of surplus]' (Tagore 1917, 102).)

There is often a conflict between what is desired and what ought to be desired, between animal life and man's life. Many things which are good for one are evil for the other. To desire what ought to be desired often demands sacrificing 'amenities of the world' on the part of the agent. Most of the time it is what he/she desires most. So he has to fight against his own desires, against himself. Tagore believes that 'this necessity of a fight within oneself has introduced an element into man's personality, which is character. From the life of desire it guides man to the life of purpose. This life is the life of the moral world' (Tagore 1917, 103).

This distinction between what is and what ought to be, what I do and what I should have done runs parallel to the most fundamental distinction between 'fact' and 'truth'. What we do or what happens belongs to the domain of facts, whereas 'good' as predicate belongs to the domain of surplus. Unlike ordinary predicates, it does not refer to any factual property of an object. Thus 'goodness' as a value points beyond the domain of facts. The 'goodness' which one 'ought to desire' is not reducible to usefulness. For Tagore, 'what works for better harmony and is a mark of our spiritual plenitude' is meant as 'goodness' (Tagore 2001, 37–8). To elucidate, the philosophy of Tagore advocates the philosophy of harmony. In the domain of morality, he believes,

> Whatever is beneficent is in deepest union with the whole world, in secret harmony with the mind of all humanity. (Tagore 2001, 172)

It is this deepest union that does not allow a person to use another *as a means*. If one uses another as a means then the deepest union with the whole world is disrupted. Moreover, Tagore was of the opinion: 'We do not express the whole truth about the benign if we say it is called "good" because it benefits us. The truly benign serves our need and it is beautiful: that is, it has an unaccountable attraction that surpasses its use.' (2001, 173). What surpasses its use is also beyond significant expression. Thus, ethics is 'an attempt to run up against significant language' and it gets manifested in creative actions. The goodness of an action depends on the way a human being survives on its surplus and the manner in which he is related to other human beings. That is, if by performing an action a man rises above his physical, material ego and its desires, and transcends himself to the spirit of surplus, he does something good; for to transcend to the spirit of surplus means to be united with 'universal man' or 'the man of one's heart'. In order to transcend to the spirit of surplus one has to 'turn his own passions and desires from tyranny into obedience' (Tagore 1923, 81). To put it simply, for Tagore, to be moral means to rise above one's emotions and passions, to be happy and in tune with the whole world. One can hear the echo of this in Wittgenstein's *Notebooks 1914–1916*:

> How can man be happy at all, since he cannot ward off the misery of this world? Through the life of knowledge. ... The life of knowledge is the life that is happy in spite of the misery of the world. The only life that is happy is the life that can renounce the amenities of the world. To it the amenities of the world are so many graces of fate. (Wittgenstein 1961a, 81)

Commentators are puzzled regarding the interpretation of such passages. Cyril Barrett is of the opinion that 'it has to be admitted that Wittgenstein is pretty *isolated* in his view. He is *not in line with hedonists or utilitarian or emotivists or ethical relativists*' (1991, 34). Here, I argue that although the Tractarian view of ethics does not fit at all with the conventional views of Western morality, yet it meshes nicely with that of Tagore's as far as the transcendentality and inexpressibility of ethics is concerned. I will discuss this in detail while elaborating the theme of the *King of the Dark Chamber* in Chapter 5 of this book, which in turn will clarify why Wittgenstein got attracted to the play.

Ethics as Mystical and Nonsensical

> T6.522: There are indeed things that cannot be put into words. They make themselves manifest. They are what is mystical.
> T6.44: It is not how things are in the world that is mystical, but that it exists.
> T6.45: To view the world sub-specie-aeterni is to view it as a whole—a limited whole. Feeling the world as a limited whole—it is this that is mystical.

In our earlier discussion, we have seen how Wittgenstein distinguished between what can be talked about and what cannot. Here, he is adding that what cannot be talked about falls under the head 'mystical'. 'The mystical' is related to a particular type of viewing of the world—viewing it as a limited whole. It is interesting to note that ethics for Wittgenstein as well as Tagore fits in with all these characterizations.

About 'the mystical', Wittgenstein says:

> T6.44: It is not how things are in the world that is mystical, but that it exists.

Elsewhere, he says:

> It is the experience of seeing the world as a miracle. (Wittgenstein 1965, 11)

Here, Wittgenstein is equating wonder at the existence of the world with the treating of the existence of the world as a miracle. Moreover, he associates this with aesthetics at the same time. In *Notebooks 1914–1916*, Wittgenstein writes,

> Aesthetically, the miracle is that the world exists. (Wittgenstein 1961a, 84e)

He maintains that his seeing the world as a miracle—wondering at its existence—is not the scientific way of seeing things; for he also says:

> The truth is that the scientific way of looking at a fact is not the way to look at it as a miracle. (Wittgenstein 1965, 11)

Now the question arises: Which way of looking at the world makes it a miracle?

According to Wittgenstein, this is the way of seeing the world sub specie aeterni (T6.45). For Wittgenstein, then, seeing the world as a miracle and taking its existence as mystical is the same thing as what he speaks of in T6.45, seeing it as a limited whole or seeing it sub specie aeterni. We can see that this is closely connected with things Wittgenstein says in *Notebooks 1914–1916*. There he says:

> The usual way of looking at things sees objects, as it were, from the midst of them, the view *sub specie aeternitatis*, from outside. In such a way that they have the whole world as a background. Is this it perhaps. ... In this view the object is seen together with space and time instead

of in space and time. The thing seen *sub specie aeternitatis* is the thing seen together with the whole logical space. (Wittgenstein 1961a, 83e)

It seems that to view a thing sub specie aeterni means viewing it as the most significant thing, which is not at par with other things in the world, it comes to the fore and the whole world goes to the background. This viewing from eternity is, however, peculiarly common to both ethical and aesthetical viewpoints.

Most importantly, for Wittgenstein 'the wonder that the world exists' serves as an example of 'absolute value judgment'. To him, it is experience par excellence and it is mystical; it cannot be put into words. Here, one might object that the term 'wonder' is being misused. We usually wonder at a thing that is not natural, that is, the opposite of which is taken to be normal; whereas in the case of the wonder that the world exists, we cannot even conceive of the world as non-existing. Thus it is nonsense to say that I wonder at the existence of the world.

Now, what is this experience that Wittgenstein says corresponds to the expression 'I wonder at the existence of the world'? From Wittgenstein's point of view in the *Tractatus*, we can understand that it lacks sense. Yet, for Wittgenstein, it corresponds to an experience that he considers both absolutely valuable and beautiful. What experience does he have in mind?

Even as a metaphor it goes far beyond our comprehension. Here I would like to point out that we can make some sense of the Wittgensteinian notion of absolute value judgements and the examples he uses in order to elucidate his most cryptic point—why ethics, truly speaking, cannot be put into words—one should look at the poems of Rabindranath Tagore.

Hence, I will bring in some of Tagore's poems to elucidate Wittgenstein's notion of absolute value judgements. The first poem I will refer to is 'The Awakening of a Stream'.[4] This poem depicts joys, unbounded joys, experienced by the poet for the existence of the world. It is the typically mystical experience to which he refers again and again in various contexts. Regarding this experience, he says in his Hibbert lectures:

When I was 18, a sudden spring breeze of religious experience for the first time came to my life and passed away leaving in my memory a direct message of my spiritual reality. One day while I stood watching at early dawn the sun sending out its ray from behind the trees, I suddenly felt as if some ancient mist had in a moment lifted from my sight, and the morning light on the face of the world revealed an inner radiance of joy. The invisible screen of the common place was removed from all things and all men and their ultimate significance was intensified in my mind. (Tagore 1953a, 93–4)

Another important insight we find in another poem where he speaks of the wonderful experience of the whole world embracing his heart is the following: 'I don't know how my heart unfolded and embraced the whole world today.'[5] It is true that one cannot picture the event of the world embracing one's heart or awakening of one's 'vital consciousness', but still one is attempting to express something that is inexpressible in the Tractarian sense. In this way, one commits oneself to nonsensicalities from the point of view of the *Tractatus*. Still they are important because they are artistic representations of 'viewing the world sub specie aeterni'; it seems as if the Tractarian ethical viewpoint has been nicely articulated in the poems of Tagore. Wittgenstein, while elucidating the experiences representative of absolute value judgments, states:

I will mention another experience straight away which I also know and which others of you might be acquainted with: it is, what one might call, the experience of feeling *absolutely* safe. (Wittgenstein 1965, 8)

Here also the term 'safe' has been misused. Because the term 'safe' can be used meaningfully only if I can compare it to or contrast it with other words depicting the imminent danger from which one can claim to be safe. I can meaningfully say that I am safe in my room in the sense that a leopard cannot attack me, and I am safe if I had Chikungunia but it did not relapse; but I cannot use the term 'safe' while saying 'I am always safe'. If I do that, I am misusing the language. Explaining this, Wittgenstein says: 'It is the state of mind in which one is inclined to say "I am safe, nothing can injure me whatever happens"'. This is connected with the idea of 'I am safe in the hands of God' (Wittgenstein 1965, 10). Now 'being absolutely safe' does not exclude the possibility of misery to the individual. Rather he can face all kinds of misery without being affected by it. Here in order to elucidate why Wittgenstein considers this example, I would like to narrate an incident from his life where he himself went through a mystical experience. Wittgenstein had some kind of mystic experience some time before he completed *Notebooks 1914–1916*. It is also suggested, on the basis of an account by Erich Heller in volume 72 of *Encounter* in 1959 (quoted in Nieli 1987, 69), that the occasion for at least one such experience was the performance of the play *Die Kreuzeischreiber* by the Austrian dramatist Ludwig Anzengrüber around 1910. There, Ludwig heard a character saying that nothing bad could happen to him no matter what went on in the world. The scene with the recurring line 'nothing can happen to you' together with the account of a religious awakening brings immediately to mind the story of Wittgenstein's change in attitude towards religion as told by Wittgenstein to Norman Malcolm (Nieli 1987, 69–70). One might feel the presence of the Indian concept of *Stithaprajña*[6] here. Cyril Barrett says:

> This notion of being absolutely safe is an oriental notion which Wittgenstein imbibed from Schopenhauer. (Barrett 1991, 54–5)

It is true that Wittgenstein was influenced by Schopenhauer, but he read Schopenhauer at the age of 19; whereas when he was writing 'A Lecture on Ethics' in 1929, it was not Schopenhauer but Tagore's writings that impressed him a lot. I do not want to say that Wittgenstein took these ideas from Tagore because so far we do not have any evidence of an acknowledgement of or indebtedness to Tagore in any of Wittgenstein's writings; but what is evident is that there are affinities between the ideas of the two great minds as far as these experiences are concerned. For example, one can cite a poem from Tagore:

> Even if there is a tempest, the headache is not yours, enjoy the fury of the waves and do not worry. Let the night and deep darkness descends, the helmsman secures the boat and will row you across to safety. (Tagore 1914f, Song no. 53)

The helmsman is none other than God and you are absolutely safe, whatever happens, in the hands of God.

A third experience of the same kind is that of feeling guilty and again this was described by the phrase that God disapproves of our conduct.

Next, I would like to point to an inconsistency in the text as far as these absolute value judgements are concerned. Wittgenstein is maintaining on the one hand that 'it is clear that ethics cannot be put into words' and that 'Ethics is transcendental' (Wittgenstein 1922, T.6.421), and on the other hand he is talking about ethics as consisting of absolute value judgements. Not only that, he is offering us examples of absolute value judgements. Regarding art and aesthetics also, he says on the one hand that it is closely connected with the mystical and 'the mystical' is something of which nothing can be spoken about and 'silence is the only possible expression of the mystical, seen sub-specie-aeterni' (Mualem 2002, 69). Whereas in *Notebooks 1914–1916*, he declares:

Art is a kind of expression. Good art is complete expression. (Wittgenstein 1961a, 83e)

How does one negotiate this inconsistency? From Wittgenstein's point of view, it might be said that because of this it was so difficult to understand what absolute judgements are like. It is simply an attempt to *point to* the inexpressible of which one can have a glimpse only through a poem. Wittgenstein asked himself this question in *Notebooks 1914–1916*:

Now try to ask: whether THAT can be expressed which cannot be EXPRESSED? But is there no domain outside the facts? Is language the only language? (Wittgenstein 1961a, 52e)

This means that he also felt that the factual language is not the only language for factual language cannot apprehend 'what is higher'. So there must be some language which can at least 'point to the higher'. Engelmann's memoirs and characterization of Wittgenstein here give us clues regarding the language that can at least point to the transcendental, to the higher. I quote:

He [Wittgenstein] relates the act of showing to poetry. (Engelmann 1967, 83)

Engelmann again remarks,

Poetry can produce a profound artistic effect beyond (but never without the immediate effect of its language). (Engelmann 1967, 84)

The 'profound artistic effect' that goes beyond the 'effect of its language' seems to mean that poetry can show far more than it can possibly say, or, more sharply formulated, poetry says nothing and yet it manages to manifest things that can only be shown. That is why he felt that the poem of Uhland conveyed the unutterable truth only by not uttering it in any explicit way. This is also the reason why the poems of Rabindranath Tagore could capture the essence of what Wittgenstein intended to *point to* and also why Wittgenstein was so fond of the poems and plays of Tagore. It is true that there are differences in their attitudes to language; still, in spite of their differences there are contexts that overlap.

Now coming to their points of divergences, one can suggest that contrary to Tagore, Wittgenstein termed both ethics and aesthetics nonsensical as they attempted to express something that is inexpressible; the way they make use of language contributes to its misuse. In 'A Lecture on Ethics', Wittgenstein comments that 'certain misuse of language runs through all ethical and religious expressions' (Wittgenstein 1965, 9) because of which they all are termed 'nonsensical'. He was not hesitant also to declare in his letters how reverential he was towards these nonsensicalities.

Although he denies the sensicalities of those propositions, which do not fall within the domain of natural science (that is, which do not picture any possible situation of the world), what he thinks most important is what we must pass over in silence or show without words. For him, what leads to nonsensical expressions is the longing to reach out and a passion for the absolute. It is this desire to know the reality that makes us unsatisfied with saying what can only be said. Whether or not this feeling is communicable, Wittgenstein feels in him this tendency deeply. So this drawing of a boundary around the sphere of what can be said significantly is not done to condemn or ridicule those who have attempted to cross the boundary. And this tendency of crossing the threshold of language and factual meaning is evident in the writings of the poet where he maintains that truth is inexpressible in ordinary scientific language; though it gets manifested in Art, which includes drawing, painting, sculpture, music, and dance.

It is true that Tagore will not allow his 'truth' to be 'nonsensical' as he did not approach it from a linguistic point of view. But his reverence for silence as depicting the sense of the world comes very close to the heart of Wittgenstein.[7] We cannot sensibly express our communication with reality in words, this is sensibly inexpressible. One can reach there silently and 'lay down one's silent harp at the feet of the silent' (Tagore 1913, Poem no. 53).

In the next section, the sameness of ethics and aesthetics will be discussed.

Ethics and Aesthetics are One and the Same (T6.421)

In the previous section, I have discussed at length issues regarding ethics in both the thinkers, but I have not specifically said anything about aesthetics in Wittgenstein or in Tagore. Hence, I would like to introduce views on aesthetics of both the thinkers at the beginning. This section is divided in the following three subsections:

1.   Early Wittgenstein and Aesthetics
2.   Rabindranath Tagore and Aesthetics
3.   Tagore and Wittgenstein: Convergence of Ideas on Aesthetics

Early Wittgenstein and Aesthetics

Malcolm points out that the most frequent topic of discussion at Wittgenstein's places was aesthetics (Malcolm 1958, 53). It is now widely known that he donated a huge sum from his inheritance to literary/aesthetical persons in need. Wittgenstein also wanted to get his book (*Tractatus*) published in a notable literary journal entitled *Der Brenner* as he believed that the major impetus of the work was literary and ethical, which for him was also aesthetical.

Besides philosophy, Wittgenstein carried out an investigation concerning rhythm in music at the psychological laboratory of Cambridge. He had hoped that the experiments would throw light on some questions of aesthetics that interested him. Wittgenstein was 'exceptionally musical', even if one judged by the highest standards. He played the clarinet and for a time he wished to become a conductor. He had a rare talent for whistling. It was a great pleasure to hear him whistle through a whole concert, interrupting himself only to draw the listener's attention to some detail of the musical texture (Von Wright 1967, 17). M.O.C. Drury in 'Some Notes on Conversations with Wittgenstein' (1984) also mentions his complete absorption in classical music. Engelmann, in his memoir, informs about Wittgenstein's passionate attachment to literature.

I quote from Engelmann:

> Wittgenstein was enraptured by Mörike's immortal story, Mozart's journey to Prague, and in it specially by the passages describing musical effects in words; 'coming as from remotest starry worlds, the sounds fall from the mouth of silver trombones, icy cold, cutting through marrow and soul; fall through the blueness of the night', he would recite with a shudder of awe. (Engelmann 1967, 85)

Rudolf Haller offers a list of poets and writers 'who may have contributed to his understanding' from Germany and other places, which include Johann Wolfgang von Goethe, Friedrich Schiller, Gotthold Ephraim Lessing, Matthias Claudius, Eduard Mörike, Ludwig Uhland, Wilhelm Busch, and certainly Georg Christoph Lichtenberg, from Switzerland Gottfried Keller, and from Austria Franz Grillparzer, Johann Nestroy, and Rainer Maria Rilke. But others should also be mentioned: for instance, Russian writers (especially Dostoevsky and Tolstoy), and *the famous Indian poet, Rabindranath Tagore* (Haller 2003, 93).

Aesthetics in Tractatus Logico-Philosophicus

The important point regarding aesthetics in the *Tractatus* is at the close of the proposition T6.421, in the form of a parenthetical remark: '*Ethics and Aesthetics are one and the same.*'

Apparently though, these two discourses are different. Usually ethics deals with actions that can be judged as good or bad, just or unjust, depending on whether it fulfils or fails to fulfil the ethical norm or criteria. In that sense, the approach of ethics is more general and objective whereas the approach of aesthetics is rather subjective. Aesthetic attributes are not generally applicable to human actions; rather they apply to individual items of the world, right from the domain of the appearance of human beings to the domain of plants, animals, and insects as well as the non-living universe. Ethics, thus, deals with action, whereas aesthetics deals with 'contemplation'. Moreover, it is possible, we are told, to bypass the aesthetic in a way in which we cannot bypass the ethical: aesthetic awareness is rarely forced upon us and aesthetic situations do not seem to affect our lives significantly. However, ethical situations in Sartre's words, 'spring up around us

like partridges' and even if a person decides to ignore an ethical matter then that decision is itself an ethical one (Collinson 1985, 266). So
why mix the two domains? Why think that the two are 'one and the
same'? There are controversies regarding the ontological identity of
these subjects of discourses because Pears and McGuinness's translation provokes one to think in such terms.[8]

The original sentence in the German language is: 'Ethic und
Aesthetic sind Eins.' Pears and McGuinness translate *eins* as 'one and
the same' though *eins* usually means 'one'. 'One' does not necessarily
connote ontological identity, rather according to some interpreters, it
might hinge on the concept of unity. Moreover, there are interpretations that translate *eins* as representing unity and inter-dependencies
(Stengel 2004, 610–25).

However, there is one reference in Wittgenstein which provides us
with a clue as to how to interpret this *eins*. In 'A Lecture on Ethics',
delivered in 1929, he says,

> Now I am going to use the term Ethics in a slightly wider sense, in a
> sense in fact which includes what I believe to be the most essential part
> of what is generally called Aesthetics'. (Wittgenstein 1965, 4)

In order to give a rough idea as to what it is that ethics is concerned
with, in contrast with the Moorean definition of ethics as the enquiry
into what is good, Wittgenstein says, 'I could have said Ethics is
the enquiry into what is valuable, or, into what is really important,
or I could have said Ethics is the enquiry into the meaning of life,
or into what makes life worth living, or into the right way of living'
(Wittgenstein 1965, 8).

Here, he is explicit that the two subjects are not identical as the
definition of ethics includes only a part of aesthetics; it might be 'the
most essential part', but still it is not the whole of it. Hence, he is not
obliterating the basic distinction between the two subjects but pointing to some fundamental points of affinities and interdependencies
of the two.

However, we can here refer to Engelmann, Wittgenstein's closest
associate at an early period of his life, who writes about this sentence:

> I guess that the statement of the *Tractatus*, 'Ethics and aesthetics
> are one,' is one of the most frequently misunderstood propositions
> of the book. Surely it cannot be assumed that this wide-ranging and

profound thinker had meant to say that there is no difference at all between ethics and aesthetics! But the statement is put in parentheses, said by the way, as something not really meant to be uttered, yet something that should not be passed over in silence at that point. And this is done in the form of a reminder recalling to the understanding reader an insight which he is assumed to possess in any case. (Engelmann 1967, 143)

Here, following David Olson Pook, I suggest that one should take Wittgenstein (and Engelmann, for that matter) at their word. Ethics and aesthetics are one, and yet at the same time Wittgenstein certainly did not mean to say that there is no difference between them (Pook 1994, 65–6).

Now why did Wittgenstein affirm that they are one? What are the connections between the two? From his various remarks one can infer that the connections lie (a) in their being values, hence being inexpressible, (b) in their being related to viewing 'sub specie aeterni', (c) with the 'right view of the world', (d) in their being linked to happiness, and finally (e) in their being 'the miracle', 'the wonder that the world exists'.

Ethics and aesthetics being values, hence being inexpressible

Earlier sections have portrayed the famous Tractarian distinction between saying and showing and also have shown how the domain of values, which includes both ethics and aesthetics, transcends the domain of facts. Hence, ethics and aesthetics are beyond the scope of pictorial representation. They lie outside the boundaries of scientific language; hence, they should be passed over in silence. We know from Engelmann's memoir and letters from Ludwig Von Ficker that the book's (Tractatus Logico-Philosophicus) point is an ethical one. It is at the same time aesthetical. As he mentions in the preface, 'Its purpose would be achieved if it gave pleasure to one person who read and understood it' (Wittgenstein 1922, 3).

Ethics and aesthetics being related to viewing 'sub specie aeterni'

There are so many items that, in accordance with the philosophy of the Tractatus, belong to the domain of the ineffable, but Wittgenstein did not refer to them as being 'one and the same'. Why did he think that ethics and aesthetics are one? We get a clue in *Notebooks 1914–1916*.

> The work of art is the object seen *sub specie aeternitatis* and the good life is the world seen *sub specie aeternitatis*. This is the connection between art and Ethics. (Wittgenstein 1961a, 83)

Viewing sub specie aeterni thus provides the link between these two disciplines. Now, what is this 'viewing sub specie aeterni'? One finds references to this Latin phrase 'sub specie aeternitatis' in the writings of Baruch Spinoza.[9] Spinoza uses it while elucidating his concept of 'intellectual love of God'. Wittgenstein did not use sub specie aeternitatis (Wittgenstein 1961a, 83e) all the time. He uses sub specie aeterni (T6.45) as well. However, all these expressions mean the same—'viewing from eternity'.

In *Culture and Value* we find Wittgenstein explaining what he means by 'viewing sub specie aeterni':

> It seems to me that there is a way of capturing the world *sub specie aeterni*. ... It is as though thought flies above the world and leaves it as it is, observing it from above, in flight. (1998 [1980], 5–7)

Explaining 'viewing sub specie aeterni' in terms of 'viewing from above in flight' might remind us that Ludwig was an aeronautical engineer at the beginning of his career. And it provides us also with an insight that such viewing leaves everything in the world 'as it is'. It cannot bring about any change in the facts or events of the world. And when you see from above, everything seems to be at the same level.

Now what happens when one views an object 'from eternity'? That object becomes the whole world .Wittgenstein elucidates, 'The thing seen *sub specie aeternitatis* is the thing seen together with the whole logical space' (Wittgenstein 1961a, 83e). Logical space in the *Tractatus* indicates the domain of possibilities, of those which are actual, constitute the world. Again, the world is also equivalent to reality, which consists of both positive and negative states of affairs, that is, it comprises the whole logical space. Hence, if the object viewed sub specie aeterni is viewing it together with the whole logical space then it implies that it constitutes the whole world.

He explains it with the example of a stove.

> As a thing among things, each thing is equally insignificant: as a world each one equally significant. If I have been contemplating the stove, and then am told but now all you know is the stove, my result does indeed seem trivial. For this represents the matter as if I had studied the stove as one among the many things in the world. But if I was contemplating the stove, it was *my world* and everything else colourless by contrast with it. (Wittgenstein 1961a, 83e)

When I view the stove aesthetically or from eternity it becomes the whole world. Such viewing enables us to see the other (person or object) as the whole world. Similarly, if one views the world ethically then also it 'waxes and wanes as a whole' and becomes a completely different world (Wittgenstein 1961a, 73e). Thus, viewing from eternity enables us to see and know that each one of us belongs to the world as a whole, where everybody is on the same level.

Moreover, Wittgenstein is pointing out that viewing sub specie aeterni or aesthetically is actually contemplating. Since contemplation makes its object 'the whole world for me', there is no distinction between ethics and aesthetics; as in art, an object can become the whole world and in good life, the world is viewed aesthetically. Such aesthetical viewing makes the object the whole world, hence, as such, distinction between art and good life, between aesthetics and ethics merges. Both become one. This is common in 'traditional accounts of aesthetic contemplation where it is typically one in which the whole of consciousness is inhabited by the object contemplated' (Nieli 1987, 71).

It is fascinating to learn at this point that Tagore also says the same thing about viewing an object from the point of view of aesthetics. He says that we find a rose beautiful when we feel the unity of a rose coinciding with the unity of the universe, and thus it takes us beyond temporality. This unity aligns itself with the inner unity of oneself along with the unity of the universe (Tagore 1923c, 82).

Wittgenstein elucidates this point ('the work of art is the object seen *sub specie aeternitatis*') clearly in *Culture and Value*. There he talks about the distinction between looking at things in the normal course of life and looking at them as works of art. These two might in fact be the very same sort of things, such as seeing a man performing some ordinary and unremarkable activity as we pass by, and seeing these same mundane things done on stage in theatre. In this example, Wittgenstein is not imagining a sequence of a play but merely the framing of such activity by the conventions of theatre. He says, 'We should be observing something more wonderful than anything a playwright could arrange to be acted or spoken on the stage: life itself. But we do see this everyday without its making the slightest impression on us! True enough, but we do not see it from that point of view' (Wittgenstein 1980d, 4–6).

A work of Art, he goes on to say, forces us to see *in the right perspective, but in the absence of Art, the object is just a fragment of nature like any other* (Wittgenstein 1980d, 6).

Ethics and aesthetics as providing 'the right view of the world'

Now, what is this 'right perspective' or 'right viewing'? Wittgenstein was not very explicit. He queries in an entry in *Notebooks 1914–1916*:

Is it the essence of the artistic way of looking at things, that it looks at the world with a happy eye? (Wittgenstein 1961a, 86e)

What does the phrase 'happy eye' connote? How can one possess such happy eyes?

Of course, Wittgenstein speaks of transformation of an unhappy world into a happy world, which has to do with the transformation of the boundaries and not the facts of the world (Wittgenstein 1961a, 74e). Now, does the above quotation suggest that only the artistic way of looking at things can bring about relevant changes in one's attitude to the world? We find a clue again in *Notebooks 1914–1916*. He says:

The world is given me, i.e. my will enters into the world completely from outside as into something that is already there. (Wittgenstein 1961a, 74e)

So it is my will that, penetrating into the world, makes it my world. The world becomes my world because of the penetration of my will. Thus by an exercise of a good will, an unhappy world can be changed into a happy world, an evil world into a good world.

As he says:

> If the good or bad exercise of the will does alter the world, it can alter only the limits of the world, *not the facts, not what can be expressed by means of language*. In short, the effect must be that it becomes an altogether different world. It must, so to speak, wax and wane as a whole, as if by accession or loss of meaning. (Wittgenstein 1961a, 74e; emphasis mine)

So we see good exercise of will changes the unhappy world into a happy one by changing the limits of the world, by making the world wax and wane as a whole. Viewing the world sub specie aeterni is thus connected with the exercise of good will. This exercise of goodwill is connected with 'happy eyes'. Wittgenstein makes connection between this and a good life explicit when he says:

> Good life is the world viewed sub specie aeterni. (Wittgenstein 1961a, 73e)

So one's viewing the world from eternity and one's exercise of will provides one with happy eyes and makes 'the world' his own. Aesthetic perception thus is a shift away from the everyday relationship with what is perceived so that the object is seen and known in a way that is at once more vivid and more detached than the everyday relationship. We are to think of the ethical as also sharing this attitude (Collinson 1985, 268). This, for early Wittgenstein, was 'the right perspective'.

Ethics and aesthetics as being linked to happiness

An important question troubles us at this point: Why should Art always be confined to a 'happy eye'? What about the artistic expression of the ugly, the terrible, and 'the tragic'? Wittgenstein somehow seems to anticipate this question and in the entries of the following day, he says:

> For there is certainly something in the conception that the end of art is the beautiful. And the beautiful is what makes us happy. (Wittgenstien 1961a, 86e)

Here, Wittgenstein is connecting the idea of Art with that of beauty. How is Art connected with the beautiful? The beauty in Art cannot be in what is depicted or presented, for ugly and painful things are often the subject matter of art; it seems that Wittgenstein here is using the word 'beautiful' in the sense that it incorporates both good and evil, beautiful and ugly. It is quite possible that Wittgenstein's thought here continues from the idea of beauty as something beyond mere material possession and as something that transcends loss or worldly interests. Wittgenstein's notion of beauty seems to come from the notion of harmony. A work of Art constructs a perspective from which many different and even conflicting elements can be brought into some unified and harmonious whole (Wilde 2004, 174). This harmonious view of the world and life comes from viewing the world as a limited whole, as mentioned in the *Tractatus*. And this contributes to a good ethical life, thus to the merging of ethical and aesthetical viewpoints once again. Surprisingly, we find the harmony of the terrible and the beautiful even in the writings of Tagore, and we will discuss this in the next section.

But for early Wittgenstein, this cannot be expressed in sensible terms to anyone.

Wittgenstein says this to Waismann:

> If I needed a theory in order to explain to another the essence of the ethical [*and also of the aesthetical*], the ethical would have no value at all. (Waismann 1979, 116–17)

Any attempt to theorize ethics or aesthetics, for Wittgenstein, would be 'to run up against the boundaries of language'. But one can live ethically by having an ethical/aesthetical attitude towards the world. We find reflections of such attitude in the 1920s during the years he spent as a teacher in lower Austria. Those were years 'representative of ethical commitment'. Those were years also of aesthetical commitment, as reflected in the design and architecture of the house he built for his sister. He himself distinguished between a 'good architect' and a 'bad architect' by saying that a bad architect falls prey to temptations, whereas a good one resists it. Finally, his aesthetical thoughts were expressed in his own declarations:

> Work on philosophy—like work in architecture in many respects— is really more work on oneself. On one's own conception. On how one sees things. (And what one expects of them.) (Wittgenstein 1980d, 24)

Ethics and aesthetics being connected with 'the wonder that the world exists'

Finally comes the proposition 'the miracle is that the world exists', which serves as the paradigm example of both *ethics* and *aesthetics*. Wittgenstein elucidates: 'Das Künstlerische Wunder ist,daß es die weltgibt' (Wittgenstein 1961a, 86e). Pears and McGuinness translate this remark as: 'Aesthetically the miracle is that the world exists.' McGuinness in his book, *Approaches to Wittgenstein* (2002, 27), translates it as 'for an artist (or for art) the miracle is that the world exists'.

It has been discussed earlier that the wonder that the world exists serves as an example of absolute value judgements. Here, Wittgenstein uses the same example as the example of an aesthetical judgement. It shows the underlying connection between ethics and aesthetics. And the peculiarity of this example lies in the fact that it falls into the domain of the mystical, the ineffable. In earlier sections, it has been shown how it gets beautifully articulated in the poems of Rabindranath Tagore. It gives us an inkling of why Wittgenstein chose to read the poems of the latter while explaining the *Tractatus* to the members of the Vienna circle.

However, the discussion of the above five points reveals that viewing sub specie aeterni is the connecting link between ethical and aesthetical discourses. It is an overview of the world taken from outside. It is, thus, connected with the sense of the world. The sense of the world with which ethics is related also lies 'outside the whole sphere of what happens and is the case'. For whatever happens in the world is accidental; there is always the possibility that it might not have happened. What makes it non-accidental cannot lie within the world, since if it did it would itself be accidental. Thus it is transcendental and works as 'a condition of the world'.

Such an overview differs from any factual or scientific viewpoint for the facts are within the world; and it is also for this reason that such a viewing can never be expressed in terms of causal or scientific language. In this way, factual representation functions as a cage and ethics and aesthetics can be taken as attempts to run against the boundaries of the cage. But in their attempts to transcend the boundaries ethics and aesthetics show themselves and make themselves understood. It can show that factual or propositional representation is not everything. There are items that go beyond factual representations; there are points of views that are not fragmentary or partial; but which can take an overview of the whole. Thus, we experience value as transcendental, since the facts and propositions that represent them all function at the same level (T6.41). It is interesting to note here that Wittgenstein connects this kind of viewing as 'viewing with a happy eye' because 'the beautiful is what makes happy' (Wittgenstein 1961a, 86e). The experience of value arises from such wholeness, from the perceived harmony between the individual and the world (Friedland 2006, 91–102). This experience of unity is what being happy means (Friedland 2006, 92). Seeing from the viewpoint of eternity is not to perceive the object in terms of causality or in orientation toward a certain end. With this move Wittgenstein separates the question of human value from scientific questions (Tilghman 1991, 44).

Rabindranath Tagore and Aesthetics

Tagore's aesthetics and philosophy are intertwined with each other as 'the touch of aesthetic inspiration' pervades not only his poems and songs but also his worldview, his approach to the fundamental issues of life and thought, and his philosophy and religion. In fact, 'aesthetics is the dough with which his metaphysics and other writings are baked and cooked' (Naravane 1989, 2). Still, it is very difficult to have a logical and succinct picture of his aesthetics and philosophy as the poet himself eludes us by saying:

> I am that poet
> who is a dream-like being moving about stealthily, and
> who is unable to make myself understood.
> I fail to fathom the import of my own song. Who
> could get a handle on this poet?
> (Tagore cited in Sil 2015, 36)[10]

Moreover, his approach to Art, literature, and paintings in later years had apparently undergone a radical change from that of earlier days, provoking an enigmatic confusion among his interpreters. However, his views on aesthetics will be discussed under the following heads:

1. Aesthetics in early works
2. Aesthetics in later works
3. Observations

Aesthetics in early works

For Tagore, man's uniqueness in this world consists in the fact that he is an artist. Because of his aesthetic faculty and expression, man is distinguished from other things and beings in the universe. Almost all of Tagore's deliberations on the relationship between man and the world reflected his aesthetic discernment. It becomes evident when he conveys:

> When we experience anything aesthetically, we do not experience only that object. A good poem confers dignity on land, sea and sky, on the whole of the existence. (Tagore cited in Ayyub 1970, 119)

In order to elucidate this idea, he has drawn our attention to various important distinctions between the artist and the scientist, between construction and creation, between the artist, the appreciator (*sahṛdaya rasika*), and the personal man.

The artist and the scientist   Tagore's approach to Art was beyond praxis. His approach seems to be unique when he mentions, 'The truth of art is not in substance or logic, but in expression. The world of abstract truth may belong to science and metaphysics, but the world of reality belongs to Art' (Tagore 1978, 10). In order to get what he means by reality, truth, and the truth of Art, one will have to analyse how Tagore views man in relation to nature.

For Tagore, though man exploits nature when tilling soil, gathering food, and getting material for clothes, still his being does not allow him to remain satisfied with quotidian facts. He wants to find out reason, the law behind facts. Apart from the intellectual man, there is yet another man: 'This personal man is found in the region where we are free from all necessity—above the needs, both of the body and mind—above the expedient and useful. It is the highest in man—this personal man' (Tagore 1917, 12). In this world of the personal man, Art takes place. Here, he uses the word 'personal' in a technical sense, which is derived from the concept of personality in his writings. He clarifies:

What I mean by personality is a self-conscious principle of transcendental unity within man, which comprehends all the details of facts that are individually his in knowledge and feeling, wish and will and work. (Tagore 1931c, 117)

By means of creativity, this personality of man transcends the abstraction of factual domain and triumphs over the limitations of logical reasoning. For Tagore, the reality of the world does not belong to the intellectual man with logical reasoning. Rather, the world becomes real in the domain of the personal where man feels his infinity, where he is divine. One can be conscious of personality in its narrower sense, which begins with the feeling of separateness from the world. But, as mentioned earlier, in a wider sense, it ultimately extends into the infinite, which generates the feeling of unity with all. Art expresses the delight of this unity of the finite and the infinite in man. Science is determined by the necessity, be it causal or material, whereas Art is free and belongs to the domain of 'surplus'.

Freedom and the notion of 'surplus'   It has been stated earlier that for Tagore, man's energy overflows into channels that have nothing to do with biological survival. It seeks outlet in creation of Art, literature, music, and dance. For 'man's civilization is built upon his surplus' (Tagore 1959, 20).

In this context, Tagore also distinguishes between the acts of creation and the acts of construction. For him, construction is always for a purpose. It expresses 'wants' while creation reveals a truth (the truth of relationship, the truth of harmony in the universe) through the rhythm of forms. Tagore wants to make us understand how people in their individual as well as societal lives accentuate on construction by exaggerating the role of the elements; whereas the harmony of elements and expression can bring forth creation.

Construction in its abstraction might be of use for some mundane purposes, but ultimately it becomes meaningless unless it gets tied to

creation. For him, all works of creation such as music, dance, painting, and literature reveal rhythmic forms and that is what is common
between man and God. This is what binds God and man together.
Here, one might feel tempted to compare Tagore with Plotinus and
Al-Ghazzali for treating the universe as a work of art.

Reality and truth   The artist creates his reality, which is more important than the factual reality of scientists. About this creation of reality,
Tagore is of the opinion that man can modulate the nature–human–
divine interrelationships through his creative faculty and can make
truth his own. Truth can be *real*[11] only when it is personal. Thus, he
defines Art in *The Religion of Man* as 'the response of man's creative
soul to the call of the Real' (Tagore 2008, 142). The call of the real
refers to the feeling of the unity of the real within oneself with the
real outside. In art, one expresses the delight of this unity by which
the world is realized as humanly significant. It is personal reality and
the truth of the world at the same time.

This truth is beautiful. Beauty for Tagore is 'born of man's desire
to fraternise with the outer world of life and nature' (Tagore 2001, 51).
Such a conception of beauty is different from the ordinary conception
of beauty; it is based on the philosophy of discipline and restraint.
Tagore argues, 'When man has the power to see things detached from
self-interest and insistent claims of the lust of the senses, then he sees
that what is unpleasant to us is not necessarily unbeautiful, but has its
beauty in truth' (Tagore 1978, 53).

Tagore says, 'The day when I first realised this truth, I remem-
bered Keats's words, "truth is beauty, beauty truth"' (Tagore 2001, 7).
It is interesting to note over here that Tagore assimilated this 'beauty
truth' with goodness. 'Which is really good is both useful and beautiful' (Tagore 2001, 37).

For Tagore, 'beauty cannot be the aim of art and literature unless it
is good. In goodness also we discover that wealth, that surplus which
is commensurate with the whole world' (Tagore 2001, 172).

Hence, as creative beings, we respond to the call of the real, by
creating music, dance, literature, and other art forms, which express
our realization of truth as good and beautiful.

When we are intensely aware of the equation of truth, beauty,
and goodness, we are aware of ourselves and the harmony of our

souls with the outside universe. It gives us Ānanda (joy as aesthetic experience).

The philosophy of Ānanda (joy as aesthetic experience) To Tagore, this aesthetic notion of Ānanda is metaphysical, which springs from the plenitude of our spirit when we realize our souls as being related to the universe.

To elucidate, one can take the example of a rose. One feels happy (pure aesthetic joy) when one sees a rose; one sees the beauty of harmony in its colour, smell, and contour, that is, in the form of a flower. The final meaning of Ānanda (delight) which one finds in a rose can never be in the roundness of its petals, just as the final meaning of joy of music cannot be in a phonograph record (Chakravarty 1966, 363).

In Tagore's opinion, the essence of the creative man is his capacity to feel and also to make others feel joy as aesthetic experience (Ānanda). On the one hand, we have the artist who expresses her inner *bhāva* (sentiment) in the art object. That gets fulfilment only when *sahṛdaya rasika* (a sensitive spectator who can connect with the performance with emotion) appreciates it, feels the inner *rasa* (emotion of aesthetic pleasure that develops from *bhāva*) within, and experiences Ānanda. Commentators have often interpreted Tagore as being a follower of traditional Indian aesthetics as Tagore himself refers to the concept of *ṣaranga* (six limbs of a good work of Art) of classical Indian theories on Art in his writing. These six characteristic features are the following:

Multiplicity of forms (*rūpabheda*) signifies that there are various kinds of things having various forms, which make them separate from each other. Proportion (*pramānāni*) maintains that however different they may be they must be proportionate to each other.

They should be conjoined with inner harmonious ideas (*bhāva*) and gracefulness *(lābanya)*. Not only that, they will be similar to worldly objects (*sadṛśa*) and some suggestiveness (*varnikābhanga*) should be there. Tagore accepts these characteristic features (*ṣaranga*) for good painting and other forms of art; still he retains his uniqueness in his views on aesthetics when he relates Art with emotional surplus and creativity. For him, Art arises when man expresses his emotion just for the sake of disinterested enjoyment and not for any utilitarian considerations.

Tagore believes that human feelings are the most important emotional forces, which transmute things into our living structures. Man looks at the world and absorbs it with emotions of love, hatred, wonder, fear, pleasure, pain, and so on. In Tagore's own words:

> Our emotions are the gastric juices which transform this world of appearance into the more intimate world of sentiments. On the other hand this outer world has its own juices, having their various qualities which excite our emotional activities. This is called in our Sanskrit rhetoric *rasa* which signifies outer juices having their response in the inner juices of our emotions. (Tagore 1959, 14–15)

Hence, the things that arouse our emotions arouse our feelings for our own selves. Then it feels the longing to express itself for the sake of expression. Art originates from such longing.

Aesthetics in later works

Quite in contrast with his aesthetics in his early works, the later poems and paintings of Tagore often seem to betray a sense of conflict, discord, and dissonance at the heart of existence.

Once, in his letters written in March 1930 (Tagore 1961c, 93–4), Tagore explained candidly that in earlier years he used to feel intense joy when he observed the world of nature. His inspiration for creation, constituting the centre of his life and the world, used to come from the outside world. But later in life, when 'the twilight dust of weariness descends with the waning of vitality, ... he entered this passionate desire to paint and to draw. That was in a way a return to that world of pure visible form. ... The movement was no more inwards from outside but outwards from inside' (Tagore 1961c, 94). One gets an inkling of such changes much earlier in the poems of *Balākā* (The Crane, 1916), where the poet celebrates humanist ethos and also salutes youthful love, beauty, and restlessness. Next, we detect *Palātakā* (The Fugitive, 1918), which expresses the 'poet's concern with the multiple mundane trials and tribulations, and the weal and woes of human life, that is a part of universal life' (Sil 2015, 42).

During the last 15 years of his life, he came into contact with younger modern poets of Bengal who were pioneering a movement that unhesitatingly depicted the weight of sin and sorrow, sexuality, evil, and the complexity of intellectual experiences. Tagore noticed this movement in Bengal as well as in continents around the world. He observed the stark changes in outer form and tone in their works of art. He also took note of the desperate disbelief and intellectual quality of the products of this movement.

He often critiqued this modernism by identifying the modern with the crude. In his novel *The Home and the World*, Sandip, a spokesperson for Modernism, states 'Yes I am crude, because I am *real*. I'm flesh, I'm instinct, I'm hunger, I'm shameless, unkind' (Tagore 1916b, 68). Here, Sandip admits that respecting our instinct as *real* is modernity.

Although Tagore expresses his resentment at the emphasis on the trivial, the grotesque, or the unholy in various writings, still one does not fail to notice the distinctive features of modernism in his writings of this period. As he writes about the trivial in 'Nabajātak' (1939),

> Mustard oil splutters inside
> A pan of sizzling fish being fried.
> The weaver women brings for the young wife
> Saris bordered with a patriotic weave. (Tagore 2004, 339)

Poems composed in these years (from 'Punasca' [Postscript, 1932] to 'Śeṣlekhā' [Last Writings, 1941]) seem to reveal his encounter with the real world.

> I'm familiar with the road to the real world.
> No fancy reality could be found there.
> There the terrific and the terrible walk hand in hand. (Tagore 1990, 68)

In 'Śeṣlekhā', we find expressions of his own personal tussle:[12] Of his own uncertainty, his own lack of knowledge of being and self at the end of the day, he confessed that he has no answer for the questions that bothered him throughout his life, and of which he thought he had answers in his early life.

Much agony in his personal life, and much 'hurts and pain' out of the chaos and crisis in the outside world had made him realize that 'Truth is hard'. Truth is not only hard but also 'terrible', which seems to be in dissonance with 'the aesthetics of harmony' in his early works. Sisir Kumār Ghosh, a noted Tagore critic writes, 'Full of dramatic discords, through alternate rhythms of intensity and exhaustion, the poems unfold a history of a conflict, long and carefully concealed at the heart of Rabindrean imagination' (Ghose 1989, viii). This is evident also in his paintings drawn during the last phase of his life.

Tagore's world of painting   During the last 20 years, one notices the upsurge of Tagorean creativity in the world of painting. He began his journey with crossed out poetical lines and doodling, which somehow created 'a unique flowing design' (Som 2011, 17). He had no training in the art of drawing or painting. Hence, the unity of the designs and of the images was not premeditated.

It is no wonder that critics describe his 'gnawed battered twisted and phantasmagorical images born out of deletions as expressions of his suppressed unconscious' (Som 2011, 25). Dyson and Adhikari traced the peculiarities of Tagore's paintings (around 2,500 paintings) due to his deficiency of colour vision. Their soulful research had resulted in their interpreting Tagore as being influenced by the German Expressionists (Dyson and Adhikari 2017 [1997]).

However, if Tagore's paintings were represented as being influenced by German Expressionism, then questions arise regarding the closeness of his paintings to Surrealism as far as his un-premeditative approach is concerned. His paintings seem to be close to Postimpressionism as well. 'He himself is on record of his enthusiasm for Van Gogh, among other painters' (Bhattacārya 1989, 164).

Observations

The last writings and paintings thus force us to look at our 'sage–poet' (*ṛṣi kavi*) in a different manner. Here, one notices that 'this Tagore does not console us like the poet but places us in a land of uncertainty' (Sarkar 2011, 3).

Saranindranath Tagore talks about 'a poetics of uncertainty' in the 'late style' of Tagore's works. For him, 'it represents a shift from his earlier stance to a radically new ontology' (Banerjee 2015, 267).

These baffle us. Is there no central aesthetics and philosophy in the works of Tagore?

If one looks closely at his poems, novels, dramas, and paintings of these years, one does not fail to notice that although his creative works look at the ordinary, at the crude, harsh reality, still, he is not oblivious to the glory of the beautiful. It is true that his last days are full of symptoms of resentments and perturbations. But that is not final. He never deviates from his central aesthetics and philosophy as he writes in *Śeṣ Lekhā* (cited in Chakravarty 1966, 371) only a few months before his death:

> The clear light of consciousness
> Piercing the mist
> Reveal the undying shape of truth ...
> Let me behold before I go
> The peace of the ever constant
> In the silent realm above all worldly agitation.

In another instance,

> I have seen the light of the eternal
> Behind the illusion of calamity.
> Truth's joyous form is imaged in this dust. (Chakravarty 1966, 72)

He can see 'the light of the eternal' and the harmony of truth and joy as aesthetic experience even in his very last months.

Not only that, he is even hopeful that the Supreme Man will appear in this world.[13] In writings of this period, one can visualize his inner tensions between his central aesthetic philosophy and new ideas of modernism. Sometimes new ideas occupy for him the central place, but his being firmly rooted on a harmonious picture of the whole does not go out of sight. Because of this, he can visualize the *leelā* (a spontaneous purposeless self-manifestation) of divine dance, where his individual self merges in the flow of the life of truth, where he sees the peace of the ever-constant and 'joyous form of truth'. His uncertainty regarding the very being gets contradicted by his image of merging himself in the festival of being (Tagore 1937, Poem no. 12).

He realizes that truth is cruel but it can be loved, and it makes free those who have loved it. There is the beautiful even in the terrible throughout history and the world. In the poem, Tagore has described the terrible and the beautiful walking hand in hand, whereas in *The King of the Dark Chamber* (1914), the king was 'as matchless in beauty as in terror'. Usually man looks at life and God as being happy and benign only when he is inexperienced.

Experience teaches man that life is tough and one has to struggle to maintain his being, which makes him feel dubious about the positivity of life and God. What Tagore wants to get across is the idea that 'experience makes a man mature, bringing him to a complete understanding that life and divinity are simultaneously terrible and beautiful, eventually reconciling him with God (Lāl 2001, 99).

It has been mentioned earlier how Tagore portrays his feelings of distress at the sight of the harshness and crudeness of reality in poems of his later years; whereas during the same time he claimed absolute certainty in 'the bright eternity behind the mist of danger':

I have seen the bright eternity
behind the mist of danger and turmoil.
I know that the beautiful truth has realized itself and I place my
head on the dust (of this world).[14]

When Tagore extends his various adventures into opposites, one finds a new modern Rabindranath who is born out of his clashes between the modern and the unmodern, between harsh reality and harmonious truth, who is creative, living, and growing. He does not intend to offer 'a radically new ontology' as he still finds strength from his inner light.

He carries to his treasure-house
His final reward.
He who could put up with your deceit receives from you the right
To everlasting peace.[15]

Tagore and Wittgenstein: Convergence of Ideas on Aesthetics

From the elucidation of ideas on aesthetics discussed above, one can portray the obvious divergences of the approach of the poet and the philosopher. The poet will be reluctant to view aesthetics as non-sensical as, for him, aesthetics helps one to approach the 'real' in one's life; whereas the philosopher will be happy to delineate it as an attempt to express the inexpressible. Yet, in spite of their natural divergences, there are few important points of convergence where the views of the poet and the philosopher concur.

Wittgenstein's statement of 'Ethics and Aesthetics being one' has its counterpart in the philosophy of Tagore. For Tagore, beauty exceeds what is necessary. That is why we recognize it as wealth. He believed:

> Beauty cannot be the aim of art and literature unless it is good. When we see a brave man abandon his self-interest or sacrifice his life for the sake of moral principle, we witness a marvel that is greater than our pain and pleasure, larger than our self-interest, nobler than our lives. By virtue of this wealth, goodness does not count loss as loss, or stress as stress. It remains unhurt by any injury to self-interest. That is why goodness as much as beauty induces us to a willing sacrifice. Beauty expresses God's plenty in all the world's functions; goodness does the same in human life. Goodness has made beauty more than something to be seen with the eye. (Tagore 2001, 173)

Tagore said:

> Whatever is beneficent is in deepest union with the whole world, in secret harmony with the mind of all humanity. When we see this beautiful accord of the true and the beneficent, the beauty of truth no longer eludes our perception. Compassion is beautiful; so are forgiveness and love. ... *The image of beauty is the fullest manifestation of the good and the image of the good the consummate self of beauty.* (Tagore 2001, 172; emphasis mine)

This is the reason that they (this harmony) cannot be represented by ordinary factual language. They are the inexpressible. Like Wittgenstein, Tagore also thinks that they transcend the boundaries of language and somehow make themselves understood by means of the suggestiveness of language. He believed:

> Poets reveal the benign to the world in its ineffably beauteous form. The truly benign serves our need and it is beautiful: that is, it has an unaccountable attraction that surpasses its use. (Tagore 2001, 174)

This is why ethics and aesthetics are one and the same for both the thinkers.

However, for Tagore also, viewing from the standpoint of aesthetics is viewing from eternity. 'When we look at a rose and find it beautiful, it becomes the whole world. Its unity of form, colour, texture, and smell coincides with the unity of the universe, and thus it takes us beyond temporality. This unity aligns itself with the inner unity of oneself along with the unity of the universe (Tagore 1986, Vol. 10, 388).

Beauty for Tagore is a fundamental concept akin to that of being, surplus, and harmony, and this concept is most important in his idea of aesthetics. For Tagore, the poet is not a devotee of truth for the sake of truth, or goodness for the sake of goodness. Rather, he is a devotee of truth and goodness as they are in themselves beautiful. And because of their beauty, the poet got attracted to them. Tagore elucidates it with the example of a blade of grass. A lay man who is indifferent to nature gets no pleasure from the blade of grass. It is a trifle matter to him. He is not interested. But a botanist finds pleasure even from a blade of grass as he knows the importance of grass in the domain of plants. But an aesthetician knows how to view a blade of grass even from the point of view of spirituality, can feel himself and the world in that particular blade of grass and finds ecstasies in it (Tagore 1961d, 6).

From this it follows that from the point of view of the scientist, the truth of a blade of grass is important, but only as representative of a class. But to the aesthetician, a blade of grass is important for its being itself and nothing else. It is important not because it belongs to a class having such and such properties, not because it has some utility, but because it becomes the whole world. It comes to the fore and everything else goes to the background. It shows that it is not a fact only, it is beautiful. When we look at a blade of grass aesthetically, the covering of its 'everyday-ness', that is, its being in particular spatio-temporal framework, gets removed. The aesthetician discovers a deep harmony in the beautiful object and feels happy from the core of his heart (Gānguly 1968, 86). This harmony transcends all discords, all conflicts. For Tagore, truth, beauty, and harmony are interchangeable terms. The moment the distinction between the whole and its parts is made with regard to an art object; it ceases to be an art object (Biswas 1988, 64–5). An ordinary object can become an art object only when aesthetical contemplation on that object gifts nobility and majesty to the whole of existence. The artist through creative synthesis extends himself over the whole world and feels the union with the world in himself. Tagore elucidates:

> I exist and everything else exists. There is this union of the two in my existence. If I do not feel anything beyond my own self, I do not feel myself. (Tagore 1961d, 352)

However, this harmony, this being with the whole world, cannot be represented by ordinary factual language. Like Wittgenstein, Tagore also thinks that they transcend the boundaries of ordinary language and somehow make themselves understood by means of the suggestiveness of language in poems, music, and other art forms. He believes that 'poets reveal the benign to the world in its ineffably beauteous form. The truly benign serves our need and it is beautiful: that is, it has an unaccountable attraction that surpasses its use' (Tagore 2001, 172).

> When I see the world through music/I come to know it as my own/ then its luminous language fills the sky with love/and its dust fills with final message for the artist. (Biswas 1988, 66)
> Only the true artist can comprehend the secret of the visible world and the joy of revealing it. ... He sings not, nor does he moralise. He lets his work speak for itself and its message is: Look this is what I am, Ayamaham bho! (Neogi 1961c, 108–9)

Thus, for both Wittgenstein and Tagore, words are incapable of expressing values that incorporate truth, beauty, and goodness. In the next chapter, I argue that 'God' is a portmanteau term for these values in Wittgenstein's early works.

But this gives rise to the typical Tractarian paradoxical situation: If words are incapable of expressing values such as truth, beauty, and goodness, then what will exactly be the status of this chapter, which uses around 15,000 words to talk about these value-related discourses? From the point of view of the *Tractatus*, the chapter is nonsensical as it has attempted to express what is inexpressible. It has confused the role of what can and cannot be stated in language. But it has a point: it points to a harmonized, value-laden, poetic universe of a poet. It thus portrays the attempts to run against the boundaries of language, which, though fruitless, still deserve our deep respect and admiration.

Notes

1. Wittgenstein writes in a letter to Von Ficker: 'The book's point is an *ethical* one. My book draws limits to the sphere of the ethical from the inside, as it were, and I am convinced that this is the *only* rigorous way of drawing those limits' (Engelmann 1967, 143–4).
2. P.M.S. Hacker did not take this point seriously. He maintained that such an attempt to read the *Tractatus* as a book on ethics would amount to be a clear case of self-deception. Von Wright, Frank Ramsey, and Otto

Neurath also belong to the same line of interpretation, and ignored the importance of the last few pages of the *Tractatus*.

3. Although the lecture chronologically falls in the middle/transitional period, it still continues with the idea in the *Tractatus* as far as the distinction between saying and showing, and the notion of ethics and aesthetics are concerned.

4. 'Nirjharer Swapnobhongo'—Abu Sayeed Ayyub refers to it as 'awakening of a stream' (Tagore 1980, 67).

5. Tagore writes, 'Hridoy āji mor kemone gelo khuli, jagat āsi setha koriche kolākuli' (Tagore 1980, 71; translation mine).

6. *Bhāgvad Gita*, Chapter 2, Sloka 56, defines *stithaprajña* as follows: 'One whose mind is not shaken by adversity, who does not hanker after happiness, who has become free from blind attachment, fear and anger, is indeed the sage of steady wisdom or *stithaprajña*.'

7. 'But there where spreads the infinite sky for the soul to take her flight in, reigns the stainless white radiance, there is no day, nor night, nor form, nor colour and *never never a word*' (Tagore 1913a, Poem no. 68).

8 'This issue concerning internal relation between ethics and aesthetics is rather vague in the *Tractatus*, a fact that entails a continuous dispute among its commentators' (Chason, 34–49). Most of them tend to reject logical equivalence between aesthetics and ethics, and the remaining question is: What, then, is the common radix of the separate notions (Tilghman 46; Barrett 20; Zemach 55–7)' (cited in Mualem 2004, 200)?

9.

God loves himself with an infinite intellectual love. Prop. The intellectual love of the mind towards God is that very love of God whereby God loves himself, not in so far as he is infinite, but in so far as he can be explained through the essence of the human mind, regarded under the form of eternity (sub specie aeternitatis). In other words, the intellectual love of the mind towards God is part of the infinite love wherewith God loves himself. (Spinoza 2009, Part V, Propositions XXXV and XXXVI)

10.

Ye-āmi svapan-mūrati gopancārī, Ye-āmi āmāre bujhāte nāri, Āpan gāner kāchete āpani hāri, Sei āmi kabi, ke pāre āmāre dharite.

11. Here, one must not take *real* to mean *mind independent* from the perspective of Western philosophy.

12. Rabindranath in *Sanchaita* (as translated in Chakravarty 1966, 363):

On the bank of the Rūp-narain
I awake;
This world is not a dream.

In words of blood I saw
My being.
I knew myself
Through hurts
And pain.
Truth is hard
And never deceives.
I loved that hardness
13. Just a few days before his demise, he wrote:

The supreme man now comes
A thrill on every side
Hail hail hail to the rise of Man
The vast sky resonates. (Chakravarty 1966, 79)
14. Tagore in 'Madhumay Prithibir Dhuli' (The Sweet Dust of This Earth),
    'Arogya' (Recovery), and *Sanchaitā* (Chakravarty 1966, 283).
15. Tagore, *Śeṣ Lekhā* (1941), *Sanchaitā* (Chakravarty 1966, 373–4).

4

The Domain of the Ineffable

The Religious

The domain of the ineffable, for early Wittgenstein, subsumes religious thoughts and feelings along with those of ethics and aesthetics. Still, the discourse of religion deserved a separate segment as after the publication of *Nachlass*, much has been written on the religious views and interests of Wittgenstein. Reflections on the literature based on reminiscences, letters, anecdotes, and remarks in coded diaries make it evident that Wittgenstein was occupied with questions of a religious nature throughout his life. The same is true of Tagore. Although he did not belong to any particular creed, he was out and out a spiritual person throughout his life.

Some commentators have discussed Wittgenstein's religious views with reference to his biography[1] while there are others who discuss it in relation to his philosophy as a whole,[2] and in the process have given rise to heated controversies in the field of the philosophy of religion.

That Wittgenstein had deep reverence for religion is evident in various textual remarks, personal letters, and other remarks found in autobiographical literature. In the introduction to *Philosophical Remarks*, he wrote: 'I would like to say "this book is written to the glory of God"' (Wittgenstein 1964b, 2). In 1930, while discussing

Schlick's criterion of moral goodness, Wittgenstein stated that an action is good if it is what God wills. He chose this criterion as superior to the rationalistic criterion that a good action is good in itself and if God wills it, it is because it is good and not for any other reason. He preferred the former alternative, because it cuts off any rational or experiential explanation. He finds the second criterion shallower because it implies that we can always give an explanation in terms of facts.

Moreover, a biographical anecdote of Wittgenstein speaks a lot in favour of his 'deep admiration for sincere religious faith'. This anecdote goes something like this: Wittgenstein had one Indian student called Kanti Shah during his tenure at the University of Cambridge.

> Once in a cold afternoon after a long silent walk Wittgenstein asked: 'Are you Muslim, Kanti?' Kanti answered: 'No we are Jains.'
>
> Wittgenstein: 'Oh I read something about Jains. I learnt that Jain Tirthankars used to meditate on hilltops.'
>
> Listening to this, Kanti made some derogatory comments. Then Wittgenstein annoyingly retorted, 'They [Jain thinkers] have carried a tradition of such thinking over the period of thousands of years. You might not accept their views, but you cannot dismiss them at ease. That does not reflect the honesty of thinking.' (Ghosh 2011, 188)[3]

Again, Wittgenstein once told M.O.C Drury: 'I am not a religious man, but I cannot help seeing every problem from a religious point of view' (Rhees 1981, 94).[4] Such remarks motivate one to explore Wittgenstein's remarks on religion to enquire into his 'religious point of view'.

In this chapter, there will be an attempt to explore how both Wittgenstein and Tagore were not 'religious' in the traditional sense of the term. Also, at the same time, I would like to wade through textual remarks to discover how they 'couldn't help seeing every problem from a religious point of view' (Rhees 1981, 94). It will be surprising to note that 'this religious point of view' for both of them incorporates ethical and aesthetical points of views and provides us with an extraordinary congruence between the journeys of Wittgenstein and Tagore.

In the first two sections of this chapter, I will explore the journey from 'the religious to the spiritual' in both Wittgenstein and Tagore through the narratives of a 'Jew' and a 'Brāhmo'. In the section titled 'Remarks on Religion in the *Tractatus*: A Textual Anatomy', I will discuss the textual remarks on religion in the works of both Wittgenstein and Tagore to discover how the problems discussed therein can be seen from a religious point of view, and how they are intertwined with the ideas of ethics and aesthetics. My findings of the previous chapters will accordingly help me in the current chapter to look at Wittgenstein's remarks on religion and religious belief with basically these questions: Does his view on religion go along with those of logic and language in the *Tractatus*? Did he really look at the problems of language, life, and the world from 'a religious point of view'? If so, are we to label these remarks as 'simply' nonsense according to the criterion of sensicality in the *Tractatus*? These questions are however intimately tied to the main puzzle of the book regarding how 'the logical' is to be tied to the 'mystical'.

Journey from the Religious to the Spiritual: Narrative of a Jew

In order to trace the journey, one will have to depend on biographical literature including letters and anecdotes where the personal opinions on such matters are reflected. In this section, I have used the biographical studies of Wittgenstein by M.O.C. Drury (1984), Brian McGuinness ([1988] 2005), Ray Monk (1990), and Bela Szabados (1997, 1999).

The important question here is: Should one take personal opinions as seriously as his official philosophical views, or should one separate them from his philosophical writings? One might object: Wittgenstein's personal opinions might be extremely interesting, but it is no part of his philosophical approach to prescribe such a faith (Richter 2001). Hence, one should restrict oneself only to his philosophical writings to form an opinion about his religious point of view and not to biographical details. On the other hand, we find references to people who think 'that the study of a man's life will help us understand his work in philosophy'.[5]

In this case, we would like to take account of Wittgenstein's own views about this. He says:

> The greatness, or triviality, of a piece of work depends on where the man who made it was standing. (Wittgenstein 1984 (1980), 49)

> The greatness of what a man writes depends on everything else he writes and does. (Wittgenstein 1984 (1980), 65)

Hence, to find out where Wittgenstein was standing when he made such remarks on religion, one should rather explore his life's journey, as far as his religious beliefs and feelings are concerned.

Background

Wittgenstein, though born in a family of assimilated Jews,[6] was never a practicing Jew. As a child, he was baptized in a Roman Catholic Church and received formal instruction in Roman Catholicism. It has also been detected that young Ludwig lied about his Jewish ancestry in order to get admission in a Viennese gymnasium club, which was restricted to those of Aryan origin (Monk 1990, 14).

But by the time Wittgenstein grew up and got admitted to Realschule, he had lost his faith in Christianity. This lack of faith was not due to peer pressure, nor is it due to the impact of new teachers. Rather it was due to the influence of the imposing personality of his elder sister, Margaret or Gretl. 'As he told his friend Arvid Sjögren, he lost his childish faith after conversations with his sister Gretl' (Malcolm 1958, 20). Gretl's tendency to challenge the tradition and to welcome new ideas led her and her younger brother Ludwig to appreciate the satirical journal *Die Fackel* (1899) by Karl Kraus. Although the journal was regarded as representative of left-wing liberal ideas till 1904, gradually it shifted its focus. It focused more on moral than on political items. For Kraus then, 'Politics is what a man does in order to *conceal what he is* and what he himself does not know' (Monk 1990, 17–18; emphasis mine). This had tremendous influence on young Ludwig. He did not want to *conceal what he is*. He confessed that he could not believe the things a Christian was supposed to believe. It was difficult, he said, for him to bend the knee (McGuinness 2005, 43). Ludwig and his brother Paul were also influenced by their father who had an overpowering personality; for whom they were prepared to accept 'a world of moral absolutes which could be perceived immediately and from which any deviation was complete failure' (McGuinness 2005, 25).

When Ludwig confided about his loss of faith to Margaret, she instructed him to read Schopenhauer's *The World as Will and Representation* (1818). She thought:

> This book would be appealing to an adolescent who had lost his faith in religion and was looking for something to replace it. For while Schopenhauer recognized man's need for metaphysics, he insists that it is neither necessary nor possible for an intelligent honest person to believe in the literal truth of religious doctrines. (Monk 1990, 18)

Thus, when Russell met Wittgenstein before the First World War, he found him to be a fierce critic of religion.[7]

However, around 1911–12, Wittgenstein had a mystical experience while enjoying a play in Vienna. It was a mediocre play by a mediocre artist. But the narration of the artist that stated 'I'm absolutely safe, nothing can happen to me' struck Wittgenstein powerfully, and, so he told Malcolm, he saw for the first time, the possibility of religion (Monk 1990, 51). Major changes regarding his views about God and living the life of a spirit took place only during the war.

During this time, he began reading Tolstoy's *The Gospel in Brief* (1883) and realized a sea of changes within him. He was moved by the Christianity found in Tolstoy as it showed him the way to overcome his fear of death. To quote from his biographer, McGuinness:

> The Christianity that he found in Tolstoy seemed to him the only sure way to happiness. ... The only true life for a man is communion with that spirit. ... For a man living not the personal but the common life of the spirit, there is no death. (McGuinness [1988] 2005, 21)

Tolstoy's spirituality endowed Wittgenstein with the courage to do his duty fearlessly.

Such Tolstoyian thoughts are manifested in Wittgenstein's *Notebooks 1914–1916*, throughout the war, and of course later in *Tractatus Logico-Philosophicus* (1922).

He was also moved by the deeply religious attitude of Dostoyevsky. Wittgenstein told Drury that Tolstoy and Dostoevsky were 'the only two European writers in recent times who really had something important to say about religion' (Drury 1984, 86).

However, this spell of Tolstoyian Christianity supported by the religious commitment of Dostoevsky received a mild blow in December 1914 when Wittgenstein had bought the eighth volume of Nietzsche's collected works in Krakow. This volume includes *The Antichrist*; Nietzsche's blistering attack upon Christianity' (Monk 1990, 121). Wittgenstein was moved by Nietzsche's arguments. He himself writes about it (in his diary on 8 December 1914):

> I'm strongly affected by his hostility against Christianity. Because his writings too have some truth in them. To be sure, Christianity is the only sure way to happiness; but what if someone spurned this happiness? Might it not be better to perish unhappily in the hopeless struggle against the external world? (Cited in McGuinness 2005, 225)

This quotation shows that he got attracted to Nietzsche's ideas though he still was confident about the truth of Tolstoyian Christianity as it supported his struggle in military duties, his depression, and his loneliness.

At the end of August 1916 Ludwig came to Olmütz, a small town where intellectuals were mainly of Jewish origin. Wittgenstein here found a circle where members used to read the Bible, chiefly the New Testament, together with the intention of finding out 'a self-made religion' and 'an ethical equivalent of Christianity' (McGuinness 2005, 226–7). We also learn from Engelmann's memoir that by this time Wittgenstein was convinced that *religion is inexpressible* in scientific language. From earlier discussions, one now apperceives how religion falls into the category of the 'inexpressible' in accordance with the criterion of sensibility/sayability of the *Tractatus*. For Wittgenstein, the propositions of logic and mathematics, ethics, aesthetics, metaphysics, and religion are all 'nonsense' and 'inexpressible'.

While Wittgenstein was staying at Olmütz and finding out the ethical equivalent of Christianity, he was very much bothered about the riddle that is: How to reconcile the logical part of the *Tractatus* with the mystical, which includes ethics, aesthetics, metaphysics, and religion?

He writes in his diary;

> Have thought a lot about everything possible. But, strangely enough, cannot establish the connection with my mathematical lines of thought.

But the connexion will be established. What cannot be said cannot be said. (McGuinness 2001, 226)

It seems that here he could connect the two realms in the light of indirect ways of making manifest and he was convinced that 'the *Tractatus* itself is a way of making manifest' (Engelmann 1967, 95).

Now, does Wittgenstein's involvement with the Jewish circle at Olmütz imply his Jewish inclination? During the December of 1929, he had a feeling that he was hiding something from others, maybe it was his Jewish identity, and he felt that he was allowing people to think of him as an aristocrat, when in fact he was a Jew (Monk 1990, 279).

In 1931, he discussed the Jews and Jewishness connecting his character as a Jewish thinker with the nature of his philosophical work.

Amongst Jews 'genius' is found only in the holy man. Even the great-est of Jewish thinkers is no more than talented (myself for instance). I think there is some truth in my idea that I really only think reproduc-tively. (McGuinness 2001, 229)

In conversation with Drury, Wittgenstein claimed 'My thoughts are one hundred percent Hebraic' (McGuinness 2001, 229). Later, in 1936–7, in his confessions he stated that while three of his grandparents were Jews, he said that only one of them is a Jew.[8] Commentators such as Chatterjee (2005) and Labron (2006) emphasize how Judaic thought finds expression in some central themes of Wittgenstein's thinking, whereas Ray Monk (1990) presents Wittgenstein as 'briefly attracted to using anti-Semitic expressions in the early 1930s, but only as a way of thinking about his own failings' (Stern 2000, 238).

McGuinness (2005) contests the general idea that Wittgenstein was a Jew. For him, it is also a mistake. Without getting into the controversy whether one should regard Wittgenstein as a Jew or a Catholic, I would like to point out that the following four strands of spirituality is evident in his journey of life pictured above:

- Aversion to Institutional Religion
- Closeness to God and 'Ethical Living'
- Experiencing the Mystical
- Interconnectedness with the Universe

Aversion to Institutional Religion

To be precise, one cannot really label Wittgenstein to be a member of any organized, institutional religion. He got attached to Christianity at some point of his life; while he went to Olmütz to find his roots in Judaism at some other time. But these experiments were short-lived. Wittgenstein was not a Catholic. He said on a number of occasions both in conversations and in his writings that he could not bring himself to believe the things that Catholics believe. He said 'It is a dogma of the Roman Church that the existence of God can be proved by natural reason; now this dogma would make it impossible for me to be a Roman Catholic' (Drury 1984, 123).

Philosophers and theologians offer cosmological, teleological, onto-logical, and other arguments for the existence of God. Wittgenstein was against such rational argumentations for the existence of God as, for him, God was beyond such rationalizations. He wrote:

> A proof of God's existence should really be something by which one could convince oneself of God's existence. But I think that believers, who have provided such proofs, have wanted to give their 'belief' an intellectual analysis and foundation, although they themselves would never have come to believe through such proofs. (Drury 1984, 129)

Wittgenstein, by rejecting evidences and arguments for the exis-tence of God, showed his aversion to the concept of having reasons for religious beliefs. 'Nevertheless, he admired the Latin collects, thought the symbolisms of Catholicism "wonderful beyond words" (Drury 1984, 102) and, unlike Franz Brentano, could even conceive of a meaningful infallible Papal declaration' (Hayes 1996, 6). He abhors 'the idea that a philosophical justification for religious beliefs is nec-essary for those beliefs to be given any credence' (Drury 1984, 101).

Norman Malcolm also reported: 'Wittgenstein could not have reconciled himself to any of the Christian denominations with their required assent to various dogmas, e.g. to God the Creator, a doctrine which Wittgenstein said, played no part in his own thinking' (Malcolm 1958, 39). We find its assurance in his conversation with Drury: 'If I thought of God as another being like myself, outside myself, only infinitely more powerful, then I would regard it as my duty to defy him' (Drury 1984, 123).

For Wittgenstein, historical records are not relevant for one's belief in God or religion. 'It did not really matter, he thought, whether Jesus was a historical figure or not' (Drury 1984, 163).

We have ample evidence of historical records and philosophical arguments for Judaism and Christianity in the history of philosophy and theology. Both Judaism and Christianity are institutionalized religions where we find respective creeds, rituals, and dogmas. Wittgenstein was disinclined to adhere to any conventional religious tradition (Drury 1984, 129). This is why when Drury intended to take the profession of a clergy, Wittgenstein said, 'I can't approve; no, I can't approve. I am afraid that one day that collar would choke you' (Drury 1984, 101). He seems to have objected to the 'narrowness of the Anglican clergy for which William James was a good antidote. Drury probably did not know that Wittgenstein had himself considered taking orders in 1919—at least, according to a fellow prisoner of war, Franz Parak' (McGuinness [1988] 2005, 274).

This discussion shows why Wittgenstein told Drury: 'I am not a religious man.' By this he wanted to get across the idea that he does not believe in any religion in the sense of an institutionalized doctrine or creed. Rather he stressed on spiritual purity and ethical living as fundamental to religious belief.

Closeness to God and 'Ethical Living'

The ideal of ethical living attracted Wittgenstein right from his early years. We noticed this in his espousal of Kraus's demands for moral integrity in his school days. He was enticed by Tolstoy's writings in which Tolstoy had presented 'Christianity as a radical moral doctrine' (Hayes 1996, 4). For Wittgenstein, the salient point of religion is that it is engaged with moral activities. He believed, 'Perhaps one could convince someone of God's existence, *through a certain kind of upbringing, by shaping his life in such and such a way*' (Drury 1984, 129; emphasis mine).

Throughout his life, Wittgenstein was concerned with ethical action which he used to term as 'decent behaviour'. This is why he said to Drury: 'If you and I are to live religious lives, it mustn't be that we talk a lot about religion, but that our manner of life is different' (Drury 1984, 114). '*It is my belief that only if we try to be helpful to other people will you in the end find your way to God'* (Drury 1984, 129; emphasis mine). Hence, for Ludwig, it is ethical action, not belonging to any creed that matters in religious life. To maintain a religious life does not even require churches to fall back on.[9]

For Wittgenstein, religion of the future then will be an ethical religion. Ethics and religion are intimately related in Wittgenstein's thinking when he said, 'If something is good, then it is Divine. In a strange way this sums up my ethics' (Wittgenstein 1965, 8). This is also connected with the following entry in *Notebooks 1914–1916*: 'How can a man be happy at all, since he cannot ward off the misery of this world?' (Wittgenstein 1961a, 81). 'The only life that is happy is the life *that can renounce the amenities of the world'* (Wittgenstein 1961a, 81; emphasis mine).

For Wittgenstein, 'To live happily is to be in accord with the world', that is, if one's living is in tune with the whole world, they feel happy (Wittgenstein 1961a, 75). Wittgenstein's biographers tell us how Wittgenstein himself lived such a happy life by renouncing the amenities of the world.

Moreover, he believed that decent behaviour as ethical living leads one towards his own inner God. So he advises, 'Oh don't depend on circumstances. Make sure that your religion is a matter *between you and God only'* (Drury 1984, 117; emphasis mine).

That God in early Wittgenstein is related to one personally is evident in his equation of God with the meaning of life and also with the meaning of the world (Wittgenstein 1961a, 73–4) and he ties this with 'the simile of God as father' (Wittgenstein 1961a, 73). God is closely related to us as our father. Interestingly, Tagore highlights this idea of the simile of God as father as being common with the ideas of the East. He opines, 'Christ's idea has something in common with the ideas of East, and with the idea of India. That of God as a father, related to human beings in a bond of love, a father, friend and a lover. God, according to Christ was related to us in a spiritual relationship of love' (Tagore 2008, 29).

Thus, closeness to God as an indispensable feature of spirituality is discernible in both Tagore and Wittgenstein. For him, such bonding and closeness to God can be grasped not by reasoning but by experiences or feelings of *the mystical*, which he expresses as 'how extraordinary that anything should exist' or 'how extraordinary that the world should exist' (Wittgenstein 1965, 8).

Experiencing the Mystical

'The mystical' is related to a particular type of viewing of the world (T6.45): 'To view the world *sub specie aeterni* is to view it as a whole—a limited whole. Feeling the world as a limited whole—it is this that is mystical' (Wittgenstein 1922, 73). He clarifies (T6.44), 'It is not how things are in the world that is mystical, but that it exists'. It is interesting to note that this particular example of the mystical, 'I wonder that the world exists', serves, for him, as an example of absolute value judgement on the one hand and also a paradigm example of aesthetic judgement on the other. Moreover, an analysis of the statement will reveal in a moment that it is actually a statement of religious experience 'it is the experience of seeing the world as a miracle' (Wittgenstein 1965, 11).

To him, wondering at the existence of the world is an experience par excellence; it cannot be put into words. It is another way of saying that it is a wonder that God created this world and one is in this world. Wittgenstein clubbed ethics, aesthetics, and religion together. Hence experiencing the mystical is something which is common to ethics, aesthetics and religion. Viewing from eternity (sub specie aeterni) thus provides the link between ethics, aesthetics, and religion. Wittgenstein explains: 'It seems to me that there is a way of capturing the world *sub specie aeterni*. ... It is as though thought flies above the world and leaves it as it is, observing it from above, in flight' (Wittgenstein 1984 (1980), 5–7).

Moreover, 'The thing seen *sub specie aeternitatis* is the thing seen together with the whole logical space' (Wittgenstein 1961a, 83e). He explains it with the example of a stove: 'But if I was contemplating the stove [the stove is not one among the many things in the world], it was *my world* and everything else colourless by contrast with it' (Wittgenstein 1961a, 83e; emphasis mine).

When one contemplates the stove aesthetically or from eternity, it becomes the whole world. Similarly, if one views the world ethically then also it 'waxes and wanes as a whole' (Wittgenstein 1961b, T6.43) and becomes a completely different world. Thus viewing from eternity enables one to see and know that each one of us belongs to the world as a whole, where everybody is on the same level. It is interesting to note here that Tagore also says the same thing about viewing an object from the point of view of aesthetics.

He says that we find a rose beautiful when we feel the unity of a rose coinciding with the unity of the universe, and thus it takes us beyond temporality. This unity tunes with the inner unity of oneself along with the unity of the universe (Tagore 1959, 82). Thus 'experiencing the mystical' leads one to feel his interconnectedness with the universe.

Interconnectedness with the Universe

In some of the cryptic passages of *Notebooks 1914–1916*, Wittgenstein speaks of the interrelatedness of man, world, and God.

> There really is only one world-soul, which I for preference call my soul and as which alone I conceive what I call the souls of others. (Wittgenstein 1961a, 49e)

> What do I know about God and the purpose of life? I know that the world exists. (Wittgenstein 1961a, 72e)

> God is how things stand
> How things stand is God. (Wittgenstein 1961a, 79e)

It is difficult to interpret what he exactly means by 'world-soul', though one does not fail to notice the interrelationship of God and the existent world. But there is an inconsistency here.

In accordance with the theory of language and meaning of the *Tractatus*, God is not a fact among other facts of the world. And he says that emphatically, *God does not reveal himself in the world* (T6.432). Is God then *in* the world (Wittgenstein 1961a)? Or is it impossible for God to be *in* the world? (T6.432)?

How to negotiate this inconsistency? For me, when Wittgenstein is saying 'how things stand is God', he is stating something that one can experience only when he/she views the world from eternity. For Wittgenstein, viewing the world from eternity connects ethics and aesthetics with God, the sense of life and the world. It helps us to see God or meaning of life and the world in every mundane object or fact. This is another way of saying: 'God is how things stand.' Thus the world as a totality of facts, as being contingent and relative, is devoid of value and significance. But however contingent the facts of the world are, they somehow reveal the necessary and the sublime. This world and this life is not totally insignificant or devoid of value for the early Wittgenstein, as the significant and the insignificant, the necessary and the contingent, the sublime and the trivial are intertwined with each other. The doctrine of showing reveals in an indirect way what is not in the world hence cannot be represented in the language (Verbin 2010, 475–6).

Wittgenstein used to think that this kind of viewing the world from eternity is viewing the world aright, where the interconnectedness of God, man, and the world is manifested.

Journey from the Religious to the Spiritual: Narrative of a Brāhmo

I have divided this section into the following strands of spirituality, which permeate Tagore's journey of life:

- Aversion to Institutionalized Religion
- 'Religion of an Artist'
- Feelings of Interconnectedness with the Universe
- Closeness to God and 'Lord of Life'
- Experiencing 'the Mystical'

Background

Rabindranath Tagore was born to an elite Brāhmo (who were believers of a monotheistic religion based upon the philosophy of the Upaniṣads) family of Bengal. His father, Devendranāth Tagore, headed the Ādi Brāhmo Samāj, and Rabindranath was made the secretary of the Samāj in 1884. With the strength and vigour of a 23-year-old youth, he disbursed his duties as a secretary in an enthusiastic manner for some time. In order to prove the importance of the philosophy of Ādi Brāhmo Samāj, he had to argue with revivalist Hindu thinkers such as Śaśadhar Tarkachurāmoni and Bankim Chandra Chattopādhyāy on the one hand, and with the members of Nababidhān (New Brāhmo Samāj) on the other. During 1900–1, we find clear articulations of his thoughts about Dharma in *Naivedya* (1901) where he has not departed from Upaniṣadic ideals and Māharṣi's influence as far as devotion to a personalized God is concerned. As an example, we can refer to poem no. 95 of *Gītāñjali*, which is the combination of poems 89 and 90 of *Naivedya*.

> When in the morning I looked upon the light I felt in a moment that I was no stranger in this world, that the inscrutable without name and form had taken me in its arms in the form of my own mother. (Tagore 1913a, 61)

This idea of a personalized God came to him through reading the Upaniṣads and Devendranāth's book *Brāhmodharma* (1850). Most of the poems written in 1896–1906 reveal the religious ideology of Ādi Brāhmo Samāj. However, with the passage of time he got disillusioned with this religion. Not only with this religion, he was disillusioned with other institutionalized religions as well—a theme to be dealt with in the first subsection.

Aversion to Institutionalized Religion

I have divided this section into 3 sub-themes referring to Tagore's antipathy towards the religion of a Brāhmo (Brāhmodharma), of a Hindu (Hindu Dharma), and of a Vaiṣṇava (Vaiṣṇavadharma).

Brāhmodharma

In 1907, we find him reacting against Brāhmodharma as institutionalized religion. He had an aversion to all definite creeds and to religions based on scriptural authority. He argued, 'Man is defeated when the authority inside him is curbed—curbed by the existence of religion, by tradition and custom, by scripture and ritual' (Das 2007, 294). Later in life, he recounts, 'I got initiation into the religion of the family I was born in. That is also pure religion, but my mind didn't agree to curtail myself in accordance with that' (Ray 2007 [1989], 83; translation mine).

When asked about institutional religion, he clearly stated that as an abstract idea he had nothing to say against it; but concretely speaking, institutional religion is bound to give rise to sectarianism. As an example, he takes the case of Christianity. He says:

> It is extremely difficult to become truly Christian, and yet by following the easy path of belonging to a Christian sect, one seems to acquire the merit of being a Christian, and to have a right to despise even one's

betters who by chance or choice do not profess Christianity. This has invariably been the case in the religions which crystallise themselves into sectarianism. Religious communities are more often formed upon custom and held habit than upon truth. (Das 2007, 293)

In *The Religion of Man* (1931), he said:

It was through an idiosyncrasy of my temperament that I refused to accept any religious teaching merely because people in my surround-ings believed it to be true. I could not persuade myself to imagine that I had a religion because whom I might trust, believed in its value. (Tagore 1953a, 91–2)

Orthodox Hindu Dharma

Disenchanted with the religion of his family, Tagore was captivated by the idea of near Orthodox Hinduism in his 40s when he founded Brahmavidyālay at Śāntiniketan (1901). He was under the impression that Hindu religion is not an institutionalized religion. At that time he curtailed himself in accordance with the dictates of Saṃhitā. It was inculcated among the students that they will touch the feet of Brahmin teachers (*praṇām*) while saluting non-Brahmin teachers only by rais-ing their folded hands (*namaskāras*). In November 1902, he wrote a letter to the principal, Manoranjan Bandyopādhyāy, stating, 'What is contrary to institutional Hindu practices will not have any place in my school. This practise is obviously in accordance with *Saṃhitās*'.[10] This phase for Rabindranath also did not last long. Communal riots and distribution of seats of Hindus and Muslims in the Parliament made him realize that he was mistaken in thinking that it is not institution-alized! We notice his concern for using religion as an instrument for violence, when he says:

We pride ourselves on having made religion the basic principle of our life, and so we see that brutality in the name of religion is widespread in this country. In the name of God, Hindus and Muslims are killing each other like ferocious beasts. Straightforward rejection of all distor-tions of religion is far better than this kind of blind and horrifying attachment to religion ... apart from burning down all religious perver-sions in the fire of atheism and making a fresh start[—]I do not see any other solution. (Bhattacāryya 2011, 137)

Vaiṣṇava Dharma

Apart from orthodox Hinduism, Rabindranath was also influenced by Vaiṣṇavism in his early years. He came in contact with the music and lyrics of Vaiṣṇavism, which made a deep impression on his mind.[11]

E.J. Thompson had a conversation with Tagore on Vaiṣṇava influences in his writings and Tagore said:

> I found in the vaiṣṇava poets lyrical movement, and images startling and new ... They gave me form. They make many experiments in meter, And then there was the boldness of their imagery. (Basu 2007, 75)

Apart from the form, Rabindranath also adopted from the Vaiṣṇava poets the philosophy that loving devotion (*prema-bhakti*) constitutes the ideal of human–divine relationship. The *Gītāñjali* (1913), the *Gītali* (1914), and the *Gītimālya* (1914) are manifestations of his attachment to the philosophy of Vaiṣṇavas. It has often been maintained by his commentators that the Tagorean idea that the finite feels the pang of separation from 'the infinite and the infinite requires the finite for the fulfilment of love is a purely Vaiṣṇava idea'. (Roy 1970, 9). This view seems justified when one refers to the following poem in *Gītāñjali*:

> Is it thy delight to see thy creation through my eyes and to stand at the portals of my ears silently to listen to thy own eternal harmony thou givest thyself to me in love and then feelest thine own entire sweetness in me? (Tagore 1913a, 34)

While emphasizing Vaiṣṇava influences on Tagore, one should also reflect on his point of dissensions. Unlike a Vaiṣṇava devotee, Tagore thinks that the love drama between the finite and the infinite, the poet and his lord of life (*jībandevatā*) is being enacted in the perceptible world of colour, sound, and touch. To elucidate, Tagore adopted Vaiṣṇava concepts such as *milan, viraha, and avisar* but moulded them with his own ideas. God fulfils himself and expresses His best through man. God needs man as much as man needs God. The human being is the centre of God's activity. He clarifies: 'I felt that I had found my religion at last, the religion of Man, in which the infinite became defined in humanity and came close to me so as to need my love and cooperation' (Tagore 1953a, 94–5). Thus, 'A

Vaiṣṇava is eager to divinize man whereas Tagore's mission is two-fold—the divinizing of man and the humanizing of God' (Roy 1970, 10). Moreover, he differs from the Vaiṣṇavites in saying that we can enjoy the beauty and harmony of our mundane world and can have emancipation only in this world and not in Vaikuṇṭha.

He also distances himself from the Vaiṣṇava preoccupation with ritualized service of the deity (Tagore 1997, 27) and frees himself from the teachings of some organized bodies of worshippers.

'Religion of an Artist'

As evident in earlier sections, Tagore did not want himself to be attached to any institutional religion such as Brāhmodharma, Hindu Dharma, or Vaiṣṇava Dharma. He gradually developed a kind of his own inner religion. He elucidates:

> Everyone has something special called 'my religion'. But the trouble is, he does not know exactly what it means. He knows that I am Christian, I'm Muslim, I'm Vaiṣṇava, and I'm Śākta. But even if he is certain that he belongs to an established religion throughout his life, he may be mistaken. Which is his religion? Is it the religion that lies hidden in his heart and keeps on creating him secretly from inside? An inherent religion and instinct of life builds up all that is animal and living. The animal need not have any sense of that religion. Man has another being greater than his physical being—it is his humanity. The creativity that is inside this being is his religion. (Tagore 2006, 23)

It can be termed *aesthetic religion, the religion of a poet or an artist.*

This quotation suggests that Tagore was clearly distancing himself from the established religions and searching for a religion that lies hidden in his heart and creates him anew in every moment. To elucidate this idea of 'religion of a poet or an artist', we would rather go back to November of 1913, when he received the Nobel Prize in Literature. He came into contact with the intelligentsia outside of Bengal, especially those belonging to the Western country rather closely than ever before. This change had affected his thoughts on religion. Tagore believed that God is the Supreme Person. He attributed personality to God. Tagore says, 'It is not in my own individual personality that reality is contained, but in an Infinite personality'

(Tagore 1959, 58). This is a peculiar conception of God as God is not an abstract reality like the Brahman of Advaita Vedānta, a system of philosophy where the highest reality is pure consciousness, which is also beyond human articulation. Nor is He a Saguṇa Brahman. He is personal but that does not indicate that He is a finite God. We feel Him in each and all that is not only in nature but also in the family, in society, and in the state. God is the concrete spirit. Tagore realizes that this God is within us but we wrongly search for Him in the outer world. He is to be sought in one's inner world, in oneself. This search is for someone who is 'the man of his heart'. This conception of *man of one's heart* developed gradually in *The Religion of Man* (1931). Not only that, this *man* makes one feel specially connected with nature, with other human beings, and finally with the universe.

Feelings of Interconnectedness with the Universe

'When a man does not realize his kinship with the world, he lives in a prison house whose walls are alien to him' (Tagore 2008, Vol. 2, 283). Tagore's love for the world and his intimacies with nature provide the background for his view of man's relation with nature, along with man's relation with other men, and ultimately with Universal Man. Tagore says: 'I have never looked at God, man and nature as problems which can be considered in isolation from each other. I could never conceive of their occupying watertight compartments' (Tagore 1920a, 36). His philosophy presents the integral picture of God, man, and nature. Nature, for Tagore, played an important role in understanding man's relation with man, with the universe and his quest for 'the lord of life'.

For him, by recitation of Gayatri Mantra (which devout Hindus recite every morning)

> we try to realize the essential unity of the world with the conscious soul of man; we learn to perceive the unity held together by one eternal spirit, whose power creates the earth, the sky, the stars and at the same time irradiates our minds with the light of a consciousness that moves and exists in unbroken continuity with outer world. (Tagore 1913b, 9)

Nature as an integral whole is the source of man's inspiration for creations, his songs, paintings, and dances. While he creates, he becomes aware of 'the surplus' of excess emotional energy, which does not get satisfied with simple preservation. It seeks an outlet in the creation of art, literature, music, and dance. While creating, man becomes aware also of his power to go beyond the factual/scientific world, to go beyond his 'physical finitude'. He writes:

> Whenever I feel the unity of the creative power within myself, I also feel connected to the infinite creativity of the universe. Like the sun, the moon and the stars, I become aware of an abiding creative power within me which is in control of my desires and disappointments. (Tagore 2006a, 332)

This feeling of 'abiding creative power' within oneself makes one realize the 'self-conscious principle of transcendental unity within man' (Tagore 2008, Vol. 3, 134), and feel close to one's God and 'Lord of Life'.

Closeness to God and 'Lord of Life' (*jībandevatā*)

Who is this 'Lord of life'? Is it our traditional God of religion? Can we label this account of personality as religious?

He himself was not very sure of it. His confusion can be sensed in the following excerpt:

> I cannot claim I am able to understand and absorb religion in its general sense. But I can say with certainty that there is something that is living in me. It is a feeling of mystery, not a dogma. It is a distinct awareness in the mind. I can sense that my life's joys and sorrows and my faith will together give my life a certain harmony. I don't know whether the scriptures are true or false. What I do know is that they mean nothing to me. (Tagore 2008, Vol. 2, 323)

In his mature life he was once interviewed regarding his own view of God and religion and surprisingly he brought out similarities between his own religion and that of the New Testament, saying: 'God according to Christ was related to us in a spiritual relationship of love' (Tagore 2008, 294). He finds in the New Testament's concept of God reflections of his own idea of closeness to the personal God as father, friend, and lover.

> The important idea in the gospels is that human beings can be and are related to an Infinite person. That they are not like so much driftwood,

that they have an individual personal route in an infinite personality, which we name God. I believe in this New Testament idea of God. (Tagore 2008, 294)

When he was asked: How do you know that there is a God? His reply was:

My personality constantly seeks union with other personalities and on the day when I realise a perfection of unity with them, it is glad and 'is filled with delight'. If this craving of my personality for supreme satisfaction exists, my poetic imagination must invent, and my reason demand a foundation of unity somewhere, where my whole being can obtain permanent shelter, where I can feel happy, find contentment and be at peace. In this realm of thought argument is no longer of much use. Men on this earth have from time to time procured or experienced direct evidence of God in and through our own Personality. (Tagore 2008, 295)

For Tagore, the personal God of religion is the supreme personality as experienced in religious exaltation. This feeling tells us that 'our personal "I" must have perfect relationship with the infinite personality' (Rādhākriśnan 1961, 58). Tagore talks about such mystical experiences of religious ecstasies in *The Religion of Man*.

Experiencing the Mystical

As stated earlier, Tagore was not a believer in scriptures, nor was he in favour of rational argumentations to prove the existence of God. For him, it is a matter of experience, a matter of feelings. Tagore talked about such mystical religious experiences in his Hibbert lectures. He says:

When I was 18, a sudden spring breeze of religious experience for the first time came to my life and passed away leaving in my memory a direct message of my spiritual reality. One day while I stood watching at early dawn the sun sending out its ray from behind the trees, I suddenly felt as if some ancient mist had in a moment lifted from my sight, and the morning light on the face of the world revealed an inner radiance of joy. The invisible screen of the common place was removed from all things and all men and their ultimate significance was intensified in my mind. (Tagore 1953a, 93–4)

Thus spiritual ecstasy resulted from his 'perfect relationship with the infinite personality' which lay within himself. It lifted the veil of difference between the self and other, between man, nature, and spirit. This blissful experience goes beyond the factual and it helps one stand on an equal footing with other religious beliefs, practices, and experiences.

Tagore draws a line of demarcation between a religious man and a theologian by saying:

> The principal creative forces which transmute things into our living structure, are emotional forces. A man where he is religious is a *person* but not where he is a mere theologian. *His feeling for the divine is creative.* But his mere *knowledge* of the divine cannot be formed into his own essence because of this lack of the emotional fire. (Tagore 1917, 22–3)

Tagore, a poetic genius, understandably emphasizes the role of emotion in transmuting inanimate things into stream of consciousness, and also the role of creativity in identifying a religious man as a person. Theologians on the other hand are entangled with their knowledge and argumentations and miss the mark of being persons.

It also explains why Tagore was attracted to the Bāuls,[12] who were by no means theologians.

Regarding Bāul songs, he says, in *The Religion of Man*:

> What struck me in this simple song was a religious expression that was neither grossly concrete, full of crude details, nor metaphysical in its rarefied transcendentalism. At the same time it was alive with an emotional sincerity. It spoke of an intense yearning of the heart for the divine who is in Man and not in the temple or scriptures, in images and symbols. The worshipper addresses his songs to man, the ideal. (Tagore 1931c, 108)

He expresses it in a song as well: 'Temples and mosques obstruct thy path, and I fail to hear thy call or to move' (Tagore 1931c, 108–9).

Finally his declaration, 'I do not know if I can be called religious in the current sense of the term, not claiming as my possession any particular idea of God, authorized by some time honoured institutions' (Tagore 2008, 294), reminds us of the declaration of Wittgenstein to M.O.C Drury: 'I am not a religious man; but I cannot help seeing every problem from a religious point of view.'[13]

Tagore's life, thus, manifests a journey from the outer to the inner, from organized, institutionalized religion to spirituality or a religion of one's own. It also shows that Tagore cannot be called religious in the traditional sense of the term. This reveals an extraordinary congruence with the journey of Wittgenstein's life.

Remarks on Religion in the *Tractatus*: A Textual Anatomy

Remarks on religion are conspicuously rare in the *Tractatus*. Of the four remarks (T3.031, T5.123, T6.372, and T6.432), three are made to prove a point of logic and there is only one remark that is relevant for religion, which is, 'God does not reveal himself in the world' (T6.432).

Not only that, for early Wittgenstein, religion belonged to the domain of nonsense (*unsinnig*) and of which one should be silent. This probably acted as a catalyst for the denial of metaphysics and religion altogether on the part of logical positivists. This section, therefore, is divided into two subsections; the first one is on dissension with logical positivists, which will show what it (Wittgenstein's view on religion) is not. And the second is on what it is, that is, interrelation of ethics, aesthetics, and religion, and their ineffability.

Dissension with Logical Positivists

Rudolf Carnap, the foremost champion of logical positivism, wrote in his autobiography that he was strongly influenced by the *Tractatus* of Wittgenstein and it was because of him that he decided to give up 'his live-and-let-live attitude towards metaphysics, abandon the model of multi-dimensional universe, and take up the cause of revolutionary positivism against the "pseudo-problems" of metaphysicians' (Nieli 1987, 64). But when the logical positivists personally interacted with him in the meetings organized by Schlick in the summer of 1927, they realized that they were totally mistaken in their interpretation of *Tractatus* and of the author of it. About this, Carnap wrote:

> When we were reading Wittgenstein's book in the circle, I had erro-
> neously believed that his attitude towards metaphysics was similar to
> ours. I had not paid sufficient attention to the statements in his book
> about the mystical, because his feelings and thoughts in this area were

too divergent from mine. Only personal contact with him helped me to
see more clearly his attitude at this point. (Carnap 1963, 34)

His attitude, Carnap thinks, was that of a creative writer or of a 'religious
prophet', not of a logical positivist by any means. In his own words:

> His [Wittgenstein's] point of view and his attitude towards people
> and problems, even theoretical problems were much more similar
> to those of a creative artist than to those of a scientist, one might
> almost say similar to those of a religious prophet or a seer. When
> he started to formulate his view of some specific philosophical prob-
> lem, we often felt the internal struggle that occurred in him at that
> very moment. ... When finally ... his answer came forth, his statement
> stood before us like a newly created piece of art or a divine revelation.
> (Carnap 1963, 25)

That he had a soft corner for metaphysics and religion was also
experienced by the members of the Vienna Circle at that time. This
made them realize that they did not give enough importance to the
mystical part of the *Tractatus*. Carnap tells us:

> Schlick and I ... had no love for metaphysics or metaphysical theology.
> ... Once when Wittgenstein talked about religion, the contrast between
> his and Schlick's position became strikingly apparent. Both agreed
> of course in the view that the doctrines of religion in their various
> forms had no theoretical content. But Wittgenstein rejected Schlick's
> view that religion belonged to the childhood phase of humanity and
> would slowly disappear in the course of cultural development. When
> Schlick, on another occasion made a critical remark about a metaphysi-
> cal statement by a classical philosopher (I think it was Schopenhauer),
> Wittgenstein surprisingly turned against Schlick and defended the phi-
> losopher and his work. (Carnap 1963, 26–7)

Not only logical positivists, British Wittgensteinian scholars also
were not comfortable with the idea that Wittgenstein had deep reverence for religion. It was like saying that to admit the author of the
Tractatus as a religious person was no less scandalous than to treat
René Descartes as an empiricist! That is why they were not even
ready to admit that Wittgenstein linked his own religious ideas with
those of Heidegger and Kierkegaard. Waismann's conversation with

Wittgenstein held on 30 December 1929 records the author of the *Tractatus* saying the following:

I can well understand what Heidegger means by *Being and Angst*. Human beings have a drive to run up against the boundaries of Language. Think for example the astonishment that anything exists (the wonder that the world exists). This astonishment cannot be expressed in the form of a question and also there is no answer at all. All we can say can a priori be only non-sensical; nevertheless we dash ourselves against the boundaries of language. Kierkegaard also had seen this throwing of oneself and even described in a very similar way as throwing oneself against a paradox. (Waismann 1965, 68)

This passage has long been a scandal to British Wittgensteinian scholars. When it first appeared in *The Philosophical Review* in 1965, the first sentence referring to Heidegger was not included. It subsequently appeared in *Wittgenstein and the Vienna Circle* (Barrett 1991, 22).

So far we have discussed what his views are not; next we will discuss what exactly his discussion on religion connotes.

The Domain of the Ineffable: The Ethical, the Aesthetic, and the Religious

In accordance with Figure 1.1, which represents the distinction between the sensible and the nonsensible, the sayable and the showable, religion along with ethics and aesthetics come under the head of 'an attempt to express the inexpressible'. Hence, the stray remarks in *Notebooks 1914–1916*, the *Tractatus*, and 'A Lecture on Ethics' may be regarded as Wittgenstein's 'personal thrust against the limits of language' and not as providing us with a consistent theory of religion.

That the discourse of ethics and religion are intimately related in Wittgenstein's mind is evident, when he said, 'If something is good, then it is divine. In a strange way this sums up my ethics '(Wittgenstein 1965, 3). 'Only the supernatural can express the supernatural'. Not only that, it also follows that the three examples that Wittgenstein chose as examples of absolute value judgements are, in fact, indicative of religious experiences. The first one was 'I wonder that the world exists'. It is another way of saying that it is a wonder that God created this world and I am in this world. The poem of

Tagore, which captures its main ideas, is actually an awakening of religious experience. The second experience talks about 'feeling safe in the hands of God' and the third experience of the same kind is that of feeling guilty and again this was described by the phrase, 'God disapproves of our conduct.' Here, Wittgenstein did not distinguish between ethical or religious experiences. Later, he talked about viewing sub specie aeterni, and by this notion he connected the ethical with the aesthetical. Wittgenstein connected this ethical and aesthetical experience with God and religious experience in his discussion with Waismann. Waismann once asked Wittgenstein: Is viewing the world sub specie aeterni or a limited whole, connected with the ethical? Wittgenstein said:

> Men have felt a connection here and they have expressed it in this way; God the Father created the world, while the Son of God (or the Word proceeding from God) is that which is ethical. That the Godhead is thought of as divided and again, as one being, indicates that there is a connection here. (Waismann 1965, 16)

It follows that Wittgenstein believed in the connection between the existence of the world and the ethical. Cyril Barrett interprets it thus:

> For Wittgenstein, the ethical, the happy life is being in harmony with the world as a whole and with its happenings, and thus with the will of God. Hence there is an ascent towards God from the ethical through the world, to the Son and the Father. (Barrett 1991, 47)

The final sentence suggests:

> Just as Father and son are one Godhead [that is, the ethical (son) and creator of the world (Father) are one and the same God], so the world and the ethical are one, and mutually interdependent in this sense. (Barrett 1991, 47)

Interestingly, the merging of ethics and religious experience is found in the writings of Tagore as well. For him, we reach God through our consciousness of what ought to be desired. This God is not the God of theologians or metaphysicians. Tagore terms it as 'man as ultimate reality' or 'Mānav Brahma'. As we find in his writing: 'God incarnates the highest accomplishment of Goodness. Man realizes his humanity, his personality in this incarnation. Man has reached his own God by depending on the magnanimity of his humanity'

(Ganguly 1968, 127; translation mine). God, to Tagore, is harmony qua harmony. He reveals the harmony of the individual self with the Universal Self. This harmony is transcendental and not factual. Automatically, it goes beyond factual representation; it is in this way inexpressible. But it gets manifested in moral and spiritual actions. He says:

> The moral side represents training in unselfishness, control of desire; the spiritual side represents sympathy and love. They should be taken together and not be separated. (Ganguly 1968, 104)

Wittgenstein also speaks of the inexpressibility of God and religious experiences. He says:

> How the world is, is for the higher, perfectly indifferent. God does not reveal himself in the world. (T6.432)

In accordance with the theory of language and meaning of the *Tractatus*, one can interpret the above quote thus: God is not a fact like other facts of the world. God is transcendental. Wittgenstein here wants to say that God does not reveal himself as a fact or an event or a state of affair that forms part of the world. God, therefore, like value, is outside the world. Now, there are other important passages on God in *Notebooks 1914–1916*.

It is interesting to note over here that for Tagore ethics, aesthetics, and religion belong to the domain of surplus. And he believes that we can reach God through moral consciousness. His God is also not the God of theologians. Individual man realizes oneself in his feeling of harmony with the Universal Man. Man can unite with the Universal Man only because he can create. Man reveals himself by means of his creative works. God is revelation in itself. He is also revealed in his creation. God is personal when he creates. Because of this similarity, man can unite with God. Such union in effect manifests the union of the finite with the infinite, the outer with the inner, which is demanded by the philosophy of Tagore. But this conception of Mānav Brahma, which he often expresses as 'the man of the heart', where the union of the finite with the infinite manifests itself, differs widely from a theological conception of God. Nor is it the God of metaphysics, which the Advaitin terms as 'Saguṇa Brahman'. This peculiar conception of God or religion presupposes a journey from faith in organized religion to faith in spirituality for Tagore. Not only Tagore, Wittgenstein also had to undertake a long journey before he settled down for a new kind of spirituality, often represented in his talks and writings.

We have mentioned earlier that remarks on religion are scarce in the *Tractatus* but they abound in his *Notebooks 1914–1916*.

> What do I know about God and the purpose of life? (Wittgenstein 1961a, 73e)
> Something about the world is problematic, which we call its meaning. (Wittgenstein 1961a, 74)
>
> To pray is to think about the meaning of Life. (Wittgenstein 1961a, 73)
> To believe in God means to see that life has a meaning. (Wittgenstein 1961a, 74)
> God does not reveal himself in the world. (T6.432)

The quotations suggest that God in the early writings of Wittgenstein is somehow related to the meaning of life and the world, which is also problematic. Since meaning of life is something higher and not 'in the world', God as the meaning of the world cannot be in the world. Now, what exactly is the meaning of the world?

> The meaning of life, i.e. the meaning of the world, we can call God.
>
> And connect with this the comparison of God to a father. To pray is to think about the meaning of life.
>
> I cannot steer the happenings of the world according to my will: I am entirely powerless.
>
> I can only make myself independent of the world—and thus, in a certain sense master it—only in so far as I renounce any influence over its happenings. (Wittgenstein 1961a, 73–4)

If one attempts to read these passages with Wittgenstein's autobiographical remarks he made in his diary during this time, one finds out that the simile of God as father is definitely in accordance with the New Testament. And these comments are made in July 1916 while he was in Olmütz. Engelmann tells us that they were discussing the Bible, chiefly the New Testament, with the intention of finding out 'a self-made religion', 'an ethical equivalent of Christianity'. Here, Wittgenstein equates life with the world, the world which is beyond one's control. In interpreting this passage, I agree with Barrett who maintains that 'the meaning of life has nothing to do with scientific explanation, whether physical, chemical, biological, historical, psychological or sociological'. The meaning of life is simply what Wittgenstein says it is: the sense of the world; 'Life and world are one and the same'. The sense of the world cannot lie within the world; it must lie outside it (Barrett 1991, 97).

In the Tractarian project there are many things that lie outside the world. Here, one might ask: Why cannot one of these be the sense of the world? I think Cyril Barrett is right when he answers this question in the following way:

> I think that they are, in Wittgenstein's view, in their different ways. They make sense of the world. Something else is needed for a full explanation of the world. And that we call God. So God gives sense to the world or in Wittgenstein's own terms, is the sense of the world, the meaning of life. But what does that mean? It could mean that God is not a being, but the name we give to explanations of facts at a higher level. 'God' is a composite or portmanteau word for ethical, aesthetic and other values with which we grace the world. (Barrett 1991, 97)

In accordance with the philosophy of the *Tractatus*, the world is the totality of facts and the meaning of life/God, thus, is not a fact among other facts, and hence cannot be 'in the world'.

But in *Notebooks 1914–1916*, Wittgenstein comments in a pantheistic overtone:

> God is how things stand
> How things stand is God. (Wittgenstein 1961a, 79e)

We know that from the point of view of the *Tractatus*, facts state how things stand. Hence, these remarks entail that God is in the world and God can be termed as a fact. Now, how to negotiate this inconsistency? Commentators such as Brian Clack interpret that this remark is pantheistic. For me, though these remarks sound like those of pantheism, they are still not to be treated as 'pantheistic', as Wittgenstein here is talking about the view that one can have only when he/she views the world from eternity. This is actually 'seeing the world aright'. Under normal circumstances, God is not 'in the world' but the world viewed from eternity, showing that the sublime is manifested in the mundane and they are intertwined. This is also not logically inconsistent as they are viewed from two different perspectives. To elucidate, Wittgenstein in the *Tractatus* distinguishes very carefully between contingent and necessary, relative and absolute. The domain of facts and the world as their totality belong to the domain of the relative and the contingent. On the other hand, there is the domain of the sublime, the necessary and the significant. They are not 'in the world'. In the *Tractatus* logic, ethics, aesthetics, meaning of life and the world, and God, all belong to this domain. Thus, the world as a totality of facts, as being contingent and relative, is devoid of value and significance. But the important point to note over here is that no matter how stringent these distinctions are and how contingent the facts of the world are, they somehow manifest the necessary and the sublime. This world and this life are not totally insignificant or devoid of value for early Wittgenstein, 'as the significant and the insignificant, the necessary and the contingent, the sublime and the trivial are intertwined with each other. The doctrine of showing reveals in an indirect way what is not in the world hence cannot be represented in the language' (Verbin 2010, 475–6).

I have discussed in Chapter 3 that the connection between ethics and aesthetics, art and ethics, is through 'viewing from eternity'. Here, I would like to add that for Wittgenstein, viewing from eternity connects ethics and aesthetics with God, the sense of life, and the world. It helps us to see the world in a right way, that is, to see God or meaning of life and the world in every mundane object or fact. This is another way of saying 'God is how things stand'. This is also connected with leading a 'happy life' by transcending the mundane life and all its miseries.

An entry in *Notebooks 1914–1916* from August 1916 asks: 'How can a man be happy at all, since he cannot ward off the misery of this world?' (1961a, 81). He himself offers a way out of this: The life of knowledge is the life that is happy in spite of the misery of the world. The only life that is happy is the life *that can renounce the amenities of the world*. We know from his biography that Wittgenstein himself lived such a happy life by renouncing the amenities of the world.

It reminds us also of Tagore's saying that our *śāstras* too instruct us. We must practice self-control, not for the sake of piety alone but also for the sake of happiness: *sukhārthi saṃyato bhabet*. That is, if you want to have your desire fulfilled, keep it in check, if you want to enjoy beauty, be calm by quelling the lust of your appetite and purifying yourself (Tagore 2001, 167).

For Wittgenstein, 'to live happily is to be in accord with the world' (Wittgenstein 1961a, 74e). That is, if one's living is in tune with the whole world, one feels happy; if not, then unhappy. What he means is that if we can accept whatever happens in the world, be it happiness, be it misery, without any grudges, then it will ensure a perfectly contented and happy world. 'A man who is happy must have no fear. Not even in face of death. Only a man who lives not in time but in the present is happy' (Wittgenstein 1961a, 74e). Fear in the face of death is the best sign of a false life, that is, a bad life (Wittgenstein 1961a, 75e). McGuinness thinks that this is what drew Wittgenstein so passionately to the music of Schubert, for in Schubert 'one can encounter the contrast of the misery of his life and the absence of all bitterness' (McGuinness 1988, 124).

This happy and contented life does not advocate asceticism or rejection of the world. Once. he told M.O.C. Drury that future religion will not be ascetic in the sense that people will go without food or drink. Seeing the world rightly is not a matter of contemplating some discrete sphere of truths; rather, it is seeing that a blade of grass, a speck of dust, 'earth's lowly delight', will bring forth 'heaven's glorious light'. Surprisingly, one notices the same insight in Tagore's poem. I quote:

> Liberation through ascetic denial? No. Not for me,
> I'll taste the sweetness of freedom through countless bonds of Joy
> In this very jar of clay you pour again and again,
> Your wines of different colours and flavours
> I'll not shut the doors of senses—no, never,
> Your joy, oh God, will ever remain real for me
> In the midst of all the earthly joys of colour song and scent. (Tagore 1977, 47–8)

In some other works,

> Blessed am I, I have searched for heaven's glorious light Blessed am I,
> that I have loved this lowly earth's delight. (Naravane 1977a, 49)

Now we can see that the God of the *Tractatus* is not a traditional God of theologians.[14] In fact the *Tractatus* is a critique of the traditional metaphysical and theological conception of God, which claims that the existence of God can be proved by observational/factual reasoning and that at the same time they will be necessary. That is, 'they make "substantial trans-empirical" truth claims for the factual propositions constituting the argument' (DeAngelis 2007, 103).

Wittgenstein argued against this in the *Tractatus*. And it is precisely in this sense that Wittgenstein claimed that he is not a religious man.

While answering earlier queries regarding the relationship of religion, logic, and language, one might now suggest that Wittgenstein's views on religion actually were not contrary to those of logic and language in the *Tractatus*. They were at par, not 'in the world', but 'the conditions of the world'. Once one understands this, one finds no problem in grasping in which sense Wittgenstein sees the problems of language, life, and the world from a 'religious point of view'.

In earlier chapters, readers are apprised of the fact that a discussion about religion, spirituality, God, or religious consciousness would fall into the domain of the 'nonsensical' from the perspective of early Wittgenstein, as they are not concerned with depicting the state of affairs or facts. They are 'beyond' this world; though they can nevertheless manifest themselves through the world. And this beyond in the field of religion manifests the imperceptibility of God 'in the world'. Not only that, this 'beyond' manifests itself in being one with ethics and aesthetics on the one hand and in a 'profane spirituality' on the other. This nonsensicality, however, is not paradoxical as it talks about two distinct points of views; and viewing the world from the point of view of eternity provides one with the 'right view' of the world, which is somehow inexpressible from the point of view of mundane facts. One might bring an analogy from the Advaita Vedānta system of Indian philosophy here and explain that a pantheistic world view is the view from the transcendental (Pāramārthika) point of view and that 'God does not reveal himself in the world' is from the empirical (Vyāvahāra) point of view.[15] All these points will be more succinct once we focus on the play *The King of the Dark Chamber* (1914) by Tagore, which, we know, had an impact on young Wittgenstein, as far as his views on religion and spirituality are concerned.

Notes

1. See Janik and Toulmin (1973), McGuinness (2005 [1988]), and Ray Monk (1991).
2. For writings on the parallels between Wittgenstein's philosophy of religion and his general philosophical method, see Malcolm (1993), and Shields (1993).
3. This anecdote was narrated by Ram Chandra Gandhi to Tayeb Mehta and Sankha Ghosh at Śāntiniketan on 28 August 1984 where both Gandhi and Mehta were visiting fellows at the Viśva-Bhārati University (as cited in Ghosh 2011, 188).
4. This remark had caused a huge uproar among Wittgenstein scholars and there had been an attempt to read it in his later writing: *Philosophical Investigations*. Norman Malcolm wrote his last book on this: *Wittgenstein: A Religious Point of View* (1993), which was critiqued by Peter Winch. Both were critiqued by Kai Nielsen and thereafter huge ink has been spilled on this topic, though there is very little evidence of reading this remark in the context of the *Tractatus*.
5. Robert Wesley, 'What Manner of Man Was Wittgenstein?' Available at: http://www.roangelo.net/logwitt/manner.html (last accessed on 12 June 2020).
6. Wittgenstein's paternal great grandfather was Moses Meier, a Jewish land agent. His grandson, Herman Christian Wittgenstein, married Fanny Figdore, also Jewish, who converted to Protestantism just before they married. Moreover, Wittgenstein's maternal grandfather was also a Jew. His paternal grandparents were born Jews but both were baptized before their marriage in the Lutheran church. His maternal grandfather was reared a Catholic while his maternal grandmother was Catholic. This is why Ludwig's family was a family of assimilated Jews (Monk 1990, 9–12).
7. Bertrand Russell reports Otto Moreline in a letter dated 17 March 1912:

   He is far more terrible with Christians than I am. He had liked F, the undergraduate monk, and was horrified to learn that he is a monk. F came to tea with him and W at once attacked him ... as I imagine, with absolute fury. (cited in Monk 1990, 34)

8. In 1935, the German government enacted the Nuremberg laws, which specified that only those people with three or more Jewish grandparents were to be classified as Jews; those with one or two Jewish grandparents were classified as different grades of mixed race. In 1936 and 1937, Wittgenstein confessed to friends and family that he had misrepresented the extent of his Jewish descent, claiming that one grandparent had been a Jew, when actually three of them were.

9. In his conversation with Drury, he asserts:

    For all you and I can tell the religion of the future will be without
    any priests and ministers. I think one of the things you and I have
    to learn is that we have to live without the consolation of belonging
    to a church. ... The religion of the future will be extremely ascetic;
    and by that I do not mean just going without food and drink. (From
    Letter by Bertrand Russell to Otto Moreline, 17 March 1912, cited
    in Monk 1990, 34)

10. A letter written to M. Bandyopādhyāy on 5 December 1902 (as cited in
    Ray 2007 [1989], 67; translation mine).

11. Tagore writes in his autobiography:

    I came across a copy of *Gitā Govindā* when I was out in the company
    of my father and was enjoying trips in the Ganges. My knowledge of
    Sanskrit was meagre then, but I could understand the significance
    of many words as my knowledge of Bengali was sound. That *Gitā
    Govindā* I have read so many times and enjoyed. (Tagore 1968, 79)

12. 'A bāul is a wandering minstrel singing philosophical songs about the
    common ways of life' (Tagore 2006b, 325).

13. Wittgenstein's ability to see every problem from a religious point of view
    despite being non-religious will be dealt with in the next section.

14. From a poem entitled 'Prabhat' in *Chaitali* (translated in Naravane 1977b,
    49).

15. In the philosophy of Advaita Vedanta, there are three levels of reality.
    They are 'Pratibhāsika', 'Vyāvahārika', and 'Pāramārthika. Reality in
    Pratibhāsika level is ephemeral, like dreams. Dream experiences are not
    real in the sense that they get contradicted by waking experiences. They
    are not totally unreal such as square circles as we can dream of only
    those things that we have seen in the phenomenal world. Reality at the
    Vyāvahārika level is empirical reality, the reality which is seen in day to
    day life. Thus empirical reality is the totality of facts, causes, and effects.
    Pāramārthika is the Ultimate Truth Level, where there are no distinctions.
    Empirical reality as the totality of facts gets contradicted by the realiza-
    tion of the Ultimate Truth. All merge into Supreme Consciousness and
    become one. In the *Tractatus*, when one sees the world from the point
    of view of eternity, there are no distinctions between the contingent and
    the necessary, the profane and the sacred, facts and values. It can only
    happen when you reach the highest level.

5

The King of the Dark Chamber and the Remarks of Early Wittgenstein

An Interpretation

The secular spirituality of Tagore and Wittgenstein has already been ascertained in the previous chapter. However, the so-called 'religious points of views' of both the thinkers will be apparent to the readers, if one reflects on the symbolic play *Rājā* (*The King of the Dark Chamber*), by Tagore. In this chapter, I juxtapose the content of *The King of the Dark Chamber*, the play by Rabindranath Tagore (which was Wittgenstein's favourite), with the cryptic passages on ethics and religion from *Notebooks 1914–1916, Tractatus Logico-Philosophicus*, and 'A Lecture on Ethics' with the intention of showing that these passages make perfect sense together in the light of the ideas contained in the play. And probably because of this, Wittgenstein was drawn so much to this particular play of Tagore.

In order to attain this objective, I have divided the chapter into three sections. In the first, the context of the play along with the famous controversy regarding its translation will be discussed. The theme of the play (the original Bengali version) along with Tagore's comments on it will be explored in the subsequent section. In the last section, there will be an analysis of the play which will show that it has counterparts in the fabric of Wittgenstein's conception of spirituality and religion explicit in the remarks in *Notebooks 1914–1916*, the *Tractatus*, and 'A Lecture on Ethics'.

Wittgenstein's Reaction to *The King of the Dark Chamber*

The King of the Dark Chamber (originally known as *Rājā* in Bengali) is a symbolic mystical play by Rabindranath Tagore that was published in November 1910. In 1919, Tagore abridged and modified the play into a new play entitled *Arūpratan*.[1] The play *Rājā* was a favourite of Tagore's. As he puts it in a letter to his friend William Rothenstein, 'I do want the message embodied in this particular play to reach your people. This play has come out of my innermost experience, almost unconsciously almost in spite of myself—I have an almost impersonal love for it.'[2] This is the time, as I have mentioned earlier, when the whole of Europe, including Germany and Austria, was going through 'Tagore mania' and every lecture of his was getting translated in the German language almost immediately. *Rājā* had been translated by Hedwig Lachmann and Gustav Landuer and published by Kurt Wolff in 1919. However, from Ray Monk's biography, we learn that Wittgenstein had first read the German translation of the play in 1921, when Tagore was at the height of his fame and enormously popular in Europe, particularly in Germany and Austria. After reading the book for the first time, Wittgenstein was not impressed. He had then written to Engelmann that, despite its great wisdom, the play had failed to make a deep impression on him (Monk 1990, 409). He stated:

> It seems to me as if all that wisdom has come out of the ice box, I should not be surprised to learn that he got it all second-hand by reading and listening (exactly as so many among us acquire their knowledge of Christian wisdom) rather than from his own genuine feeling. Perhaps I don't understand his tone; to me it does not ring like the tone of a man possessed by the truth (such as, for instance, Ibsen's tone). It is possible however that here *the translation leaves a chasm* which I cannot bridge. I read with interest throughout but without being gripped. (Engelmann 1967, 47; emphasis mine) .

But he changed his mind within a few months. He re-read the play, reviewed his earlier remarks, and told Hansel, his friend, 'I believe that there is indeed something grand here' (Monk 1990, 408). In due course, it became one of his favourite books which he often lent to his friends (including members of the Vienna Circle) to read.

In this section, there will be an attempt to explore, what is it that Wittgenstein found 'grand' in this play. By this time, it is quite evident that Wittgenstein was moved by the play, as he once again read the play before he delivered his lectures on psychology, aesthetics, and religious belief at Cambridge.

Translation Controversy

Regarding the translation of *The King of the Dark Chamber* there was confusion right from the beginning. The initial version of the play published by MacMillan was translated by Kshitish Chandra Sen. Professor Śyamal Sarkār in his pioneering article, 'The King of the Dark Chamber: Text and Publication' (Sarkār 2013, 141–54), has done an 'investigative study of six extant manuscripts and typescripts of English version and has made some startling discoveries that reflect poorly on almost everybody concerned and offer chastening glimpses into a case history of bungled translation and publication' (Sarkār 2013, 141).

It was really unfortunate for Tagore to receive a copy of *The King of the Dark Chamber* in printed form from his publisher Macmillan, while he got no proofs beforehand. 'He was not consulted, he had no idea whatsoever that the play was slated for publication' (Sarkār 2013, 141). Moreover, he did not translate the play. As said earlier, a Bengali graduate of Cambridge University, Kshitish Chandra Sen, undertook to translate *Rājā* in 1912, when Tagore was in England. We know from Sarkār that Sen had been studying for the Indian Civil Services examination at that time. Sarkār narrates:

> Mr. Sen recollects that he was occupied for a mere seven days over the translation of this, a full length play. On his own admission, he dashed off lines of the concluding portion of the play even during those distracting moments when he was waiting for the train at the Euston station. (2013, 146)

From the narrative one can well imagine how casual the translation would turn out to be! However, in Sarkār's examination of Sen's manuscript, it is evident that 'Tagore had a hurried look at it and blue pencilled clusters of lines – but only in the first five scenes of the play. He also translated 12 of the songs contained in the Bengali version, for Mr. Sen appears to have left the songs out of his task' (Sarkār 2013, 146).

However, out of this casual translation made by Sen, two type-scripts were made. Tagore gave one copy to Rothenstein, probably to hear his valued opinion on this symbolical play. Tagore kept one copy with himself for improvement. Obviously, he was not happy with Sen's translation, the young student at Cambridge. Tagore was visiting the United States of America at that time. The Chicago journal, *The Drama*, had called him for a contribution, and the typescript that Tagore was carrying with him appeared in the journal with some minor revisions in May 1914. The copy that was lying with Rothenstein also got circulated in England. In 1913, Tagore received the Nobel Prize and visited England again in April. At that time, people were curious to learn about his new writings and he read *The King of the Dark Chamber* in some select private congregations. But as scheduled earlier, the play was not published as a supplement to the London's *Nation* due to the disapproval of Macmillan, the authorized publisher of the poet.

When Tagore came back, he started working on the typescript again, making some more changes in the scenes of the play. The typescript on which he was working finally had 14 scenes. He was still dissatisfied. He started working on language revisions. Then, in June 1914, he was completely taken aback when Macmillan sent published copies of the play, *The King of the Dark Chamber*. The manuscript was not ready. Tagore was not prepared to see it published. Nor did he give permission to Macmillan to publish it. Rothenstein was completely unaware of this fiasco. He liked the play and wrote about his deep appreciation in a letter to Tagore (Lago 1972, 167–8).

In reply to Rothenstein, Tagore stated:

> I was rather surprised to receive from Macmillan copies of the *King of the Dark Chamber*. I had no idea that they were going to bring it out so soon and I was not prepared for it. The manuscript that you had with you was the first draft and in the later ones the translation had undergone such a vast deal of alterations that it is quite a differing thing now.

So I was rather put out at the sudden appearance of this book with all its crudities. ... The worst of it is that I am not the translator—it was an Indian student, Kshitish Chandra Sen, who translated it for me. I have cabled to Macmillan to make correct announcements—please see that it is done properly. (Sarkār 2013, 142–3)

But Macmillan never made correct announcements even in its several reprint editions. As Sarkār points out:

Each of these reprints bears on its title page, in ten point caps, a piece of announcement which cannot escape the notice of even a casual observer glancing through the pages: TRANSLATED BY THE AUTHOR. And only at the end is printed in ten point small caps the name of Kshitish Chandra Sen as the translator of *The King of the Dark Chamber* of the volume in the 1918 reprint as also in the successive ones, in the publishers announcement of the other works of the author. (2013, 143)

But the mess does not end there. Rothenstein wrote back, 'explaining that in their haste to publish something by Tagore, Macmillan had got hold of the typescript in his possession'. He added with hindsight, 'The slang and other weaknesses of the translation always worry me a little' (Lāl 2001, 100). The other weaknesses that had entered into print were unforgivable—Rothenstein's typescripts had grammatical errors, misspellings of proper names, dropped lines, all of which were carried over into published form. Even the ellipses—which Sen had put in and Tagore did not have the time to substitute with words—did not escape print. The book caught everyone by surprise, including the New York branch of Macmillan, which consequently could not publish the American edition until September. To this day, we do not know who read the proofs.

Thus, we find MacMillan, Tagore's authorized publisher, made an unauthorized publication of the play *The King of the Dark Chamber* without the consent of the author, which should have been withdrawn immediately. Few people realize this fact though, and 'the play continues to be treated respectfully as an authorized translation such as the other Macmillan volumes' (Lāl 2001, 99–100).

While reading this English version, a sensitive genius like Wittgenstein realized that the translation is inadequate to capture the deeper significance of the play. 'The translation left a chasm' and in

order to overcome this—in order to as it were, to unearth the text—
Smythies and Wittgenstein prepared their own translation. Among
Smythies' papers was found a typed copy of their version of act II of
the play headed:

> The King of the Dark Chamber, by Rabindranath Tagore [sic] trans-
> lated from the English of Rabindranath Tagore into English used by
> L. Wittgenstein and Yorick Smythies, by L. Wittgenstein and Yorick
> Smythies. (Monk 1990, 410)

In order to find out what is 'grand' in the play and how it came
close to Wittgenstein's own ideas about God, spirituality, religion, and
religious consciousness we need an overview of the play.

Theme of the Play

The play (Bengali version) revolves around a mysterious invisible
king who, as we learn from his subjects, is benevolent and efficient
although they have doubts about his nature, beauty, and, peculiarly,
even his existence. His reticence towards being seen causes most of
the drama centring round his queen, Sudarśanā. Queen Sudarśanā is
eager to meet her king and, as a beloved wife, she desires to see him
in daylight, whereas the king so far has met her only in a dark chamber. The king warns her about the caprice of sensuality, of beauty, and
says that she will not be able to bear his sight if he reveals himself in
light, in the outside world. The king advises her to be content with
what she is receiving at present, that is, union with the king in the
darkness of his private chamber.

Apart from these two important characters there are two others:
Grandfather and Surangamā, the maid of Sudarśanā, both of whom
have unconditionally surrendered themselves to the will of the king.
Thus, they can feel when the king will arrive and they can listen to the
tune of the king's lyre. Surangamā is the messenger of the union of
the king and the queen. The Grandfather is the leader of the spring
festival and he attempts to feel the presence of mirth in nature, which
ultimately merges into the highest ecstasies of God.

But the important point is that both Grandfather and Surangamā,
though close to the king, are unable to express the nature of the
king in words. They feel the presence of the king, feel whatever the

king wants to convey, but they cannot comprehend the true nature of the king.

Apart from them, there are seven kings of whom the king of Kānchi plays a major role; King Suvarna, an imposter; Grandfather's group of boys; and subjects and foreigners who are visitors to this spring festival.

In the very first scene (of the original Bengali version, act II of the original English version [Munz and Ritter 2017, 327–36] which Wittgenstein translated along with Smythies) the king and the queen meet in the dark chamber; Surangamā works here as the mediator between the two. When the king knocks on Sudarśanā's door, Surangamā is the first to hear the knock and she is the person who opens the door for the king (rājā).

The queen begs to see the king in the light of the day. The king replies: 'You want to look at me in the midst of a thousand other things. Why? Why can you not feel me in the dark? If I show myself, the sight will overpower you. It will be painful. You'll not be able to bear it' (Tagore 1961g, 18).

Sudarśanā replies that the question of not bearing the sight of the king does not arise at all. Finally, the king promises Sudarśanā that he will reveal himself during the spring festival, but the only condition is that Sudarśanā will have to recognize the king all by herself. Sudarśanā is confident of her intelligence and love, so she thinks that she will be able to recognize her love, her king.

The next scene begins with the commencement of the spring festival. Various people from various parts of the country and also from different countries come for the festival. People are vocal about the absence of the king in his kingdom. Some feel the king is ugly and that is why he does not reveal himself. Others think that the kingdom is a perfect example of anarchy and anomie. Amid the hullaballoo, a false king takes advantage of the absence of the king and declares himself to be the king in a pompous and luxurious procession. Queen Sudarśanā now mistakes this false king to be her king and surrenders herself to the cheat. She fails to recognize the actual king in broad daylight.

On the political front, seven kings from neighbouring countries arrive in this land for spring festival. The king of Kānchi, the cleverest of them, detects that the person who is claiming to be the king is not actually so. The king of Kānchi plans to woo Sudarśanā by attacking the kingdom with the help of other visiting kings. Somehow the plan does not work out. The attacking kings have problems among themselves and became sceptical about each other. Both the false king and the king of Kānchi finally overtake the mask. And the false king asks for forgiveness from the real king. At this moment, Queen Sudarśanā and the real king meet again in the dark chamber in act VIII. Now the queen perceives the king in his terrible fiery form, not in the pleasing beautiful manner that she imagines him to be. The king appears 'like the awful night when a comet swings fearfully into our ken, black as the threatening storm cloud, black as the shoreless sea with the spectral red tint of twilight on the tumultuous waves' (Tagore 1961g, 36), but he forgives her adultery, unfaithfulness, incapability of accepting the truth, and her dearth of mental preparation to accept the king as he is. But still, the queen is not worthy of union with the king. It is true that the queen has forsaken her ego and pride, yet she is not free of them. She is not repentant; rather she makes the king responsible for her mistakes. Now she cannot stand the king nor can she stand Surangamā who has surrendered herself entirely to the king. She rejects her king and leaves the palace to move to her father's place.

This is another mistake on Sudarśanā's part. She is, thus, brought to complete despair. She feels utterly humiliated and degraded in her father's place and the kings of nearby kingdoms attack her father's kingdom just to woo her. In despair, she then casts away her pride. She now realizes that she can only be reconciled with her husband if she bows down to him with complete servility. Only when Queen Sudarśanā is brought down to the level of the servant Surangamā can she become enlightened. The play ends with her realization that everything of any real value is conferred upon her by the king, who can now say to her, 'Come, come with me now, come outside into the light.' When the final surrender comes, she feels that her experience is all the richer for the agitation and ignorance she has gone through. And so, in the end she is able to tell the king: 'Your love lives in me, nothing is mine, and everything is yours, master' (Tagore 1961g, 65).

After Sudarśanā has been saved, she remarks to the king: 'You are not beautiful, my lord—you stand beyond all comparisons!' To this the king replies, 'That which can be comparable with me lies within yourself.' If this be so, says Sudarśanā then that too is beyond comparison: 'Your love lives in me—you are mirrored into that love and you see your love reflected in me, nothing of this is mine, it is all yours' (Tagore 1961g, 65).

Author's Review of the Play

Most critiques and commentators described this play as an allegorical play where the problematic theme centres round the pride of Sudarśanā, whose uncontrollable emotions brought immense despair in her life. Even Ray Monk describes it as 'an allegorical play of religious awakening' (1990, 410), much to the displeasure of the author who vehemently opposes the idea of labelling this play as allegorical. In a letter to C.F. Andrews, the poet objects to categorizing of the play as allegorical.

'Critics and detectives are naturally suspicious,' he says:

> They scent allegories and bombs where there are no such abominations. It is difficult to convince them of our innocence. ... The human soul has its inner drama which is just the same as anything else that concerns man, and Sudarśanā is not more allegory than Lady Macbeth, who might be described as an allegory representing the criminal ambition in man's nature. (Tagore 1929, 48–9)

Let us now look at the introduction of *Arūpratan* (Formless Jewel) where Tagore himself stated the underlying theme of the play, *The King of the Dark Chamber*:

> Sudarśanā sought the Rājā externally. She sent the bridal garland to the place where things can be seen by the eyes, touched by the hands, amassed in the storehouse, where there's men and money and fame. With the vanity of intelligence she must have determined that she could attain success in life externally by the strength of intelligence alone. Her companion *Suraṅgamā* told her that it would not be wrong to know the Lord in all respects through externals, but only after He is known in the interior secret chamber where He comes Himself and summons: however it would be wrong to call '*rājās*' those who delude the eyes through *Māyā*. Sudarśanā did not heed these words. She surrendered herself in her mind to *Suvarṇa* on seeing his beauty. Then— how a fire started on all sides of her; how a battle over her ensued among a group of many false external *rājās* as soon as she left the *Rājā*

internal; how her introduction to her own *Rājā* occurred in the midst of that conflagration; how her vanity was destroyed by the shock of sorrow; and eventually how after accepting defeat, leaving the palace, standing in the street, she gained the company of that Lord of hers. The Lord who can be perceived in all lands, in all times, in all forms, in the blissful rasa of one's own interior—all that has been narrated in this play. (Lāl 2001, 269)

In accordance with the intention of the author, that is, without treating it as an allegorical play and keeping his narration in mind, we would like to analyse the theme of the play in the next section.

The King of the Dark Chamber and Remarks of Early Wittgenstein: An Interpretation

In this section there will be an analysis of the theme of the play *The King of the Dark Chamber* which will, in turn, help us in interpreting the cryptic passages of *Notebooks 1914–1916* and the *Tractatus*. Now this analysis will centre on the following five leitmotifs:

1. Imperceptibility of the King
2. Importance of Feelings
3. Transformation of the World
4. The Beautiful and the Terrible
5. Philosophy of Harmony

Imperceptibility of the King

In the play, the king is invisible. No one sees him. Throughout the play the king is not physically seen. Grandfather and Surangamā who have surrendered unconditionally to the king stated clearly that they also do not have any idea of the real nature of the king. They cannot describe him in words. Keeping in mind our earlier discussion of Tagore's distinction between fact and truth, expressible and inexpressible, we can now say that the king in the play represents the infinite, one might also term it as God who belongs to the domain of truth which eludes facts. Facts cannot directly apprehend the truth. That is why the king is invisible in broad daylight. The dark chamber seems to me to be representative of dark chambers of deep feelings and emotions of man, which, although not statable in factual language, can yet apprehend the Truth. Truth is not directly statable in terms of factual language, still it can be stated by indirection, by simple bending of meanings, and by poems which can portray our feelings and emotions, by the means of which we can somehow apprehend the manifestation of truth.

The imperceptibility of the king in the play implies that he is neither an object nor a fact of the world. Nor is he a metaphysical entity in so far as he is not an abstraction, as he is dearly related to people, as he is within people's heart.

People can relate to him as Grandfather and Surangamā did.[3] This seems to be quite different from the traditional orthodox ritualistic conception of God. That the author is critical of the ritualistic orthodoxy is obvious in his sarcasm on Kaundilya's remarks:

> My father spends his whole life within a circle of radius of 49 cubits drawn with a rigid adherence to the injunction of the scriptures and never for a single day did he cross this circle ... ours is indeed no common country. (Tagore 1961g, 3)

All these points seem apropos to the remarks of the early Wittgenstein in *Notebooks 1914–1916*, the *Tractatus*, and 'A Lecture on Ethics'.

The imperceptibility of God in early writings of Wittgenstein

Regarding the imperceptibility of God, Wittgenstein remarks (T6.432):

> How things are in the world is a matter of complete indifference for what is higher. God does not reveal himself in the world.

It entails that God belongs to the domain of 'higher' which is somehow beyond 'how things are in the world'. Facts actually describe 'how things are in the world'; hence the domain of God is beyond the domain of facts. But why cannot God reveal himself in the world? Because the world is limited by the totality of facts and God is not a fact among other facts. God transcends these facts, hence He cannot be revealed in the world.

> To believe in a God means to see that the facts of the world are not the end of the matter. (Wittgenstein 1961a, 74e)

The conventions of our language are extraordinarily complicated. There is enormously much added in thought to each proposition and not said (these conventions are exactly like Whitehead's conventions. They are definitions with a certain generality of form). (Wittgenstein 1922, 19)

There is a suggestion here that thought and language are not co-extensive. There are many things in thought which cannot be said. Thus, as God does not reveal himself in the world, we 'cannot say' it in our ordinary language. It goes beyond our describability in factual language.

Now this God of the *Tractatus*, which goes beyond the domain of facts, is not the God of theologians or metaphysicians. Various kinds of arguments for the existence of God have occupied an important place in the literature of metaphysics and theology. The propositions which constitute the body of the arguments are all factual proposi-tions. Moreover, metaphysicians and theologians believe that these arguments are capable of proving the existence of God, that is, they make 'substantial trans-empirical' truth claims for the factual proposi-tions constituting the argument. Wittgenstein here is arguing against this long-standing tradition of confusing the domain of facts with the domain of truth. For the author of the *Tractatus*, truth is of two kinds: necessary logical truth which is senseless (devoid of factual content) and factual truth which is sensible but contingent. He thus 'left no room for metaphysical or theological or religious truths' (Nieli 1987, 103).

As has been noted in Chapter 4, in conversation with M.O.C. Drury, Wittgenstein stated clearly:

> It is a dogma of the Roman church that the existence of God can be proved by natural reason. Now this dogma would make it impossible for me to be a Roman Catholic. (Drury 1984, 123)

This is why God of the *Tractatus*, though not in the world, is also not 'outside oneself', rather God is personally related to oneself, and that is, he has a place in one's heart. The importance of the concept of God stems not from its theological significance, but rather from its relation to a particular way of living in the world. He continued:

> If I thought of God as another being like myself, *outside myself*, only infinitely more powerful, then I would regard it as my duty to defy him. (Drury 1984, 123; emphasis mine)

The concept of 'outside myself' is important as it implies that He can only be within. In the play, the king is within us, within any of us, not outside of us. Wittgenstein is also against orthodox rituality. He says Christianity does not mean saying a lot of prayers, rather taking an attitude towards life. He says:

> If you and I are to live religious lives, it mustn't be that we talk a lot about religion, but that our manner of life is different. (Drury 1984, 129)

This peculiar conception of God/king is explicit in the song of Grandfather's boys' group:

> We are all kings in the kingdom of our king
> Were it not so, how could we hope in our heart to meet him!
> We do what we like,
> Yet we do what He likes
> We are not bound with the chain of fear at the feet of a slave owning king,
> Were it not so, how could we hope in our heart to meet him?
> Our king honours each one of us,
> Thus honours his own very self
> No littleness can keep us shut up in its walls of untruth for eye,
> Were it not so, how could we hope in our heart to meet Him? (Tagore 1961g, 14)

The Importance of Feelings

Although Grandfather and Surangamā did not know anything about the king, they could feel his presence, hear him knocking at the door. Even Queen Sudarśanā used to hear his tunes, smell the fragrance of his *uttoriyo* (scarf), and even hear his loving words, that is, the king was amenable to feelings. Not only Grandfather, his disciples along with Sudarśanā could connect with the king in all situations of life as they were bound by 'the feelings of love, trust and complete surrender'.[4] They express it in a song:

> My beloved is ever in my heart
> That is why I see him everywhere

Who are you who seek him like a beggar from door to door
Come to my heart and see his face in the tears of my eyes.[5]

That means He is in our heart, He is everywhere yet nowhere (in the sense that He is found nowhere in the world as an entity). So one had to prepare oneself to respond to His call, to feel His presence in the innermost corners of our heart.

This stress on feeling is clearly visible in early Wittgenstein. In the *Tractatus* we find him saying that 'to feel the world as a limited whole is mystical' (T6.45), and that ethics, aesthetics, and religion come under the head of the mystical. Obviously for early Wittgenstein religion had to do only with the feeling of viewing the world sub specie aeterni, that is, of 'feeling the world as a limited whole'. This passage reinforces the idea that religious belief is intimately connected with the feeling that facts are not enough, that there is something beyond the factual, which is of great significance and importance.

Here, one might question the status of feeling for the king/God and ask: Are such feelings 'in the world'? Ordinarily, we take feelings as mental states of affairs which are very much in the world. If it is the case then the problem arises: How can something which is 'in the world' apprehend something 'higher'? Does it not sound paradoxical? In response to this one can point out that this feeling is a special feeling of the mystical, it is feeling the world as a limited whole, feeling of viewing the world from eternity. Hence, it is not something which is 'in the world'. This feeling is somehow connected with 'a new spiritual attitude' to the world as a whole and not pictorial from the point of view of the *Tractatus*.

Engelmann, in his memoir, highlighted Wittgenstein's thoughts on 'the possibility of a new spiritual attitude', an attitude summed up by the term 'wordless faith', which Grandfather and Surangamā possessed in the play. Wittgenstein states:

> In this faith of the future there will be no verbal doctrines; for these become the source of misconstructions. Intimations of the divine, rather than talk of the divine, will be the heart of wordless faith in the future. Ideals will not be communicated by attempts to describe them, which inevitably distort, but by the models of an appropriate conduct in life. (Engelmann 1967, 135)

This stress on feeling is a way of protest against metaphysical argumentation for the existence of God. Nieli Russell argues:

> The theological emphasis falls on insight, personal revelation and divine grace as the way of knowing God—i.e., on spiritual experience—metaphysical argumentation may be seen as a great impediment in a man's search for God: When God who reveals himself in a divine encounter (say through feelings) is not arrived through any argument or demonstration. (Nieli 1987, 83)

In fact, as Nieli suggests, this argument reminds us of Augustine who read Aristotle's book *Ten Categories* in his 20s and attempted to understand God in terms of these categories. Later, he confessed that such an attempt made it difficult for him to comprehend God with whom one can have union (Nieli 1987, 84). So we can say that both early Wittgenstein and Tagore had no faith in metaphysical argumentation in favour of the existence of God. Both of them stressed on the importance of feelings as far as the presence of the divine in one's heart is concerned.

Transformation of the World

The play centres round the transformation of Queen Sudarśanā who at the beginning of the play was proud of her intelligence, of her love for the king and the king's love for her. Because of this, she was confident that she will be able to recognize the king in broad daylight during spring festival. But she failed—a huge catastrophe occurred due to her failure. She had to go through utter despair, pain, and humiliation, and then, finally her king showed himself only after she had cast away her pride and prejudices against ugliness and come out on the road as a maid of the king. Thus, complete surrender allows her to see the king, to realize him in everything.

Queen Sudarśanā in the play represents our finite selves in the domain of facts; the king represents the infinite, which belongs to the domain of truth that eludes facts. In a sense, the play is based on the relationship of finite with infinite. This is most evident in the conversation of the king and the queen.

When Sudarśanā asks the king whether he can see her, the king replies,

King: Yes I can ... when I see you I feel that the primeval darkness of the skies, churned into life by the power of my love, has been bathed in the light of million stars and become embodied in your form of flesh and blood. Aeons of thought and endeavour, the yearnings of limitless space have gone into the making of this form of yours.

Queen: Am I so wonderful?

King: Your own mirror will not reflect them. It lessens you, limits you, and makes you look small and insignificant. But could you see yourself mirrored in my own mind. How grand would you appear! In my own heart you are no longer the daily individual who you think you are— you are verily my second self. (Tagore 1961g, 52–3)

The remarks of the king are significant. He represents the queen as his second self which somehow gets lessened, limited in her smallness and insignificance. Now, how is this second self related to him? When does the second self realize that s/he is his second self? The first question has an answer in sloka 7, chapter 15 of the Śrīmadbhagavadgītā:

mamaivāṁśojīvalokejīvabhūtaḥsanātanaḥ |
manaḥṣaṣṭhānīndriyāṇiprakṛtisthānikarṣati || 15/7

Here, Śri Kṛṣṇa says *jīva* is his second self but the second self forgets about its true nature, as it gets infatuated with name, fame, and other worldly pleasures. This is what is meant by saying that the king/ our true self somehow gets lessened, limited in her/our smallness and insignificance. Now as to the question when does the second self realize that s/he is His second self, the answer seems to be: When one changes one's attitude to the world, that is, one casts one's own pride, gets over one's infatuation with material wealth and beauty, and surrenders unconditionally to the Supreme with love and trust. Such changes in one's attitude bring transformation in oneself as well as the world s/he inhabits.

When the time came when Queen Sudarśanā had self-realization, only then she became ready to meet her king. We have noted earlier that she realized that she can only be reconciled with her husband if she bows down to him with complete servility. Only when Queen Sudarśanā is brought down to the level of the servant Surangamā, can she become enlightened.

Feminists might object that Tagore masculinizes God here and this self-realization entails a complete surrender to patriarchy. But it seems that for Tagore the fundamental idea is to realize one's own divinity within oneself, be it masculine or feminine. Here, surrendering oneself does not entail surrendering to patriarchy, rather it entails surrendering to one's higher self (*baḍo ami*).

However this realization contributed to Sudarśanā's transformation (along with the transformation of her world), which constituted the basic theme of the play and which comes close to the heart of early Wittgenstein.

Apropos the distinction between the invisible king/Lord and his second self, Queen Sudarśanā, we find in early Wittgenstein the distinction between the philosophical subject and our ordinary notion of a subject or self. Usually we consider ourselves either as a body (materialists) or as a soul (idealists), or a soul enslaved in a spatio-temporal body. But for early Wittgenstein, 'The "I" is not an object' (Wittgenstein 1961a, 80e), that is, the self is not an object in the world as a body or a soul or a combination of both. He remarks:

> The Philosophical I is not the human being, not the human body or the human soul with the psychological properties, but the metaphysical subject, the boundary (not a part), of the world. The human body, however, my body in particular, is a part of the world among others, among animals plants stones, etc. etc. (Wittgenstein 1961a, 82e)

So one's own body and one's soul with psychological properties are limited and at par with other things of the world; But the 'philosophical I', not to be identified with the body or with the mind (soul with psychological properties), is somehow related to these things of the world as its boundary, as its limit.

Here the concept of the 'Philosophical I' seems to be personified in the character of the king in the play and our ordinary subject with lesser body and mind is represented by the Queen Sudarśanā. Hence, when the body, mind, or soul with psychological properties gets mirrored in the boundary, the relationship between the two gets established. Another cryptic paragraph from the *Tractatus* might be of much use to us in this regard.

> T5.631: There is no such thing as the subject that thinks or entertains ideas. If I wrote a book called 'the world as I found it' I should have

to include a report on my body, and should have to say which parts
were subordinate to my will, and which were not, etc., and this being a
method of isolating the subject or rather of showing that in an important sense there is no subject, for it alone could not be mentioned in
that book.

Here one finds a denial of the thinking subject, whereas in the
previous paragraph there was a mention of a philosophical subject
who does exist. Not only that, here comes the notion of will and the
willing subject. In interpreting these passages referring to conflicting
accounts of the self or the subject, we find that there are references to
three different kinds of subjects in the writings of early Wittgenstein,
namely (a) the thinking subject which does not exist; (b) the philosophical subject which does exist as the boundary, the limit of the world;
and (c) the ethical subject that also exists as the bearer of good and evil.

Wittgenstein denies the thinking subject as Cartesian soul-
substance, which is in the world and which is an object of experience.
Almost in a Humean manner, he discards the thinking self by saying
that he confronts every object in the world but not the 'I'. No one can
have such a special experience of the 'I'. Above all, if someone writes
a book containing 'the world as I found it', it will mention everything
in the world but not the 'I'. But there are references to the existence of the metaphysical subject and the ethical subject. Now, how
are these subjects related? Wittgenstein was not very explicit about
the relationship in the *Tractatus*, though in *Notebooks 1914–1916* he
comments:

> As the subject is not part of the world, but a presupposition of its exis-
> tence, so good and evil are predicates of the subject and not properties
> in the world. (Wittgenstein 1961a, 82e)

This remark suggests that the 'Philosophical I' is the same as the
ethical subject or the willing subject. Supposing that these two subjects are ultimately the same, the question arises: How is this subject
related to the world? It is obvious that it is not in the world but as will,
it is somehow related to the world. Wittgenstein elaborates on this on
4 November 1916:

> The will is an attitude of the subject to the world. The subject is the
> willing subject. (Wittgenstein 1961a, 86e)

And also on 5 August 1916, he remarks:

> If the will did not exist, neither would there be that centre of the world, which we call the I, which is the bearer of ethics. (Wittgenstein 1961a, 82e)

Here one might wonder how something that is not in the world could be 'the centre of the world'. In fact, the phrase 'centre of the world' has been used to indicate the importance of the notion, not to mention it as being the component of the world. Regarding the relationship between the ethical/philosophical subject and the world, Wittgenstein states in a cryptic passage of the *Tractatus*:

> T6.43: If the good or bad exercise of the will does alter the world, it can alter only the limits of the world, not the facts—not what can be expressed by means of language.
> In short the effect must be that it becomes an altogether different world. It must, so to speak, wax and wane as a whole.
> The world of the happy man is a different one from that of the unhappy man.

It is confusing at its appearance as on the one hand the will is independent of the world, it cannot alter facts of the world, but on the other hand it alters the limit of the world. Not only that, by altering the limits of the world, it can contribute to an altogether different world. To make it clear one can suggest that the ethical/metaphysical subject cannot bring about any change in the domain of facts since it itself is not a fact and it is completely powerless against the happenings of the world. But then how can it bring about changes in one's world? By changing one's will, that is, by changing one's attitude to the world, one can transform one's unhappy world to a happy one or happy world to an unhappy one. And this is something that cannot be portrayed by factual language as it is not concerned with facts but can only be shown in language. But how does this change occur in one's life? 'Getting to the centre actually gets you the world, dispassionately as it were. That is, the emotional surrender to Him bears rich fruit: it does not lead to denial of the world as in Vedanta and the mystic tradition, but to celebration of life itself since you are no longer affected by it.'[6] The life of Queen Sudarśanā in *The King of the Dark Chamber* shows us how changing one's attitude to the world can transform one's unhappy world into a happy one. In the concluding scene of the play, when the queen is ready to receive the king as he actually is in himself, he joins her in her dealings with the world. Certainly, her world 'waxes and wanes as a whole' (T6.43) with changes of her inner world incorporated. The king, we must note, does not impose himself upon the queen. He does not come to rescue her when the palace is set on fire by a king from another country, the king does not abandon her either.

'Instead, he waits for her to find the way to life existentially herself ushering in the moment his presence would be truly relevant.'[7] It was only her feelings that changed, nothing else. That changed the boundary of the world, making an unhappy world a happy one. But that did not alter the arrangements of the totality of facts, which constitute the world.

This notion of transformation of the world is very important because Wittgenstein also intends the reader's world to be transformed once he understands the book rightly. It helps one understand the most oracular paragraph at the end of the book (Wittgenstein 1922).

T6.54: My propositions serve as elucidations in the following way: anyone who understands me eventually recognises them as non-sensical, when he has used them—as steps to climb up beyond them (he must, so to speak, throw away the ladder after he has climbed up it). He must transcend these propositions and then he will see the world aright.

The implication is that when the reader uses the book as a ladder and sees the world rightly, he is in no need of the ladder as his world is transformed. But what exactly is this 'seeing the world rightly' which transforms one's world? Which kind of seeing can change one's life and world completely? We find a clue to answer these questions in *Notebooks 1914–1916*.

In *Notebooks 1914–1916* on 1 August 1916, Wittgenstein says:

How things stand is God
God is how things stand. (Wittgenstein 1961a, 74e)

Here, Wittgenstein does not need to be taken as going against the *Tractatus*, which holds that anything higher (which includes ethics, aesthetics, and religion) must lie outside of the world. One might apprehend some inner contradiction here as Wittgenstein speaks in almost the same breath that God is beyond the domain of facts and again in a pantheistic overtone equates God with how things stand. Here, Sitansu Chakrabarty argues, 'Interpreting that the totality of facts i.e., the world as a whole is the holding ground for the value, may not help because the totality is not outside of the world' (Chakrabarty 2012, 8). In the *Tractatus*, one has to go beyond the world to look for the value. However, once one has reached the mystic state, has gone beyond the ordinary world, the world they look back upon is never the same again. With the mystic transformation having taken shape in the subject, the facts (that is, how things stand) have got a touch of value on them, as indicated in T6.43.

In this interpretation, the world that the person sees right when he has climbed up all the stairs is the pantheistic world on the one hand and the solipsistic on the other, that is, 'how things stand is God' on the one hand and 'I am my world' on the other. The equation goes like this: I am my world, this world as it stands is God, and there are three Godheads: me, my world, and God. In the *Tractatus*, Wittgenstein wanted to draw a limit to thought, which he could not do; instead he drew a boundary on the limits of language, which are somehow to be co-extensive with the boundaries of sensible thought. Once you draw the boundary, you are somehow apprised of what lies there outside the boundary. The *Tractatus* shows that what lies on the other side of the boundary are the domain of values, which include ethical, aesthetic, and religious values. Thus, the limits of logic and language are determined by the totality of possible states of affairs and the totality of elementary propositions. What transcends these limits is the mystical union of three Godheads: me, my world, and God. One cannot say this. An attempt to say this will be nonsensical; yet it is not insignificant. In fact, this is most important, as one who has this experience can view the world pantheistically. This right view of the world can be seen in the songs of Grandfather and his group of disciples as we have mentioned earlier:

My beloved is ever in my heart
That is why I see Him everywhere,
He is in the pupils of my eyes
That is why I see Him everywhere.

The Beautiful and the Terrible

Another important digression from our ordinary conception of king/ God occurs when we learn that the king is not benevolent all the time, he is also malevolent at some other times; he is not only beautiful, he is at the same time terrible. He favours his subjects no doubt; there he does not make any discrimination, but he also behaves cruelly with his devoted and dedicated subjects. For example, Grandfather had lost five children one after another but he did not want to complain about this to the king. His argument is: 'Shall I lose my king too because I have lost my children? Don't take me for such a big fool as that' (Tagore 1914e, 25).

Again, take the case of Bhadrasen, the humble devotee. Citizens of the country complain: 'Look at the justice of our king! That Bhadrasen is reduced to such a state of penury that even the bats that infest his house find it a too uncomfortable place' (Tagore 1914e, 26).

Lāl rightly interprets this as follows:

> Tagore follows through the course of the play the spiritual maturation and enlightenment of humankind from a one-dimensional conception of God to an all inclusive one. Man's originally innocent or myopic vision of life and divinity, as happy and benign is usually shattered at some point by a confrontation with the harshness and pitiless cruelty of reality, which leads him immediately to question God and negate life sometimes as a result embracing false ideals—as exemplified in this play by the impostor king, Suvarṇa. Experience makes a man mature bringing him to a complete understanding that life and divinity are simultaneously terrible and beautiful, eventually reconciling him with God. The spiritual allegory of growth from the state of innocence through experience to the state of full acceptance is by no means original, but Tagore's treatment of it shows a characteristically simple and unfettered purity. (Lāl 2001, 99)

It is surprising that the poet here asks us to accept both good and bad, pleasure and pain, tragedy and happiness, as the core of human life and experiences without associating those with the fundamental law of karma prevalent in Indian philosophical and religious tradition. That is, he is not offering a rational principle of justification for evils in life. As the evil, the terrible, the tragedies, form harmonious wholes with the beautiful, with the pleasant in our lives, one will have to accept these facts of life. Once someone accepts these, she becomes happy and nothing else can make her cry or unhappy. At the end we find Grandfather uttering these words:

> Grandfather: I have known him now—I have known him through my griefs and joys—he can make me weep no more now. (Tagore 1914e, 56)

Tagore's God does not interfere either with the natural law or with moral law. These laws have their tradition (*paramparā*), like the iron chain; whatever disaster is caused by the natural law or however hurt the devotees feel; the king interferes neither with natural laws nor with moral law. Whatever has to happen, will happen. We will have to accept it so that we will be in accord with the world. Being in accord with the world implies being in harmony with the world which will give us happiness in turn.

Such an attitude comes very close to what Wittgenstein stated in *Notebooks 1914–1916*.

> I cannot bend the happenings of the world to my will. I am completely powerless. I can only make myself independent of the world—and so in a certain sense master it by renouncing any influences on happenings. (Wittgenstein 1961a, 73)

We have experienced such attitude in the behaviour of Bhadrasen and Queen Sudarśanā at the end of the play.

Now here one might wonder: if God is indifferent to my good or evil, if He cannot bring about any change in my life and experience, and if I have to accept whatever comes to my life, then God becomes nothing other than fate. Wittgenstein also thinks along the same line when he says:

> In order to live happily I must be in agreement with the world. And that is what 'being happy' means. I am then, so to speak, in agreement with that alien will on which I appear dependent. That is to say 'I am doing the will of God'. (Wittgenstein 1961a, 75)

In another instance:

> However this may be, at any rate we are in a certain sense dependent and what we are dependent on we can call God.
> In this sense God would simply be fate. (Wittgenstein 1961a, 74)

For Wittgenstein, the recipe for 'living happily' is to accept the world and whatever ills it may throw at us, not to rage against our sufferings and our pains, but to acquiesce in them. That is, one should not be carried away by emotions and passions but rather should remain calm in all situations. So Wittgenstein's stoicism recommends both the acceptance of pointless suffering and (crucially) the happy acceptance of death. 'Fear in the face of death is the best sign of a false, i.e., bad life. Hence if suffering, frustration and ultimately death can be accepted by us, we will be living in agreement with the world and with fate: we will in other words, be doing the will of God' (Clack 1999a, 45).

Philosophy of Harmony

Central to this play, *The King of the Dark Chamber*, is the philosophy of harmony of smiles and tears, joys and sorrows, good and bad, and life and death, which is nicely represented in the following song sung by Grandfather and his disciples:

> Smiles and tears, emeralds and diamonds,
> swing in fate, Good and bad vibrate to the rhythm,
> keeping time, Birth and death dance at one another's
> heels.
> What happiness, what happiness, what happiness,
> For freedom and confinement dance all day and night
> I flow with these waves, joyful at their heels. (Lāl 2001, 101)

Pleasure/pain, good/bad, life/death, and smiles/tears—all these binaries had revealed a great wonderful harmonious picture in the aesthetic vision of Grandfather and of Tagore, his creator. This happiness/joy (*ānanda*) is an aesthetic notion in Tagore as happiness/joy is not pleasure; pleasure is opposed to pain but joy/happiness is not opposed to pain. It accommodates pain and pleasure both in the above song. Good and bad have the same weightage, and dignity, both are equally true. The beauty that Queen Sudarśanā sees in her king is there in him. Again, the unwavering cruelty that Suraṅgamā experiences is also true. Thus, meditating on the beautiful aspects only will not help anyone reach the king/God. To have that, one will have to stand face to face with God. And to face God one has to have a strong character and mental maturity, and one has to train one's mind to bear and love the hardest truth. The poet says it beautifully in *Sanchaitā* (Chakravarty 1966, 363): 'Truth is hard, and it never deceives. I loved that hardness'—almost in a Spinozistic manner. The truth is cruel but it can be loved, and it makes free those who have loved it. There is the beautiful even in the terrible throughout history and the world. One will have to acquaint oneself with the terrible, otherwise to know the king/lord will be incomplete' (Ayyub 1973, 46–7; translation mine).

Wittgenstein's idea of the happy life, which follows from being dependent on an alien will (as we have seen earlier), includes within itself the idea of harmony. He says: 'The happy life seems to be in some sense more harmonious than the unhappy' (Wittgenstein 1961a, 78e). The unhappy life cannot accommodate the terrible within the beautiful and gets infatuated by the glitter of a mundane materialistic life (as seen in the case of Sudarśanā in the early part of the play). According to early Wittgenstein, This happy and harmonious life can only be had by those who can transcend the limits of language and those of the world (the scientific world as the totality of facts) (Wittgenstein 1961a, 73–5).

Now, one can transcend the limits of the scientific world only when one's attitude to the world gets changed, only when one's life and the world gets transformed completely, which Wittgenstein describes as 'waxing and waning as a whole' (T6.43).

All this reveals to us why it would be normal for Wittgenstein to be philosophically drawn to *Rājā* (*The King of the Dark Chamber*), while we find some passages in *Notebooks 1914–1916* as well as the *Tractatus* that make sense together in the light of the ideas contained in the play that fascinated the philosopher.

Notes

1. The play was staged in 1914, originally in Bengali language. Later, its popularity grew international and it is said to have been staged in the Moscow Art Theatre as early as 1918 (*Modern Review*, January 1925). The *London Times* (13 November 1920) billed a production of the play in Frankfurt on 27 November 1920 as the first long play by Tagore attempted in a European theatre. A news brief in *The Times* (26 May 1922) announced *The King of the Dark Room* on 27 May 1922 at the Nouveau Theatre, Paris: 'The first of Rabindranath Tagore's plays to be given in

France. Later it has been staged repeatedly around the world' (as cited in Lāl 2001, ix–x).
2. Tagore to William Rothenstein, 17 June 1913 (cited in Lago 1972, 113.)
3. Śitanśu Chakraborty, 2012, 'Tagore Wittgenstein Interface: The Poet's Activism and Virtue Ethics', draft version of a paper presented at IIAS, Shimla, in March, p. 8.
4. Fn 3, p. 9.
5. Fn 3, p. 21.
6. Nirmalangshu Mukherjee, University of Delhi, commented while going through the first draft of the chapter at IIAS, Shimla in 2013.
7. Fn 3.

Conclusion

Our journey through the threshold of sensible language and meaning has come to an end. Here, the expectation is that the conclusions
reached so far ought to be presented clearly. But it is particularly
difficult to imagine 'presenting a conclusion' to a study about 'the
inexpressible' of which one should better have been silent. The idea
of putting forward a theory and, thus, contributing to scholarship
at the end of the work fits well with the scientific scheme of factual
investigations. The texts of both Tagore and Wittgenstein contribute
to a stance that is subversive to the scientific scheme. Both of them
were in favour of 'showing' the inexpressible or the *avyakta* through
poems, literature, and music.

Hence, my endeavour in drawing the conclusion will be an attempt
to articulate what has so far been manifested by the chapters of the
book, even at the risk of being 'nonsensical' from the point of view of
the *Tractatus*. The argument in the first chapter attempted to express
how the inexpressible, *'the feeling* of the world as a limited whole' for
Wittgenstein of the *Tractatus*, constitutes the 'truth' of Tagore where

> Feeling yearns to become a part of form.
> But form desires to surrender itself to feeling.[1]

Thus, we notice a kind of philosophy of harmony in the *Tractatus*
which includes harmony of fact and form, of form and feeling, and

above all, a harmony of expressible and the inexpressible, the sayable and the showable. In a way this also shows in an important manner that 'the logical' and 'the mystical' are not antithetical. They are the 'conditions of the world'.

Now this harmony, the blending of the infinite and the finite, the formless and the formed, the visible and the invisible, is the key concept of the philosophy of both Tagore and Wittgenstein. But we have to accept that it is also at the same time beyond description or narration in terms of scientific factual language. As these are not sayable in ordinary scientific language, their unsayability and the mode of silence forms the important key theme in the *Tractatus* and also in the poems of Tagore.

The second chapter has treated the paradoxicality of the position of Wittgenstein as he has said a lot of things about what cannot be said in the book—'instead of keeping mum he has written a whole philosophical book' (Ramsey 1931, 238). Although, at the end, he declares that whatever he has said in the book is nonsensical, in the preface he proclaimed that the truth he found in this book is unassailable and definitive.

However, I agree with Engelmann that there is no paradox in Wittgenstein's admonition to silence at the end. That admonition is meant for the scientists and philosopher's alike but not for the poets, musicians, or artists. Here we should remember that Wittgenstein wanted to treat the *Tractatus* as a literary work at the same time![2] Through the literary work, we can apprehend the unutterable. The unutterable is unutterably contained in their utterances; one can also say that in these art forms, the inexpressible manifest themselves. Here comes the method of indirect communication. Both Wittgenstein and Tagore are prompted to use this method to state 'which cannot be stated'. Both deny the priority of 'scientific and factual paradigms' in matters concerning the ethical, aesthetical, religious, and metaphysical.

Wittgenstein himself really did consider the admonition to silence to be the crucial insight that philosophy provides. He passionately believes that what we cannot talk about is most important. In fact, when Wittgenstein wrote to Ludwig Von Ficker that what he did not write in the book is most important, it was something that was most revolutionary for the readers and commentators. Because it implies that the *Tractatus* ultimately does not concern logic or language but rather those matters that the treatise rules out from being talked about—namely ethics, aesthetics, metaphysics, and religion.

Accessing 'the beyond' is, thus, not paradoxical as it can be done via indirect means, via bending of meanings, through indirection and suggestiveness of language with which we are familiar in the context of Tagore from Chapter 1. Thus, in my interpretation, the *Tractatus* is an attempt to show the threshold of language and meaning. The scientific language in the *Tractatus* is limited, bounded by the totality of elementary propositions. But the matter does not end there. The *Tractatus* wants to convey through language its boundary, its limit, and also, in a paradoxical sense, a glimpse of what lies on the other side of the boundary. To the Wittgenstein of the *Tractatus*, on the other side of the boundary is the realm of values, the domain of God, the meaning of life and the world. Regarding all these things, Wittgenstein opines, philosophers should remain silent. Thus, the unutterable, regarding which one should remain silent, is beyond the argumentation of defenders or critics. It is beyond the words of our ordinary language. Here, one might say that it has, so to speak, got its own language, which shows us the nature of the deepest interconnection between 'the logical' and 'the mystical'. As on the one hand, the unutterable lies in the relations between language and the outside world, so on the other hand does it lie in the relation between language and the world of values.

Both Chapters 3 and 4 are concerned with the domain of the ineffable, which incorporates the ethical, the aesthetic, and the religious. The three discourses for early Wittgenstein are interconnected; hence, whatever is ethical is also aesthetic and religious and vice versa. The discourse of ethics was extremely important because it is 'the enquiry into the meaning of life' or 'into what makes life worth living', or 'into the right way of living' (Wittgenstein 1965, 3). One can say, in Kantian terminology, the world of ethics, aesthetics, and religion belong to the world of noumena, and hence are distinguished from the phenomenal realm of facts. Yet, the difference between the two realms is not absolute; one gets manifested in the other, and there is a yearning to manifest and be manifested on the part of both counterparts. This is the beauty of tackling the problem of ontology in the *Tractatus*.

Both Tagore and Wittgenstein agree that words in our everyday language are incapable of expressing the higher truth. Tagore also wanted to stress that facts are inadequate tools for the expression of truth.

As we have discussed in Chapter 3, the Tractarian view of ethics does not fit at all with the conventional views of Western morality; still it meshes nicely here with that of Tagore's as far as the transcendentality and inexpressibility of ethics is concerned. '[Thus] by keeping ethics free from the primarily discursive and rationalizing aspects of our human intelligence, it [the *Tractatus*] paves the way for a particular view of the world (sub-specie-aeterni), of ourselves and others, which does have practical and moral consequences' (Stockhof 2002, 246).

Wittgenstein sets out his notion of 'the mystical' which comprises ethics, aesthetics, and religion right from a concrete experience, a particular way of viewing the world, namely the mystical experience of the world as a limited whole. Here the possibility is that some might have this experience, some might not. For those who do not have any such experience 'the entire procedure fails'. Here, I completely agree with Martin Stockhof that it is because of this that his views on ethics, aesthetics, religion, and the mysticals did not have a serious impact on the philosophical scene. In fact, its strong emphasis on the relationship between contingency and meaningfulness, and its dismissal of the possibility of genuine philosophical knowledge fostered a way of dealing with ethics negatively in philosophical literature.

However, any attempt to theorize ethics or aesthetics or religion, for Wittgenstein, is 'to run up against the boundaries of language'. But one can live ethically by having an ethical/aesthetical attitude towards the world. We find reflections of such an attitude in the 1920s during the years he spent as a teacher in Lower Austria. We also notice that Wittgenstein's view of how to live did exercise considerable influence in the context of personal relationships. It is possible as his anti-intellectual stance shows that factual or propositional representation is not everything. There are items which go beyond factual representation; there are points of views which are not fragmentary or partial, but which can take an overview of the whole. Thus, we experience value as transcendental. It is interesting to note here that Wittgenstein connects this kind of viewing as 'viewing with a happy eye' because 'the beautiful is what makes happy' (Wittgenstein 1961a,

86e). The experience of value arises from such wholeness, from the perceived harmony between the individual and the world (Friedland 2006, 91–102) This experience of unity is what being happy means (Friedland 2006, 92). Seeing from the viewpoint of eternity is not to perceive the object in terms of causality or in orientation towards a certain end. With this move Wittgenstein in a strict sense separates the question of human value from scientific questions (Tilghman 1991, 44). For Tagore also, viewing from the point of view of aesthetics is viewing from eternity. When we look at a rose and find it beautiful, it becomes the whole world. Its unity of form, colour, texture, and smell coincides with the unity of the universe, and thus it takes us beyond temporality. This unity tunes with the inner unity of oneself along with the unity of the universe (Tagore 1923c, 82).

From this it follows that from the point of view of the scientist, the truth of a blade of grass is important, but only as representative of a class. However, to the aesthetician a blade of grass is important for its being itself and nothing else. It shows that it is not a fact only, it is beautiful. When we look at a blade of grass aesthetically, the covering of its 'everydayness', that is, its being in a particular spatio-temporal framework, gets removed. And the aesthetician discovers a deep harmony in the beautiful object.

Hence, we see the philosophy of harmony of 'the form and the formless' for both the thinkers, which gets manifested in Chapter 1, is now being connected with the harmony of the ethical, aesthetical, and religious viewpoints in Chapter 3 and Chapter 4. In Chapter 4, we discovered both the philosopher and the poet traversing the journey from the outer to the inner, from 'the religious' to 'the spiritual', to one's own religion where there is no formal creed, ritual, or sermons. Here, for Wittgenstein, religion begins with experiences, one's own religious experiences, not with theory. This experience has the potentiality of 'transforming one's world', making unhappy worlds into happy ones.

According to early Wittgenstein, this happy and harmonious life can only be had by those who can transcend the limits of language and those of the world (the scientific world as the totality of facts). Now, one can transcend the limits of the scientific world only when his attitude to the world gets changed, only when his life and the world gets transformed completely, which Wittgenstein describes as 'waxing and waning as a whole'.

This experience, though personal, is connected with the objective world by being unattached to the world. This viewing the world as a limited whole, where the formless manifests itself through the forms, can thus reconcile solipsism with pantheism without even getting into a logical muddle. It still might sound paradoxical and nonsensical from the point of view of the *Tractatus*. Even Tagore apprehends its paradoxicality from the point of view of the scientists. He says that '[a] scientist refuses to accept the paradox of the infinite assuming finitude' (Tagore 1923c, 83), but he has his way out of this paradoxicality by accepting it as it is. I would like to conclude by taking recourse ultimately to Tagore, who maintains:

> It is the paradox which lies at the root of existence. It is as mysterious yet as simple as the fact that I am aware of this wall, which is a miracle that can never be explained. (Tagore 1923c, 84)

Notes

1. From Rabindranath Tagore's Poem no. 17 in *Utsarga* (cited in Naravane 1964, 123–4).
2. 'The work is strictly philosophical and at the same time literary,' Wittgenstein observes in a letter to Ludwig Von Ficker (cited in Engelmann 1967, 78)

Bibliography

Anscombe, G.E.M. 1959. *An Introduction to Wittgenstein's Tractatus*. London: Hutchinson University Library.

Ard, D.J. 1978. *Language, Reality and Religion in the Philosophy of Ludwig Wittgenstein*. Hamilton, Ontario: McMaster University.

Aronson, Alex. 1943. *Rabindranath through Western Eyes*. Allahabad: Kitabistān.

Arrington, R.L., and M. Addis, eds. 2001. *Wittgenstein and Philosophy of Religion*. London: Routledge.

Ayyub, Sayeed. 1970. *Poetry and Truth*. Kolkata: Jadavpur University.

———. 1973. *Pantho Joner Sokhā*. Kolkata: Dey's Publishing.

Baker, G. P. 2004. *Wittgenstein's Method: Neglected Aspects*. Edited and introduced by Katherine J. Morris. Oxford: Blackwell.

Baker, G. P., and P.M.S. Hacker. 1984. *Scepticism, Rules and Language*. Oxford: Blackwell.

———. 2005 (1980). *Wittgenstein: Understanding and Meaning*, Vol. 1 of *An Analytical Commentary on the Philosophical Investigations*. Oxford: Blackwell.

———. 2009 (1985). *Wittgenstein: Rules, Grammar and Necessity*, Vol. 2 of *An Analytical Commentary on the Philosophical Investigations*. Oxford: Blackwell.

Bandyopādhyāy, H. 1969. *Rabindradarśan* (in Bengali). Calcutta: Sāhitya Samsad.

———. 1976. *Śāntiniketaner Bhāsanmaalaa* (in Bengali). Calcutta: Pustak Bipani.

————. 1977. *Rabindra Śilpatattva* (in Bengali). Calcutta.

Banerjee, C. 1946. *Rabi Raśmi* (in Bengali), Vols I–III. Calcutta: A.K. Mukherjee & Co.

Banerjee, Debashis, ed. 2015. *Rabindranath Tagore in the Twenty First Century: Theoretical Renewals*. Springer: India.

Banerjee, H. 1971. *Rabindranath Tagore*. New Delhi: Publication Division.

Barrett, C. 1991. *Wittgenstein on Ethics and Religious Belief*. Oxford: Wiley-Blackwell.

Bartley III, William Warren. 1973. *Wittgenstein*. Philadelphia: Lippincott.

Basu, Amitabha. 1999. *Lyrics to Love from the Poet of the World*. California: Rainbow Printing.

Basu, Somendranath. 1974. *Rabindranatake Tragedy* (in Bengali). Calcutta: Tagore Research Institute.

Basu, T.K. 2007. 'The Sources of Philosophy of Rabindranath Tagore', in *Indian Poetry in English: Roots and Blossoms*, Part 1. Edited by S.K. Pal and A. Prasad. New Delhi: Sarup and Sons.

Biletzki, Anat. 2003. *(Over)Interpreting Wittgenstein*. Leiden: Kluwer.

Bisi, P.N. 1974. *Madhusudantheke Rabindranath* (in Bengali). Calcutta: Karuna Prakashani.

Bhattacharya, J. 1977. *Rabindrakabitāśatak Prathamdaśak* (in Bengali). Calcutta: Kabi o Kabita.

Bhattacārya, Jagadish. 1996. *Kavi Mānasi*, Vol. 1. Kolkata: Vārabi, Kolkata.

Bhattacārya, Lokenath. 1989. 'Paintings of Rabindranath Tagore: A Breath Taking Dimension of a Totality', in *Rabindranath Tagore in Perspective: A Bunch of Essays*. Calcutta: Viśva Bhārati.

Bhattacāryya, Sabyasāchi. 2011. *Rabindranath Tagore: An Interpretation*. New Delhi: Penguin Books.

Biswas, Gautam. 1988. 'Personal Man and Aesthetic Truth: An Approach to Rabindranath Tagore's Philosophy of Art', in *Rabindranath Tagore and the Challenges of Today*. Edited by Bhudeb Chaudhuri and K.G. Subramanyan. Shimla: Indian Institute of Advanced Study (IIAS).

Black, Max. 1967. *A Companion to Wittgenstein's Tractatus*. Ithaca: Cornell University Press.

Block, Irving, ed. 1981. *Perspectives on the Philosophy of Wittgenstein*. Oxford: Blackwell.

Canfield, John V., ed. 1986. *The Philosophy of Wittgenstein*, Vols 1–15. New York: Garland Publishers.

Carnap, Rudolf. 1935. *Philosophy and Logical Syntax*. London: Routledge and Kegan Paul Ltd.

————. 1963. 'Intellectual Autobiography', in *The Philosophy of Rudolf Carnap*. Edited by P.A. Schlipp. La Salle, Illinois: Open Court.

Cavell, S. 1969. *Must We Mean What We Say?* New York: Charles Scribner's Sons.

———. 1979. *The Claim of Reason: Wittgenstein, Skepticism, Morality, and Tragedy.* Oxford: Oxford University Press.

———. 1990. *Conditions Handsome and Unhandsome.* Chicago: University of Chicago Press.

Chakrabarty, Sitansu S. 2012. *Tagore Wittgenstein Interface: The Poet's Activism and Virtue Ethics.* Draft version of paper presented at IIAS, Shimla.

Chakravarty, Amiya. 1966. *A Tagore Reader.* Boston, MA: Beacon Press.

Chatterjee, Ranjit. 2005. *Wittgenstein and Judaism: A Triumph of Concealment.* Germany: Peter Lang Publishing.

Chaudhary, B. 1930. *Kāvye Rabindranath* (in Bengali), 3rd ed. Calcutta: Mitra O Ghosh.

Chaudhary, P.J. 1963. *Rabindranather Saundaryadarśan* (in Bengali). Calcutta: Mukherjee & Co.

Chuchill, J. 1994. 'Wonder and the End of Explanation: Wittgenstein and Religious Sensibility', in *Philosophical Investigations* 17(2): 388–416.

Clack, B.R. 1999a. *An Introduction to Wittgenstein's Philosophy of Religion.* Edinburgh: Edinburgh University Press.

———. 1999b. *Wittgenstein. Frazer, and Religion.* New York: Palgrave Macmillan.

Collinson, Diané. 1985. 'Ethics and Aesthetics are One', in *British Journal of Aesthetics* 25(3): 266–72.

Conant, James. 1991. 'Throwing Away the Top of the Ladder', in *Yale Review* 79(3): 328–64.

———. 2002. 'The Method of the *Tractatus*', in *From Frege to Wittgenstein, Perspectives on Early Analytic Philosophy.* Edited by E.H. Reck. Oxford and New York: Oxford University Press.

Conant, James, and Cora Diamond. 2004. 'On Reading the Tractatus Resolutely: Reply to Meredith Williams and Peter Sullivan', in *Wittgenstein's Lasting Significance.* Edited by M. Kölbel and B. Weiss. London: Routledge.

Copi, I.M., and R.W. Beard, eds. 1966. *Essays on Wittgenstein's Tractatus.* London: Routledge.

Crary, Alice, ed. 2007. *Wittgenstein and the Moral Life.* Cambridge, MA: MIT Press.

Crary, Alice, and Rupert Read, eds. 2000. *The New Wittgenstein.* London: Routledge.

Creegan, C.L. 1989. *Wittgenstein and Kierkegaard.* Michigan: University of Michigan.

Das, K. 1960. *Rabindrapratibhārparicaya* (in Bengali). Calcutta: Satish Ray, Punthighar.

Das, S.K. 1971. *Tagore and the Perennial Problems of Philosophy.* Calcutta: Rabindra Bhārati University.

Das, Sisir Kumar, ed. 2007. 'Tagore on Institutional Religion', in *English Writings of Rabindranath* Tagore, Vol. 4. New Delhi: Sahitya Academy.

Dasgupta, Sasibhusan. 1961. *Upanishader Patabhumikay Rabindra Manas* (in Bengali). Calcutta: A. Mukherjee and Co Pvt Ltd.

Dasgupta, S.N. 1948. *Rabindranath the Poet and the Philosopher.* Kolkata: Mitra and Ghosh.

DeAngelis, William James. 2007. *Ludwig Wittgenstein—A Cultural Point of View: Philosophy in the Darkness of This Time.* Burlington, VT: Ashgate Publishing.

Diamond, C. 1991. *The Realistic Spirit.* Cambridge: MIT Press.

————. 1997. 'Realism and Resolution: Reply to Warren Goldfarb and Sabina Lovibond', in *Journal of Philosophical Research* XXII(1): 75–86.

————. 2000. 'Ethics, Imagination and the Method of Wittgenstein's Tractatus', in *The New Wittgenstein.* Edited by A. Crary and R. Read. London: Routledge.

Drury, M.O.C. 1967. 'A Symposium', in *Ludwig Wittgenstein: The Man and His Philosophy.* Edited by K.T. Fann. New Jersey: Humanities Press, Dell Publishing Co.

————. 1984. 'Some Notes on Conversations with Wittgenstein', in *Recollections of Wittgenstein.* Edited by Rush Rhees. Oxford: Oxford University Press.

Dyson, K.K.; and S. Adhikari. 2017 (1997). *Ranger Rabindranath: Rabindranath Sahitye O Chitrakalay Ranger Vyavahar.* Kolkata: Ananda Publishers.

Edwards, James C. 1985. *Ethics without Philosophy: Wittgenstein and the Moral Life.* USA: University Press of Florida.

Engelmann, Paul. 1967. *Letters from Ludwig Wittgenstein: With a Memoir.* Edited by B.F. McGuinness. Translated by L. Furtmüller. Oxford: Basil Blackwell.

Fogelin, R. J. 1976. *Wittgenstein.* London: Routledge & Kegan Paul.

————. 2009. *Taking Wittgenstein at His Word: A Textual Study.* Princeton: Princeton University Press.

Friedland, Julian. 2006. 'Wittgenstein and the Metaphysics of Ethical Value', in *Ethica* 5(1): 91–102.

Gangopādhyāy, S. 1975. *Rabindradarśan* (in Bengali). Calcutta: Viśva Bhārati.

Ganguly, Sachindranath N. 1968. *Rabindra Darshan.* Śāntiniketan: Viśva Bhārati.

Genova, Judith. 1995. *Wittgenstein: A Way of Seeing.* New York: Routledge.

Ghose, Sisir Kumār. 1989. *The Later Poems of Tagore.* New Delhi: Sterling Publishers Private Ltd.

Ghosh, Sankha. 2011. *Bot Pakurer Phena.* Kolkata: Ekush Satak.

Ghosh, Taraknath. 1962. *Rabindranather Dharmacintā* (in Bengali). Calcutta: Orient Book Company.

Gibson, John, and Wolfgang Huemer, eds. 2004. *The Literary Wittgenstein.* London: Routledge.

Glock, Hans-Johann. 1996. *A Wittgenstein Dictionary.* Oxford: Blackwell.

Griffin, Nicholas, ed. 2002. *The Selected Letters of Bertrand Russell: The Private Years, 1884–1914.* London and New York: Routledge.

Griffiths, A.P. 1991. *Wittgenstein: Centenary Essays.* Cambridge: Cambridge University Press.

Gupta, N.K. 1968. *Rabindranath* (in Bengali). Calcutta: Aurbindo Patna Mandir.

Hacker, P.M.S. 1972. *Insight and Illusion: Themes in the Philosophy of Wittgenstein.* Oxford: Clarendon Press.

———. 1986. *Insight and Illusion,* revised edition. Oxford: Oxford University Press.

———. 1990. *Wittgenstein: Meaning and Mind, Mind,* Vol. 3 of *An Analytical Commentary on the Philosophical Investigations.* Oxford: Blackwell.

———. 1996a. *Wittgenstein: Mind and Will,* Vol. 4 of *An Analytical Commentary on the Philosophical Investigations.* Oxford: Blackwell.

———. 1996b. *Wittgenstein's Place in Twentieth-Century Analytic Philosophy.* Oxford: Blackwell.

———. 2000. 'Was He Trying to Whistle It?', in *The New Wittgenstein.* Edited by A. Crary and R. Read. London: Routledge.

———. 2001. *Wittgenstein: Connections and Controversies.* Oxford: Oxford University Press.

Haller, Rudolf. 2003. 'Wittgenstein: Poetry and Literature', in *Writing the Austrian Traditions: Relations between Philosophy and Literature.* Edited by Wolfgang Huemer and Marc-Oliver Schuster. Edmonton, Alberta: Wirth Institute for Austrian and Central European Studies.

Hayes, John. 1996. 'Introduction', in *The Danger of Words and Writings on Wittgenstein* by M.O.C. Drury. Edited by David Berman, Michael Fitzgerald, and John Hayes. New York: Thoemmes Continuum Press.

Hesham, Muhammad. 2008. '"Language of Eternal Silence": A Reading of Poems by Rabindranath Tagore (1861–1941)'. Available at: https://www. academia.edu/26094466/_Language_of_eternal_silence_A_Reading_of_ Poems_by_Rabindranath_Tagore_1861_1941 (accessed 24 June 2020).

High, D.M. 1967. *Language, Persons, and Belief.* Oxford: Oxford University Press.

Hintikka, M.B., and J. Hintikka. 1986. *Investigating Wittgenstein.* Oxford: Blackwell.

Hudson, W.D. 1968. *Ludwig Wittgenstein: The Bearing of His Philosophy Upon Religious Belief.* London: Lutterworth Press.

———. 1975. *Wittgenstein and Religious Belief.* London: Macmillan Press.

Hyman, J. 1997. 'Wittgensteinianism', in *A Companion to Philosophy of Religion*. Edited by P.L. Quinn, and C. Taliaferro. Oxford: Blackwell Publishers.

James, W. 1982. *The Varieties of Religious Experience*. New York: Penguin.

Janik, Allen. 2011. 'Wittgenstein, Ethics and the Silence of the Muses', in *Egon Schiele Jahrbuch*, Vol. 1. Edited by Johann Thomas Ambrozy, 108–18. Vienna: Wien Kultur.

Janik, Allan, and Stephen Toulmin. 1973. *Wittgenstein's Vienna*. New York: Simon and Schuster.

Kahane, Guy, Edward Kanterian, and Oskari Kuusela, eds. 2007. *Wittgenstein and His Interpreters*. Oxford: Wiley-Blackwell.

Kampchen, Martin. 1991. *Rabindranath Tagore and Germany*. Calcutta: Max Mueller Bhavan.

Keats, John. 1919. 'Ode on a Grecian Urn', in *The Oxford Book of English Verse 1250–1900*. Edited by A.T. Quillar-Couch. Oxford: Clarendon Press.

Keightley, A. 1976. *Wittgenstein, Grammar and God*. London: Epworth Press.

Kenny, A. 1973. *Wittgenstein*. Cambridge, MA: Harvard University Press.

Kerr, F. 1997. *Theology after Wittgenstein*. Oxford: Basil Blackwell.

Klagge, James C. 2001. *Wittgenstein: Biography and Philosophy*. Cambridge: Cambridge University Press.

———. 2010. *Wittgenstein in Exile*. Cambridge, MA: MIT Press.

Kripke, S. 1982. *Wittgenstein on Rules and Private Language: An Elementary Exposition*. Oxford: Blackwell.

Kuusela, Oskari. 2006. 'Nonsense and Clarification in the Tractatus—Resolute and Ineffability Readings and the Tractatus' Failure', in *Acta Philosophical Fennica* 80: 35–65.

———. 2008. *The Struggle against Dogmatism: Wittgenstein and the Concept of Philosophy*. Cambridge, MA: Harvard University Press.

Kuusela, Oskari, and Marie McGinn, eds. 2011. *The Oxford Handbook of Wittgenstein*. Oxford: Oxford University Press.

Labron, Tim. 2006. *Wittgenstein's Religious Point of View*. London: Continuum.

Lago, Mary, ed. 1972. *Imperfect Encounter: Letters of William Rothenstein and Rabindranath Tagore, 1911–1941*. Cambridge: Harvard University Press.

Lāl, Ānanda. 2001. *Rabindranath Tagore: Three Plays*. Oxford: Oxford University Press.

Lazenby, Mark J. 2006. *The Early Wittgenstein on Religion*. London: Continuum.

Lewis, David. 1986. *On the Plurality of Worlds*. Oxford: Blackwell.

Malcolm, N. 1958. *Ludwig Wittgenstein: A Memoir*. Oxford: Oxford University Press.

———. 1986. *Nothing is Hidden, Wittgenstein's Criticism of His Early Thought*. Oxford: Blackwell.

———. 1989. *Nothing is Hidden*. Oxford: Blackwell.

———. 1993. *Wittgenstein: A Religious Point of View?: Edited with a Response by Peter Winch*. Ithaca, NY: Cornell University Press.

McCutcheon, F. 2001. *Religion within the Limits of Language Alone*. Aldershot: Ashgate Publishing.

McGinn, Colin. 1984. *Wittgenstein on Meaning*. Oxford: Blackwell.

McGinn, Marie. 1997. *Routledge Philosophy Guidebook to Wittgenstein and the Philosophical Investigations*. London: Routledge.

———. 2001. 'Saying and Showing and the Continuity of Wittgenstein's Thought', in *The Harvard Review of Philosophy* 9(1): 24–36.

———. 2009. *Elucidating the Tractatus*. Oxford: Oxford University Press.

McGuinness, Brian. 1981. 'The So-Called Realism of Wittgenstein's *Tractatus*', in *Perspectives on the Philosophy of Wittgenstein*. Edited by I. Block. Oxford: Basil Blackwell.

———. 2001. 'Wittgenstein and Jewishness', in *Wittgenstein, Biography and Philosophy*. Edited by James C. Klagge. Cambridge: Cambridge University Press.

———. 2002. *Approaches to Wittgenstein: Collected Papers*. London: Routledge.

———. 2005. *Young Ludwig: Wittgenstein's Life, 1889–1921*. Oxford: Clarendon Press

———. 2005 (1988). Wittgenstein, a Life: Young Ludwig (1889–1929). Oxford: Clarendon Press.

Miller, Alexander, and Crispin Wright, eds. 2002. *Rule-Following and Meaning*. Chesham, UK: Acumen Press.

Monk, Ray. 1990. *Ludwig Wittgenstein: The Duty of Genius*. New York: Macmillan.

Mounce, H.O. 1981. *Wittgenstein's Tractatus: An Introduction*. Oxford: Blackwell.

Moyal-Sharrock, Danièle, ed. 2004. *The Third Wittgenstein: The Post-investigations Works*. London: Ashgate.

———. 2007. *Understanding Wittgenstein's on Certainty*. London: Palgrave Macmillan.

Moyal-Sharrock, Danièle, and William H. Brenner, eds. 2005. *Readings of Wittgenstein's on Certainty*. New York: Palgrave Macmillan.

Mualem, Shlomy. 2002. 'Borges and Wittgenstein on the Borders of Language', in *Variaciones Borges* 14: 61–78.

———. 2004. 'The Imminence of Revelation: Aesthetics and Poetic Expressions in Early Wittgenstein and Borge', in *Variaciones Borges* 18: 197–217.

Mukherjee, A.K. 1975. *Upanishad: In the Eyes of Rabindranath Tagore*. Calcutta: Dasgupta and Co.

Mukhopādhyāy, P.K. 1940–1956. *Rabindra Jīvanī o Rabindra Sāhityapraveśak* (in Bengali), Vol. I–IV. Calcutta: Viśva-Bhārati.

Munz, Volker A., and Bernhard Ritter. 2017. *Wittgenstein's Whewell's Court Lectures: Cambridge, 1938–1941, From the Notes by Yorick Smythies*. West Sussex: Wiley Blackwell.

Nandi, S.K. 1960. *Rabindradarsan Anvikshan* (in Bengali). Calcutta: Sirbhumi Publication.

Naravane, V.S. 1961. *Rabindranath Tagore: A Philosophical Study*. Allahabad: Central Book Depot.

———. 1964. *Modern Indian Thought*. Bombay: Asia Publishing House.

———. 1977a. *Introduction to Rabindranath Tagore*. London: Macmillan.

———. 1977b. *The Philosopher: Introduction to Rabindranath Tagore*. Madras: Macmillan Co. of India Ltd.

———. 1989. 'Tagore's Aesthetics Concepts of Harmony and Personality', in *Rabindranath Tagore in Perspective: A Bunch of Essays*. Calcutta: Viśva Bhārati.

Nieli, Russell. 1987. *Wittgenstein: From Mysticism to Ordinary Language: A Study of Viennese Positivism and the Thought of Ludwig Wittgenstein*. New York: State University of New York Press.

Nielsen, Kai, and D.Z. Phillips. 2005. *Wittgensteinian Fideism?* Norwich: Hymns Ancient and Modern Ltd.

Pears, David F. 1987. *The False Prison: A Study of the Development of Wittgenstein's Philosophy*, Vols I and II. Oxford: Oxford University Press.

Perloff, Marjorie. 1999. *Wittgenstein's Ladder: Poetic Language and the Strangeness of the Ordinary*. Chicago, IL: University of Chicago Press.

Phillips, D.Z. 1968. *Belief, Change and Forms of Life*. New York: Palgrave Macmillan.

———. 1982. *Faith after Foundationalism*. New York: Routledge.

———. 1993. *Wittgenstein and Religion*. New York: Palgrave Macmillan.

Phillips, D.Z. and K. Nielsen. 2005. *Wittgensteinian Fideism?* London: SCM Press.

Phillips, D.Z., and Peter Winch, eds. 1989. *Wittgenstein: Attention to Particulars*. Houndmills: Macmillan.

Phillips, D.Z., R. Rhees, and M. Von der Ruhr, eds. 2005. *Religion and Wittgenstein's Legacy*, Ashgate Wittgenstein Studies. Oxford: Routledge.

Pichler, Alois, and Simo Säätelä, eds. 2005. *Wittgenstein: The Philosopher and His Works*. Norway: Wittgenstein Archives, University of Bergen.

Pitcher, George. 1964. *The Philosophy of Wittgenstein*. London: Prentice Hall Inc.

Pitkin, Hannah. 1972. *Wittgenstein and Justice: On the Significance of Ludwig Wittgenstein for Social and Political Thought*. Berkeley, CA: University of California Press.

Plant, B. 2005. *Wittgenstein and Levinas*. London: Routledge.

Pook, David Olsen. 1994. 'Working on Oneself: Wittgenstein's Architecture, Ethics and Aesthetics', in *Symplokē* 2(1): 48–82.

Rādhākriśnan, S. 1961. *The Philosophy of Rabindranath Tagore*. Vadodara: Good Companions.

Ramsey, Frank. 1931. 'General Propositions and Causality', in *The Foundations of Mathematics and Other Logical Essays*. Edited by R.B. Braithwaite. London: Routledge and Kegal Paul Ltd.

Ray, Satyendranāth, ed. 2007 (1989). *Dharmachinta*. Kolkata: Granthalay Pvt. Ltd.

Rhees, R. 1970. *Discussions of Wittgenstein*. London: Routledge and Kegan Paul.

———. 1981. *Ludwig Wittgenstein: Personal Recollections*. Oxford: Basil Blackwell.

Rhys, E. 1917. *Rabindranath Tagore: A Biographical Study*. London: Macmillan.

Richter, Duncan. 2001. 'Missing the Entire Point: Wittgenstein and Religion', in *Religious Studies* 37(2):161–75.

Ricketts, Thomas. 1996. 'Pictures, Logic, and the Limits of Sense in Wittgenstein's *Tractatus*', in *Cambridge Companion to Wittgenstein*. Edited by H. Sluga and D. Stern. Cambridge: Cambridge University Press.

Roy, B.G. 1970. *The Philosophy of Rabindranath Tagore*. Calcutta: Progressive Publisher.

Roy, N.R. 1983. *Rabindra Sāhitya Bhūmikā* (in Bengali). Calcutta: Book Emporium.

Roy, P. 1983. *Rabindranather Dharmadarsan* (in Bengali). Calcutta: Gopa Prakāshani.

Rundle, Bede. 2004. *Why There Is Something Rather than Nothing*. Oxford: Oxford University Press.

Sarkar, Pabitra. 2011. 'Foreword', in *Tagore's Paintings: Versification in Line* by Sovon Som. New Delhi: Niyogi Books.

Sarkar, S. 1948. *Rabindrakavyatrayi parikalpana* (in Bengali). Calcutta: Kaniyalal Sarkar.

Sarkār, Śyāmal Kumār. 2013. 'The King Of the Dark Chamber: Text and Publication', in *Collected Papers on Rabindranath Tagore*. Kolkata: Dey's Publishing.

Scheman, Naomi, and Peg O'Connor, eds. 2002. *Feminist Interpretations of Ludwig Wittgenstein*. University Park, PA: Pennsylvania State University Press.

Schönbaumsfeld, G. 2007. *A Confusion of the Spheres*. Oxford: Oxford University Press.

Sengupta, S.C. 1948. *The Great Sentinel: A Study of Rabinranāth Tagore*. Calcutta: A. Mukherjee.

———. 1959. *Rabindranath* (in Bengali). Calcutta: N. C. Sarkar.

Shanker, S.G., ed. 1986. *Ludwig Wittgenstein: Critical Assessments*, Vols 1–5, Beckenham: Croom Helm.

Sherry, P. 1977. *Religion, Truth and Language Games*. UK: Palgrave Macmillan Press.

Shields, Philip R. 1993. *Logic and Sin in the Writings of Ludwig Wittgenstein*. Chicago: University of Chicago Press.

Sil, Narasingha P. 2015. 'Rabindranath Tagore's Aesthetics Revisited'. In his *Rabindra Miscellany*, 31–48. Available at: https://www.parabaas.com/rabindranath/articles/Rabindra%20Miscellany.pdf (accessed on 7 April 2020).

Singh, Uday Narayan. 2014. 'Redrawing the Boundaries', in *Muse India*, Issue 54: March–April.

Sluga, Hans D., and David G. Stern, eds. 1996. *The Cambridge Companion to Wittgenstein*. Cambridge: Cambridge University Press.

Som, Sovon. 2011. *Tagore's Paintings: Versification in Line*. New Delhi: Niyogi Books.

Spinoza, B. 2009. *The Ethics*. Translated by R.H.M. Elwes. The Project Gutenburg. Available at: https://www.gutenberg.org/files/3800/3800-h/3800-h.htm (accessed 7 April 2020).

Stengel, Katherine. 2004. 'Ethics as Style: Wittgenstein's Aesthetic, Ethics, and Ethical Aesthetics', in *Poetics Today* 25(4): 610–25.

Stern, David. 2000. 'Was Wittgenstein a Jew?' In *Wittgenstein: Biography and Philosophy*. Edited by James C. Kluge. Cambridge: Cambridge University Press.

———. 2004. *Wittgenstein's Philosophical Investigations: An Introduction*. Cambridge: Cambridge University Press.

Sterrett, Susan. 2005. *Wittgenstein Flies a Kite: A Story of Wings and Models of the World*. London: Penguin Books (Pi Press).

Stockhof, Martin. 2002. *World and Life as One: Ethics and Ontology in Wittgenstein's Early Thought*. Stanford: Stanford University Press.

Stroll, Avrum. 1994. *Moore and Wittgenstein on Certainty*. New York: Oxford University Press.

Sullivan, Peter M. 2000. 'The Totality of Facts', in *Proceedings of the Aristotelian Society* 100(1): 175–92.

Sullivan, Peter, and Michael Potter, eds. 2013. *Wittgenstein's Tractatus: History and Interpretation*. Oxford: Oxford University Press.

Szabados, Bela. 1997. 'Wittgenstein's Women: The Philosophical Significance of Wittgenstein's Misogyny', in *Journal of Philosophical Research* 22: 483–508.

———. 'Was Wittgenstein An Anti-Semite? The Significance of Anti-Semitism for Wittgenstein's Philosophy', in *Canadian Journal of Philosophy* 29(1): 1–27. 1999.

Tagore, Rabindranath. 1913a. *Gītāñjali (Song Offerings)*. London: Macmillan.

———. 1913b. *Sādhanā: The Realisation of Life*, originally written in English. London: Macmillan.

———. 1913c. *The Crescent Moon*. London: Macmillan.

————. 1913d. *The Hungry Stones and Other Stories.* Translated by several writers. London: Macmillan.

————. 1914a. *Der Gärtner (The Gardener).* Translated by Hans Effenberger. Leipzig: Kurt Wolff.

————. 1914b. *Ein Spiel in einem Aufzug (Chitrā).* Translated by Elizabeth Wolff Merck. Leipzig: Kurt Wolff.

————. 1914c. *Hohe Lieder (Gītāñjali).* Translated by Marie Luise Gothein. München: Kurt Wolff.

————. 1914d. *Sādhana: The Realization of Life.* London: Macmillan & Co.

————. 1914e. *The King of the Dark Chamber.* New York: Macmillan Publishers.

————. 1915. *Der Zunehmende Mond (The Crescent Moon).* Translated by Hans Effenberger. Leipzig/München: Kurt Wolff

————. 1916a. *Balākā* (in Bengali). Calcutta: Indian Publishing House.

————. 1916b. *Ghare Baire (The Home and the World).* London: Macmillan and Co Ltd.

————. 1916c. *Stray Birds.* Translated from Bengali to English by the author. New York: The Macmillan Company.

————. 1917. *Personality (Lectures Delivered in America).* New York: Macmillan.

————. 1918a. *Das Postamt, Ein Bühnenspiel (The Post Office).* Translated by Hedwig Lachmannand Gustav Landuer. Leipzig/München: Kurt Wolff

————. 1918b. *Erzählungen (Hungry Stones and Other Stories).* Translated by Annmarie Von Puttkamer. München: Kurt Wolff.

————. 1918c. *Fruchtlese (Fruit-Gathering).* Translated by Annmarie Von Puttkamer. Leipzig: Kurt Wolff.

————. 1918d. *Nationalismus (Nationalism).* Translated by Helene Meyer-Franck. Leipzig: Neuer Zeist Verlag.

————. 1919a. *Der König der dunklen Kammer (The King of the Dark Chamber).* Translated by Hedwig Lachmann and Gustav Landuer. Leipzig/München: Kurt Wolff.

————. 1919b. 'The Message of the Forest', in *The Modern Review,* XXV(5): 453–4.

————. 1920a. *Āmār Dharma.* Calcutta: Viśva-Bhārati.

————. 1920b. *Das Heim und Die Welt (The Home and the World).* Translated by Helene Meyer-Franck. München: Kurt Wolff.

————. 1920c. *Das Opfer und Andere Dramen (Sacrifice and Other Plays).* Translated by Helene Meyer-Franck and Heinrich Meyer-Benfey. München: Kurt Wolff.

————. 1920d. *Der Frühlingskreis: Drama in Vier Akten.* Translated by Emil Engelhardt. München: Kurt Wolff Verlag.

————. 1920e. *Die Gabe der Liebenden (Lover's Gift and Crossing).* Translated by Helene Meyer-Franck. München: Kurt Wolff.

————. 1920f. *Nationalism.* London: Macmillan.

————. 1921a. *Der Gast Japans. Der Sonnenuntergang des Zeitalters* (*Essay on Japan*). Translated by Helene Meyer-Franck. Leipzig: Verlag Neue der Geist.

————. 1921b. *Die Nacht der Erfüllung* (Mashi and Other Stories). Translated by Helene Meyer- Franck. München: Kurt Wolff.

————. 1921c. *Der Schiffbruch* (The Wreck). Translated by Helene Meyer-Franck. München: Kurt Wolff.

————. 1921d. *Der Weg zur Vollendung* (Sādhana). Translated by Helene Meyer-Franck. München: Kurt Wolff.

————. 1921e. *Gesammelte Werke* (Collected Works). Vols I and II (Poetry), III (Plays), IV (Short Stories), V and VI (Novels), VII and VIII (Essays and Aphorisms). Edited by Heinrich Meyer-Benfey and Helene Meyer-Franck. München: Kurt Wolff.

————. 1921f. *Glimpses of Bengal*. London: Macmillan.

————. 1921g. *On Constructive Work—A Letter*. March. Calcutta.

————. 1921h. *Persönlichkeit* (Personality). Translated by Helene Meyer-Franck. München: Kurt Wolff.

————. 1921i. *Thoughts Relics*. Revised edition 2008. Virginia: Wilder Publications.

————. 1921j. *Verirrte Vögel* (Stray Birds). Translated by Helene Meyer-Franck. München: Kurt Wolff.

————. 1922. *Creative Unity*. London: Macmillan and Co. Ltd.

————. 1923a. *Lover's Gift and Crossing*. London: Macmillan.

————. 1923b. *Meine Lebenserinnerungen* (Reminiscences). Translated by Helene Meyer-Franck. München: Kurt Wolff.

————. 1923c. *Personality (Lectures Delivered in America)*. London: Macmillan and Co. Ltd.

————. 1924. *Letters from Abroad*. Madras: Ganesh & Co.

————. 1925a. *Gora: Roman in Zwei Bänden* (Gora: A Novel in Two Volumes). Translated by Helene Meyer-Franck. München: Kurt Wolff.

————. 1925b. *Talks in China*. Calcutta: Viśva-Bhārati.

————. 1926. *One Hundred Poems of Kabir*. Translated by Rabindranath Tagore, with assistance of Evelyn Underhill. London: Macmillan.

————. 1927. *An Eastern University*. Śāntiniketan: Viśva-Bhārati.

————. 1928a. *City and Village*. Śāntiniketan: Viśva-Bhārati.

————. 1928b. *Fireflies*. New York: Macmillan.

————. 1928c. *The Growth of Viśva-Bhārati 1920–21*. Śāntiniketan: Viśva-Bhārati.

————. 1929 (1924). *Letters to a Friend*, Revised edition of *Letters from Abroad*. Edited with two introductory essays by C.F. Andrews. New York: Macmillan.

————. 1931a. *Address at Śāntiniketan*. Calcutta: Viśva-Bhārati.

————. 1931b. *Child*. London: Allen and Unwin.

————. 1931c. *The Religion of Man Being the Hibbert Lectures for 1930*. London: George Allen and Unwin.

————. 1932. *Mahatamaji and the Depressed Humanity*. Calcutta: Viśva-Bhārati.

————. 1933 (1917). *My Reminisces*. Translated by Rabindranath Tagore. London: Macmillan.

————. 1937. *Prantik*. Kolkata: Vishwabharati Granthalay.

————. 1941. *Crisis in Civilisation*. Calcutta: Viśva-Bhārati.

————. 1942–2004. *Cithi Patra: Collected Letters* (in Bengali), Vols I–XIX. Calcutta: Viśva-Bhārati.

————. 1944. *Samāj* (in Bengali). Calcutta: Viśva-Bhārati.

————. 1946–72 (1939–65). *Rabindra Racanāvalī: Collected Works*, Vols I–XXVIII. Calcutta: Viśva-Bhārati.

————. 1953a. *The Religion of Man*. London: Allen and Unwin.

————. 1953b. *Religion of Artist*. Calcutta: Viśva-Bhārati.

————. 1955. *Dharma* (in Bengali). Calcutta: Viśva-Bhārati.

————. 1956a. *Buddhadeva* (in Bengali). Calcutta: Viśva-Bhārati.

————. 1956b. *Sañcay* (in Bengali). Calcutta: Viśva-Bhārati.

————. 1956 (1943). *Pāścātya Bhraman* (in Bengali). Calcutta: Viśva-Bhārati.

————. 1958. *Śāntiniketan Brahmacāryāśram* (in Bengali). Calcutta: Viśva-Bhārati.

————. 1959 (1923). *Personality (Lectures Delivered in America)*. London: Macmillan and Co. Ltd.

————. 1960. *Gitavitān*. Kolkata: Viśva Bhārati Publication.

————. 1960 (1934). *Letters from Russia*. Translated by Sasadhar Sinha. Calcutta: Viśva Bhārati Publication.

————. 1961a. *Ātmaparicay* (in Bengali). Calcutta: Viśva-Bhārati.

————. 1961b. *Fruit Gathering*. London: Macmillan.

————. 1961c. *On Art and Aesthetics: A Selection of Lectures, Essays & Letters*. Edited by Prithwish Neogy. New Delhi: Orient Longman.

————. 1961d. *Rabindra Rachanabali*, Vol. 12. Calcutta: Viśva Bhārati.

————. 1961e. *Sacrifice and Other Plays*. London: Macmillan.

————. 1961f. *The Gardener*. London: Macmillan.

————. 1961g. *The King of the Dark Chamber*. Translated by Kshitish Chandra Sen. London: Macmillan and Co.

————. 1961h. *Towards Universal Man*. Edited by Bhabani Bhattachārya. Translated by various writers with introduction by Humāyun Kabir. Bombay: Asia Publishing House.

————. 1961 (1940). *My Boyhood Days*. Translated by Marjorie Sykes. Calcutta: Viśva-Bhārati.

————. 1962a. *Creative Unity* (originally written in English). London: Macmillan.

————. 1962b. *The Diary of Westward Journey*. Translated by Indu Dutt. Connecticut: Greenword.

———. 1963. *Mahatma Gandhi*. Calcutta: Viśva-Bhārati.

———. 1963–5. *Gītavitān* (in Bengali), Parts I–III. Calcutta: Viśva-Bhārati.

———. 1967a. *Āśramerrūp o bikas* (in Bengali). Calcutta: Viśva-Bhārati.

———. 1967b. *Bankim Chandra* (in Bengali). Calcutta: Viśva-Bhārati.

———. 1967c. *Chinna-patrāvalī* (in Bengali). Calcutta: Viśva-Bhārati.

———. 1968. *Jīvansmriti* (in Bengali). Calcutta: Viśva-Bhārati.

———. 1968a (1961). *Europe Jatrir Diary* (in Bengali). Calcutta: Viśva-Bhārati.

———. 1968b (1961). *Europe Prabasir* (in Bengali). Calcutta: Viśva-Bhārati.

———. 1968 (1962). *Palli Prakiti* (in Bengali). Calcutta: Viśva-Bhārati.

———. 1972. *Mānusher Dharma* (in Bengali). Calcutta: Viśva-Bhārati.

———. 1973–5 (1966–8). *Gitāben* (in Bengali), Vols I–III. Calcutta: Viśva-Bhārati.

———. 1977. 'Naivedya', in *An Introduction to Rabindranath Tagore* by V.S. Naravane. Madras: Macmillan Publishers.

———. 1978. *Sense of Beauty, Angel of Surplus*. Edited by Sisir Kumār Ghose. Calcutta: Viśva Bhārati.

———. 1980. 'Prabhāt Utsav, Prabhāt Sangīt', in *Rabindra Rachanāvali*, Vol. 1. Kolkata: Paschimbnga Sarkar.

———. 1981. *On the Edges of Time*. Second edition. Calcutta: Viśva-Bhārati.

———. 1985. *Collected Poems and Plays of Rabindranath Tagore*. London: Macmillan.

———. 1986. *Rabindra Rachanabali*, Vol. 14. Kolkata: Paschimbanga Sarkar.

———. 1988. 'Construction versus Creation', in *Lectures and Addresses by Rabindranath Tagore*. Edited by Anthony X. Soares. Madras: Macmillan Pocket Edition.

———. 1989. *Viśva-Bhārati* (in Bengali). Calcutta: Viśva-Bhārati.

———. 1990. *Selected Poems of Rabindranath Tagore*. Edited by William Radice. Delhi: Penguin.

———. 1993 (1961). *Ātmaparicay* (in Bengali). Calcutta: Viśva-Bhārati.

———. 1995 (1902). *Rabindra Racanāvalī: Collected Works*, Vols I–XXVIII. Calcutta: Viśva-Bhārati.

———. 1997 (1900). *Śikśā* (in Bengali). Revised edition. Calcutta: Viśva-Bhārati.

———. 1997. *Chithi-Potro*. Edited by K. Samanta and S. Bagchi. Kolkata: Viśva-Bhārati.

———. 2000 (1907). *Prācīn Sāhitya* (in Bengali, reprint). Calcutta: Viśva-Bhārati.

———. 2000. *Śāntiniketanvidyālaya 1901–2000*. Calcutta: Viśva-Bhārati.

———. 2001. *Selected Writings on Literature and Language: Rabindranath Tagore*. Edited by Sisir Kumār Das and Sukanta Chaudhuri. New Delhi: Oxford University Press.

————. 2002. *Poems*. Collection includes translations done by Rabindranath Tagore and translations authorized by him. Calcutta: Viśva-Bhārati.

————. 2002 (1910). *Gitanjali*. (Bengali). First edition. In *Gitabitan*. Kolkata: Tulikalam.

————. 2002 (1920). *Arupratan*. In *Gitabitan*. Kolkata: Tulikalam.

————. 2004. *Selected Poems: Rabindranath* Tagore. Edited by Sukānta Chaudhuri. New Delhi: Oxford University Press.

————. 2006a. 'Ātmaparicay', in *My Life in My Words*. Edited by Uma Das Gupta. New Delhi: Oxford University Press India.

————. 2006b. *Of Myself (Ātmaparichay)*. Translated by Devadatta Joardar and Joe Winter. London: Avil Press Poetry.

————. 2008. *The English Writings of Rabindranath Tagore*, Vols 1–4. Edited by Sisir Kumār Das. New Delhi: Sahitya Akademi.

Thompson, Edward J. 1921. *Rabindranath Tagore: His Life and Work*. Calcutta: YMCA.

————. 1926. *Rabindranath Tagore: Poet and Dramatist*. New York: Oxford University Press.

Tilghman, B.R. 1991. *Wittgenstein, Ethics and Aesthetics: The View from Eternity*. London: Macmillan.

Tinker, Hugh. 1979. *The Ordeal of Love: C.F. Andrews and India*. New Delhi: Oxford University Press.

Tuck, Donald. 1974. 'The Religious Motif in the Poetry of Rabindranath Tagore', in *Numen: International Review for the History of Religions* 22(2): 97–104.

U'hland, Ludwig. 1848. *The Poems of Ludwig U'hland*. Translated by Alexander Platt. Leipzig: Friedrich Volckmar.

Upadhyāy, Brahmabandhab. 1900. 'The World Poet of Bengal'. *Sophia*. 1 September.

Verbin, N. 2010. 'The Ladder and the Cage: Wittgenstein, Qoheleth, and Quietism', in *Common Knowledge* 16(3): 474–92.

Vesey, G., ed. 1974. *Understanding Wittgenstein*. Ithaca: Cornell University Press.

von Wright, G.H. 1967. 'A Biographical Sketch', in *Ludwig Wittgenstein: The Man and His Philosophy*. Edited by K.T. Fann. New Jersey: Humanities Press, Dell Publishing Co.

Waismann. Friedrich. 1965. 'Notes on Talks with Wittgenstein', in *The Philosophical Review* 74(1): 12–16.

————. 1979. *Wittgenstein and the Vienna Circle*. Oxford: Rowman & Littlefield Publishers.

Wehmeier, K.F. 2004. 'Wittgenstein's Predicate Logic', in *Notre Dame Journal of Formal Logic* 45(1): 1–11.

White, Roger. 2006. *Wittgenstein's Tractatus Logico-Philosophicus: A Reader's Guide*. London: Continuum.

Wilde, Carolyn. 2004. 'Ethics and Aesthetics Are One', in *Wittgenstein, Aesthetics and Philosophy*. Edited by Peter B. Lewis. Aldershot: Ashgate.

Williams, Meredith. 2002. *Wittgenstein, Mind and Meaning: Towards a Social Conception of Mind*. London: Routledge.

Winch, Peter. 1993. 'Discussion of Malcolm's Essay', in *Wittgenstein: A Religious Point of View?* Edited by Peter Winch. London: Routledge.

————. 2004. *The Idea of a Social Science and Its Relation to Philosophy*. Second edition. London: Routledge.

Wittgenstein, Ludwig. 1922. *Tractatus Logico-Philosophicus*. Translated by C. K. Ogden. London: Routledge and Kegan Paul. Originally published as 'Logisch-Philosophische Abhandlung', in *Annalen der Naturphilosophische* XIV(3/4), 1921.

————. 1929. 'Some Remarks on Logical Form', in *Proceedings of the Aristotelian Society* 9(Supplemental): 162–71.

————. 1953. *Philosophical Investigations*. Edited by G.E.M. Anscombe and R. Rhees. Translated by G.E.M. Anscombe. Oxford: Blackwell.

————. 1956. *Remarks on the Foundations of Mathematics*. Edited by G.H. von Wright, R. Rhees, and G.E.M. Anscombe. Translated by G.E.M. Anscombe. Oxford: Blackwell.

————. 1958. *The Blue and Brown Books* (*BB*). Oxford: Blackwell.

————. 1961a. *Notebooks 1914–1916*. Edited by G.H. von Wright and G.E.M. Anscombe. Translated by G.E.M. Anscombe. Oxford: Blackwell.

————. 1961b. *Tractatus Logico-Philosophicus*. Translated by D.F. Pears and B.F. McGuinness. New York: Humanities Press.

————. 1964a. *Philosophische Bemerkungen, Vorwort*. Oxford: Basil Blackwell.

————. 1964b. *Philosophical Remarks*. Edited by R. Rhees. Translated by R. Hargreaves and R. White. Oxford: Blackwell.

————. 1965. 'A Lecture on Ethics', in *The Philosophical Review* 74(1): 3–12.

————. 1966. *Lectures and Conversations on Aesthetics, Psychology and Religious Belief*. Edited by C. Barrett. Oxford: Blackwell.

————. 1967a. 'Remarks on Frazer's Golden Bough'. Edited by R. Rhees in *Synthese* 17(1): 233–53.

————. 1967b. *Zettel*. Edited by G.E.M. Anscombe and G.H. von Wright. Translated by G.E.M. Anscombe. Oxford: Blackwell.

————. 1968. 'Notes for Lectures on "Private Experience" and "Sense Data"', in *Philosophical Review* 77(3): 275–320.

————. 1969. *On Certainty*. Edited by G.E.M. Anscombe and G.H. von Wright. Translated by G.E.M. Anscombe and D. Paul. Oxford: Blackwell.

————. 1971. *Proto Tractatus—An Early Version of Tractatus Logico-Philosophicus.* Edited by B.F. McGuinness, T. Nyberg, and G.H. von Wright. Translated by D.F. Pears and B.F. McGuinness. Ithaca: Cornell University Press.

————. 1972 (1921). *Tractatus Logico-Philosophicus.* Translated by D.F. Pears and B.F. McGuinness. London: Routledge and Kegan Paul.

————. 1973. *Letters to C. K. Ogden with Comments on the English Translation of the Tractatus Logico-Philosophicus.* Edited by G.H. von Wright. Oxford: Blackwell.

————. 1974a. *Letters to Russell, Keynes and Moore.* Edited by G.H. von Wright and B.F. McGuinness. Oxford: Blackwell.

————. 1974b. *Philosophical Grammar.* Edited by R. Rhees. Translated by A. Kenny. Oxford: Blackwell.

————. 1976. *Wittgenstein's Lectures on the Foundations of Mathematics.* Edited by C. Diamond. Ithaca: Cornell University Press.

————. 1977. *Remarks on Colour.* Edited by G.E.M. Anscombe. Translated by L. McAlister and M. Schaettle. Oxford: Blackwell.

————. 1979a. *Ludwig Wittgenstein and the Vienna Circle: Conversations Recorded by Friedrich Waismann (VC).* Edited by B.F. McGuinness. Oxford: Blackwell.

————. 1979b. *Wittgenstein's Lectures, Cambridge 1932–1935.* Edited by A. Ambrose. Oxford: Blackwell.

————. 1980a. *Culture and Value.* Edited by G.H. von Wright and Heikki Nyman. Frankfurt: Suhrkamp.

————. 1980b. *Remarks on the Philosophy of Psychology,* Vol. 1. Edited by G.E.M. Anscombe and G.H. von Wright. Translated by G.E.M. Anscombe. Oxford: Blackwell.

————. 1980c. *Remarks on the Philosophy of Psychology,* Vol. 2. Edited by G.H. von Wright and H. Nyman. Translated by C.G. Luckhardt and M.A.E. Aue. Oxford: Blackwell.

————. 1980d. *Wittgenstein's Lectures, Cambridge 1930–1932.* Edited by D. Lee. Oxford: Blackwell.

————. 1984 (1980). *Culture and Value.* Edited by G.H. von Wright and Heikki Nyman. Frankfurt: Suhrkamp.

————. 1986. *Wittgenstein: Conversations, 1949–1951.* Edited by O.K. Bouwsma, J.L. Kraft, and R.H. Hustwit. Indianapolis: Hackett.

————. 1988. *Wittgenstein's Lectures on Philosophical Psychology 1946–47.* Edited by P.T. Geach. London: Harvester.

————. 1992. *Last Writings on the Philosophy of Psychology,* Vols 1–2. Edited by G.H. von Wright and H. Nyman. Translated by C.G. Luckhardt and M.A.E. Aue. Oxford: Blackwell.

————. 1993. *Philosophical Occasions*. Edited by J. Klagge and A. Nordmann. Indianapolis: Hackett.

————. 1997. *The Collected Manuscripts of Ludwig Wittgenstein on Facsimile CD Rom*. Edited by The Wittgenstein Archives at the University of Bergen. Oxford: Oxford University Press.

————. 1998 (1980). *Culture and Value: A Selection from the Posthumous Remains*. Edited by G.H. von Wright. Translated by P. Winch. Reprint, Oxford: Basil Blackwell and Co. Ltd.

————. 2003a. *Ludwig Wittgenstein: Public and Private Occasions*. Edited by J. Klagge and A. Nordmann. Lanham: Rowman & Littlefield.

————. 2003b. *The Voices of Wittgenstein: The Vienna Circle: Ludwig Wittgenstein and Friedrich Waismann*. Edited by Gordon Baker. Translated by Gordon Baker, Michael Mackert, John Connolly, and Vasilis Politis. London: Routledge.

————. 2005. *The Big Typescript: TS 213, German English Scholars' Edition*. Translated by C. Grant Luckhardt and Maximilian E. Aue. Oxford: Wiley-Blackwell.

————. 2008. *Wittgenstein in Cambridge: Letters and Documents 1911–1951*. Edited by Brian McGuinness. Oxford: Blackwell.

————. 2009a. *Philosophical Investigations (PI). Fourth edition*. Edited and translated by P.M.S. Hacker and Joachim Schulte. Oxford: Wiley-Blackwell.

————. 2009b. *Wittgenstein's Notes on Logic*. Edited by Michael Potter. Oxford: Oxford University Press.

Index

46; early life of, 113; fascination
for Tagore's poems, 1; idea of
happy life, 167; idea of sense,
20; influence of Schopenhauer
on, 82; involvement with the
Jewish circle, 116; notion of
absolute value judgements, 80;
as philosopher of language, 4;
position in the *Tractatus*, 22;
reaction to *The King of the Dark
Chamber*, 144–5; religious views
and interests of, 10; remarks
on ethics and aesthetics, 10, 69;
visit to Olmütz, 57; Waismann's
conversation with, 132–3; work
in field of philosophy, 4
Wittgenstein's Vienna (1973), 43, 52,
69, 131, 137, 140, 172

Wolff, Kurt, 144
Wonder, that the world exists, 79–80,
88, 94, 120, 133
world and life, harmonious view
of, 93
World as Will and Representation, The
(1818), 114
writings of Tagore: affinity with
Wittgenstein on the notion of
facts, 28; bending of meanings
through indirection and
suggestiveness in, 56; differences
between construction and
creation in, 44; on distinction
between fact and truth, 27–35,
48n4; German translations of, 7;
idea of realism and idealism, 29;
publication of collected works, 8

About the Author

Priyambada Sarkar is professor at the Department of Philosophy, University of Calcutta, West Bengal, India, where she also held the position of head of the department from 2003 to 2005. Her research interests include analytic philosophy, epistemology, applied ethics, and Indian ethics. She completed her PhD from King's College, London, UK. She has authored three books: *Wittgenstein and Solipsism* (2009), *Uttarparber Wittgenstein: Philosophical Investigations* (in Bengali, 2007) and *Tatparya o Vachya: Freger Bhasa-Darsaner Bhumika* (in Bengali, 2007), and has co-edited six books.

Sarkar, as co-ordinator of the Departmental Research Support Program (UGC, 2008–10) has organized multiple lectures, seminars, and conferences. She is former president of the Ludwig Wittgenstein Philosophical Society (Lucknow, India), a life member of the Indian Council of Philosophical Research (ICPR), and a life member of the British Wittgenstein Society (UK). She has been awarded a fellowship by the IIAS (Shimla, 2012–14) and She had been invited to deliver lectures at the University of Cambridge, England, University of Vienna, Austria, and Pontifical University of Rome, Italy, and Dacca University, Rangpur University, and Jahangirnagar University in Bangladesh.